CRUSADE AGAINST CRIME

Edited by JERRY D. LEWIS

CRUSADE

AGAINST

CRIME

PUBLISHED BY

BERNARD GEIS ASSOCIATES

DISTRIBUTED BY RANDOM HOUSE

Acknowledgments

The editor is grateful to the following people and organizations for their generous permission to include their work among our selections in this book:

Amy Giessner and Henry Regnery Company for "Dead or Alive" by Frederick Ayer, Jr., from his book *Yankee G-Man* © 1957 by Henry Regnery Company.

Mrs. Natalie Bates and Myron D. Davis of Esquire, Inc. for "Blood Money" by Ray Brennan, reprinted from *Coronet* (November 1948) © 1948 by Esquire, Inc., and for "Mystery in New Mexico" by William Bradford Huie, reprinted from *Coronet* (March 1950) © 1950 by Esquire, Inc.

Lois Stewart and The Bobbs-Merrill Company, Inc. for "Robbery in the Cathedral" by Francis X. Busch, from his book *Casebook of the Curious and True* © 1957 by The Bobbs-Merrill Company, Inc.

William A. Koshland, Lila Karpf and Alfred A. Knopf, Inc. for "A Baby Is Missing" by Alistair Cooke, from his book *One Man's America* © 1952 by Alistair Cooke.

Charles Schlessiger and Brandt & Brandt for "A Dead Man's Honor" by Herbert Corey, from his book *Farewell, Mr. Gangster!* (Appleton-Century-Crofts, Inc.) © 1936 by Herbert Corey.

Dodd, Mead & Company for "Death in Illinois" by Irving Crump and John W. Newton, from their book *Our G-Men* © 1937 by Dodd, Mead & Company, Inc.

Publisher Franklin S. Payne and columnist Charles Denton for "The Frugal Forger," from the *Los Angeles Examiner* © 1958 by the *Los Angeles Examiner*.

James A. McCracken and *Reader's Digest* for "No Clues" by Karl Detzer © 1957 by Reader's Digest Association, Inc.; for "Crime of the Century" by J. Edgar Hoover © 1951 by Reader's Digest Association, Inc.; and for "The FBI Goes Hunting" by Carl B. Wall © 1945 by Reader's Digest Association, Inc., condensed from *American Legion Magazine*.

Morris L. Ernst for "A Liberal Looks at the FBI," from Mr. Ernst's book *The Best Is Yet . . .* © 1945 by Margaret S. Ernst.

ACKNOWLEDGMENTS

Jack R. Cormack and Gerald Austin of the Hutchinson Publishing Group for "The Cut-Rate Kidnappers" by Leonard R. Gribble © 1953 by John Long, Ltd.

Jacqueline Korn and David Higham Associates, Ltd. for "The Oberleutnant" by Richard Harrison © 1956 by the author.

Margaret M. White and Prentice-Hall, Inc. for "The Scales of Injustice" by Asa S. Herzog and A.J. Ezickson, from their book *Camera, Take the Stand* © 1940 by Prentice-Hall, Inc.

Alex Jackinson for "Dallas' Reign of Terror" by Ken Jones, from his book *The FBI in Action* © 1957 by New American Library of World Literature, Inc.

John Seigenthaler, Administrative Assistant to the Attorney General, and Mrs. Helen Lane of Harper & Brothers for "Jimmy Hoffa vs. the FBI" by Robert F. Kennedy, from his book *The Enemy Within* © 1960 by Robert F. Kennedy.

Judge Harold R. Medina for "Guts and Loyalty," from Judge Medina's book *The Anatomy of Freedom* © 1959 by the author.

Max Wilkinson of Littauer and Wilkinson for "The Unhidden Persuaders" by Vance Packard © 1946 by The Crowell-Collier Publishing Company.

Mrs. Terry Peck and Doubleday & Company, Inc. for "I Remember John Dillinger" by Melvin Purvis, from his book *American Agent* © 1936 by Melvin Purvis, and for "The Lindbergh Tragedy" by Leon G. Turrou, from his book *Where My Shadow Falls* © 1949 by Leon G. Turrou.

Quentin Reynolds for "Round Trip to Nowhere," from Mr. Reynolds' book *The FBI* © 1954 by the author.

Doris Doland and *Look* Magazine for "Is John Jones a Communist?" by Leo Rosten, reprinted from the September 12, 1950 issue of *Look* Magazine © 1950 by Cowles Magazines, Inc.

Ronald Setter and Frederick Muller, Ltd. for "Murder in Mid-Air" by David Rowan, from his book *Famous American Crimes* © 1959 by Frederick Muller, Ltd.

Mrs. Rose Morse and the Philosophical Library for "Lady in Love" by Ronald Seth, from his book *Spies at Work* © 1954 by Ronald Seth.

Jeffrey Simmons of W. H. Allen & Co., Ltd. and Kurt Singer for "The Lady with the Dolls," from Mr. Singer's book *Women Spies* © 1951 by Kurt Singer.

Mrs. Julie D. Crum of *Ladies Home Journal* and Attorney Alan U. Schwartz for "In Defense of Wiretapping" by Dorothy Thompson © 1954 by Curtis Publishing Company.

Leah Daniels and Random House, Inc. for "The Actor from San Francisco" by Don Whitehead, from his book *Journey into Crime* © 1960 by Don Whitehead.

Ruth Stark and Anna-Marie Walsh of Holt, Rinehart & Winston, Inc.

for "The Double-edged Sword" by Charles Wighton and Gunter Peis, from their book *Hitler's Spies and Saboteurs* © 1958 by Charles Wighton and Gunter Peis.

Rose Bigman and Walter Winchell for "Rendezvous with Murder, Inc." by Walter Winchell © 1939 by New York *Daily Mirror*.

Helen Strauss and Arlene Friedman of the William Morris Agency, Inc. for "A Nice, Busy Little Bank That Ought to Be Robbed" by Evan McLeod Wylie © 1957 by the author.

Harold Ober of Harold Ober Associates for "Alias Me" by Philip Wylie © 1959 by Curtis Publishing Company.

Homer Grosvenor, *The Saturday Evening Post,* and Dr. Dale Yoder for "Manhunt" by Robert M. Yoder © 1950 by Curtis Publishing Company.

Alan Hynd for "Gold Bricks on Signal Hill" by Alan Hynd © 1946 by the author.

J. B. Lippincott Company for "Illicit Gold" by John J. Floherty, from his book *Men Against Crime* © 1946 by John J. Floherty.

Appleton-Century-Crofts, Inc. for "G.I. Burglars" by Willis George, from his book *Surreptitious Entry* © 1946 by Willis George.

The World Publishing Company for "The Case of the Insurance Conspiracy" by Sam D. Cohen, from his book *One Hundred True Crime Stories* © 1946 by The World Publishing Company.

Julian Messner, Inc. for "Homemade Money" by Harry Edward Neal, from his book *Six Against Crime* © 1959 by Harry Edward Neal.

Andrew Tully for "One-Man Narcotics Squad" by Andrew Tully © 1958 by the author.

The Bobbs-Merrill Company, Inc. for "Clues in Wood" by Henry Morton Robinson, from his book *Science Versus Crime* © 1935 by The Bobbs-Merrill Company, Inc.

To Louise, Dale, David and Dick,
And
To all those men and women who write our laws,
And
To those who enforce them,
And
To those who obey them.

The Line-up

Manhunt

by ROBERT M. YODER

One of the bandits was dead—and with him died the link to the other two. But the tireless Postal Inspectors began again on their relentless pursuit of the boastful machine gunner, the chief murderer in the notorious Bruce Case. That the Postal Inspectors' chief weapon was a printing machine did not matter in the long run—they got their man!

T HE PURSUIT OF ERNIE MORRIS—in the manhunt known as The Bruce Case—was curious in that the pursuers were stationary, patiently allowing this bandit a great deal of freedom, while the wanted man, though he didn't know it, came home to them trustingly five times. The second phase of the greatest manhunt United States Post Office Inspectors have performed brought a reversal of roles.

This time it was the pursuers who roved the entire country while the criminals enjoyed lives of the most smug respectability.

One-third of the problem had been resolved, bloodily and not to the Inspectors' satisfaction. They had identified Ernie Morris, a Kentucky gunman, as one of the three who robbed the United States mail of twenty-five thousand dollars in Guthrie, Kentucky. But on a silken and moonlit night, just

1

to the rear of a rose garden, Morris had proved with a .45 that he meant it when he said he would die fighting.

He was no good to them dead. Now, thirteen weeks after the robbery, there remained the job of finding and capturing two machine-gunning brothers who had been Morris' confederates—Floyd Bruce and his younger brother, Ray. There remained so much to be done, though no one knew it, that the case would become a classic in the one-hundred-year history of the Inspection Service.

The Bruces were only names when this operation began. The Inspectors set out cheerfully to know them very well. For one thing, Inspectors all over the country had to be advised. For another, the pursuers intended to use their great bloodless weapon, the reward circular.

As a part of their scholarly inquiry, the Inspectors listed every town the Bruces ever had visited, every man and woman the brothers visited there. This directory ran four or five pages. Here and there glinted the name of a celebrity— Bugs Moran, the Chicago bootlegger, Earl Shelton, of the Shelton gang. And from bits picked up here and there a likeness began to emerge. It was dim, at first, but the first word sent out to brother Inspectors showed the Bruce biographers were beginning to know their subject. They had, of course, never seen the Bruces.

Floyd—this fill-in said—is the older, thirty-seven. He is five feet eight, lightly built. He likes good clothes and good cars. He walks with a swagger and likes to act tough. This isn't entirely a pose. He sometimes wears his hat turned up all around; he finds fault with food and drink in restaurants. He fancies rimless glasses as a disguise, though his eyesight is very good. He is an exceptionally good automobile driver. He is something of a romanticist about crime. He might boast of a bulletproof sedan he once had, with a tricky button to open a special gun compartment. He is authentically brave and dangerously good with guns.

He will have a girl with him—this letter of introduction
went on. She may be his wife; we don't yet know. Her name
is Helen. She is twenty-two. She is slight, with dark hair and
eyes; she isn't tough looking. She comes from Pierce City,
Missouri; she lisps a little. She is fond of driving, but doesn't
drive well. She likes dogs. Mark that commonplace fact. It
caused the Bruces a great deal of grief and was a great con-
venience to the Inspectors. Now as for Ray Bruce—this bulletin went on—he is twenty-seven, plays golf, and so on.

The Bruces had been arrested, though not recently, and
mugged. The pictures were ten years old and terrible like-
nesses. They would have to do. The Inspectors issued the
first of their reward circulars. These always begin with an
eye-catching dollar sign. The standard rate is two thousand
dollars a head. So above the pictures of Floyd and Ray
blazed the simple invitation, "$4000 Reward."

It sounds ineffectual. Actually, the Inspectors were beginning a process that would undermine the Bruces as it
has undermined many another. The Inspectors were setting
out to make the Bruces famous. This would be accomplished
by circulars and more circulars and still more circulars.
Against men who rob the mail there is brought to bear the
whole Postal Service. The process begins by sending the circulars to peace officers and post offices, for posting on bulletin boards. But as more and more are printed, with better,
fresher information, they go to hotels, tourist homes, rooming houses, filling stations, garages, used-car lots, restaurants,
saloons and general stores. Just in case the Bruces wanted a
haircut in the next few months, the Inspectors also intended
to make their faces well known in barber shops. Then would
come vacation resorts and possibly grocery, cigar and drug
stores. The Inspectors have never yet put a circular in every
mailbox in the United States, but it is entirely feasible.

The circulars make a man "hot"—not simply with the

police but with the great, unarmed, curious and observant public. They confer a nerve-racking kind of renown. Floyd Bruce was a vain man who liked having it known that he amounted to something. But this kind of celebrity gave him nightmares.

Up went the circulars—not many, at first—and in came the tips.

The Bruces were "seen," of course, from coast to coast. From Chief Inspector Clifton Garner on down, ask any Inspector in the service if he had a part in The Bruce Case and he is almost certain to say something like this: "Oh, sure. I wasn't in on the main hunt. I just ran down tips. I remember waiting one night in a hillbilly cabin just because some mountain girl was sure her new boy friend was one of the Bruces. He wasn't."

Nobody came up with the right tip—at first.

About May twenty-seventh, five months after the robbery, a Mr. and Mrs. Howard P. Baxley bought the Four Points filling station four miles east of San Antonio, Texas. Baxley had a small line of groceries, bakery goods and soft drinks, and what the neighbors didn't know was that he had a hobby: he pulled a few burglaries. This Baxley was a great one to gab.

He would tell anyone who would listen how he used to be a rumrunner—yes, sir, driving that liquor all over these United States. He was a little nervous. He smoked a lot, sometimes sat up all night, kept his car parked beside a bedroom window. He worried about his digestion and his teeth, too; thought he had pyorrhea. Friendly people, the Baxleys. Baxley and his wife Helen made a good many friends.

A few days later, a Mr. and Mrs. J. C. Adams—another nice young couple—bought a chicken farm five miles south of St.

Augustine, Florida. They set to work diligently to improve the place, especially with a floodlight, an unusually stout fence and a watch dog. They weren't as sociable as the Baxleys. Mr. Adams—a fellow about twenty-seven—had a strange aversion to using the rural-delivery mailbox. He would never let his wife mail anything there, and even hated to take anything out of it. You'd have thought Mr. Adams had some grievance against the United States mail.

None of this the Inspectors knew. All summer long they ran down bum tips. That was all right with them; it meant the circulars were getting attention. They had begun to make the Bruces famous. But summer waned and the Inspectors had no trail. Inspector E. J. Holmes, of Chicago, became the "coordinator." All tips came to him. They came from California to Maine, but the one that paid off came one glowing October afternoon from a Chicago suburb.

"I'm a taxi driver," said a voice on the phone. "But I used to have a filling station near San Antonio. I sold it last spring for six hundred dollars."

"Yes?"

"To that fellow in your pictures, Floyd Bruce. He called himself Baxley."

Taking the cab driver with them, two Inspectors from Illinois raced almost nonstop 1243 miles from Chicago to San Antonio. The filling station was vacant. They found the real-estate man. The Baxleys? Why, they sold out about the middle of September. The Inspectors found the Baxleys' apartment. The Baxleys had lingered in San Antonio until October third—six days before the Inspectors' arrival.

Fortunately, Howard and Helen Baxley had been delightfully indiscreet. They had mentioned that they might go to Florida, to visit Howard's brother—thus giving the Inspectors their first line on Ray. The Baxley-Bruces were running from a murder charge. Would they so forget themselves as to send postcards to old friends in San Antonio? People being what they are, the Inspectors thought this likely. And sure enough, one day after the Inspectors' arrival, in came the cards. Floyd and Helen were in Pensacola. The happy tourists reported that their dog Tippie had behaved well on the trip. The Inspectors hurried to join them.

First, however, these lovers of detail took time to learn still more about their quarry. That dog Tippie might be useful as a means of identification. Tippie was half fox terrier and half hound, black and white. The Inspectors got a picture of her litter sister, as if they intended to send out another of their circulars, this time to all dog lovers, all kennels, and possibly all hounds and fox terriers. They never used the photo. Patient questioning established the fact that Tippie didn't look much like her sister.

"Baxley" had complained about his teeth. The Inspectors found his dentist, and made Floyd's dentition the subject of another of their circulars, this time to dentists. In a few days every dentist in the South knew that Floyd Bruce might be using any of a variety of names, but would undoubtedly be using a set of (his own) very hard teeth corresponding to Shade No. 4 on the 20th Century Shade Guide. There is a large mesial occlusal silver filling in the upper left third molar, and so on. To make it dangerous for Floyd to go to a dentist anywhere, his dental chart was published in a dentists' professional journal. The Inspectors were beginning now to chop down every cornstalk behind which the rabbits might find cover.

By October twenty-first the Inspectors knew Ray Bruce was the J. C. Adams running the chicken farm, with two hundred fifty hens and a mailbox he avoided as if it were radioactive. But their beautiful detective work won them only disappointment. They were two days too late. Ray had driven away on October nineteenth.

But his wife Edith was there, and so was Floyd's wife Helen. The Inspectors knew very little about Edith and had no good pictures with which to make her an uncomfortable celebrity. They improved their waiting hours by learning where she bought groceries and gasoline. Then they parked nearby and took snapshots with a telescopic-lens camera.

That Floyd and Ray would visit the farm seemed too much to hope, and was. Instead, Edith was trying to sell out. That would require a deed, of course, and "Adams" had signed one in advance. There weren't many prospective buyers, especially after the Inspectors got through shooing them away. The best of the lot was an affable man who thought this might be just the place for his family. He liked the size— a house and three acres—he admired the new bathroom and the new electric pump. He was ready to buy. But his lawyer, that thoroughly fictitious fuss-budget, found a defect in the title. It would require another deed. When did Mrs. Adams think her husband would be back?

Mrs. Adams didn't know, but thought she could promise another deed in thirty days. The buyer made her post one hundred dollars as a guarantee. There was no identifying the money, but you could be pretty sure these bills were long overdue at the Federal Reserve Bank in Louisville. The buyer was of course an Inspector, Sylvester Hetrick.

It was a good try, but nothing could coax Ray back to the chickens. And Edith hauled out, chickens or no chickens, on the evening of October twenty-seventh, taking Helen with her.

The Inspectors sighed. This would have been a fine place to close with the Bruces. The girls obviously were setting out to meet the boys. If they could be followed, they would lead the Inspectors to one or even both.

But the girls were too cagey to be followed in the ordinary sense. It would be necessary to accompany them invisibly. The most subtle form of fast-moving watch would have to be set. It would take men by the dozens. Still, it would be worth it.

Thus the Mesdames Bruce, and party, set out.

There were from fifteen to twenty-five Inspectors in the pack, in various localities. Trying to keep both ahead of and behind the girls shortly had the Inspectors hollow-eyed from lack of sleep. It was the Inspectors who were living like fugitives, and who looked it. Along with trailing the little car like a somewhat substantial cloud, they ran ahead at times to make sure tourist camps had a cabin for the girls.

Fortunately, it was not going to be hard for anyone to spot the car. It was a two-door coach of a common make. But the girls took Tippie. Better still—and the Inspectors blessed them for this—they took another dog as well. The second was Cappie, a mixture of chow and Airedale. Two girls and two dogs—that was going to make a nicely noticeable grouping.

Helen and Edith stopped for the night at Madison, Florida, about one hundred miles on their way, whatever their way was. So did a large retinue of Inspectors, determined that at no time in the next few days or weeks or months would Helen and Edith see the same men twice, or the same car. The Inspectors traveled in from ten to twelve cars; their police helpers used as many.

And the job was going to be as delicate as herding butterflies. To begin with, these were no innocent schoolgirls, though they looked innocent enough. Helen carried an automatic as well as a compact. The girls were alert against being followed. Each day in setting out they "shook a tail." They might head east, turn south on a side road, and end up driving west. The only way to know where they were going was to watch every turn. The Inspectors enlisted state and local police, and then called up their great reserves—the postmasters, the mail clerks, the carriers.

As the girls headed east, they passed a man sitting on a bridge, fishing. He went to a phone and reported to an Inspector who was director of traffic. When the girls turned south, they passed a man having a cool drink at a roadside stand. He put a nickel in the phone and said, in effect, "They went thataway." It meant putting men at every junction in all directions, before the girls set out in the morning. But in this difficult operation the Inspectors had the unconscious cooperation of Helen and Edith, who made it easier by driving a sedate thirty miles an hour. So as not to attract attention, of course.

The girls were in no hurry; they sometimes paused for two days, holding up a considerable procession. Starting and stopping, this curious cavalcade wound across Florida, through Alabama, into Mississippi, into Louisiana, out of Louisiana, back again. The Inspectors came to know their wards so well they could often pick the tourist camp Helen and Edith would choose.

The Inspectors checked in, one or two of them, an hour or so earlier. Sometimes they made use of a gadget Inspector L. C. Kirkpatrick had been asked to bring down from Chicago. It looked like a portable radio. What it tuned in was the conversation in the girls' cabin.

What the listeners hoped to hear, of course, was where and when this meeting with Floyd and Ray would be held. Then they could take leave of the girls and get on with the capture. All they got out of it was acute embarrassment. They heard all manner of private feminine talk. Never once did the girls say anything that would do the Inspectors a speck of good.

Every morning the watch was posted on the roads; every afternoon Inspectors raced ahead to watch the girls stop for the night. Not once did the girls show any indication that they thought themselves under surveillance, which is something of a tribute to an awkward procedure skillfully executed. But the girls did get out of sight. Their retinue lost them on November fourth in Hammond, Louisiana, but picked them up again two days later in New Orleans. The girls eluded them again on November tenth; again it took two days to bring them back under the eye. The night of the twelfth Helen and Edith took a cabin near Gulfport, Mississippi. And the hunters—pretty tired of this continuous Ladies' Day—rubbed their hands.

On other nights the Inspectors' darlings had preferred a cabin back from the road. Tonight they asked for one right on the highway. Thanks to influential friends they never knew they had, they got just what they wanted. They also got a microphone. Now, if ever, they ought to say something useful. They didn't.

But that night Helen parked the car a new way—at a sharp right angle to the highway, nosing out where it would be conspicuous. It was clearly a signal. The next day should do it.

In fiction it might. What really happened was that seventeen days of beautiful shadowing blew up in the Inspectors' faces. One of their amateur helpers let himself be hoodwinked.

The two-door coach rolled out onto U.S. 90 and headed for Mobile. This was duly reported. The girls turned around and traveled west through Bay St. Louis. They crossed a long bridge. One of the bums idling there was an Inspector, and he phoned in.

But beyond the bridge there was a fork. A postmaster was posted there. The girls turned to the left. He so reported. What he didn't see was that 200 yards down the road they took a side street back to the right fork. Nobody picked them up after that, on the day that should have brought the sleep-

less Inspectors face to face with the Bruce brothers who had
robbed the United States mail.

As the hours went on with no report, the Inspectors all but
blew their tops. The silence could mean only one thing.
Helen and Edith had left the road and at this minute were
meeting one or even both of the Bruces nearby.

Forced to guess where, the Inspectors guessed New Orleans. Driving toward Mobile would be the girls' roundabout
way of preparing for a meeting in New Orleans, and Helen
and Edith had looked at apartments there. Sore at themselves, the Inspectors went to New Orleans in a mood to tear
down every wall. Beginning at the city limits, the angry Inspectors began canvassing every street to left and right of
the route.

While the Inspectors were wearing out their tires and their
tempers, Helen and Edith turned into a woods and met
Floyd and Ray. It must have been a touching reunion.

"Why, what did we do wrong?" the girls asked in wifely
innocence.

"You travel with that screwy-looking dog and you ask
what you did wrong! Why didn't you carry a neon sign?"

"Why, we had two dogs until just this morning," one of
the wives would have remarked, just to prove there couldn't
be anything wrong with having one dog. "We had a pretty
black-and-white fox terrier. We gave her to the people at a
tourist camp."

"I gave Helen hell," Floyd Bruce said moodily some
weeks later, "and shot the Airedale."

When they shook their followers, the girls had been
heading straight for the meeting. In another hour or so they
would have led the Inspectors directly to their quarry. For
the woods in which this meeting was held—there was eloquent swearing when this became known—was just outside
Bay St. Louis.

The Inspectors found the terrier, of course, which made

them sorer. They beat the New Orleans woods for almost two weeks, getting nowhere. On November twenty-seventh, Chicago sent word that explained it. The car had been abandoned in the Chicago suburb of Cicero. The Northern Inspectors turned back North, the Southerners returned to desks they hadn't seen for a month or more. They had come very, very close. But it was one of those misses that hurts far worse than a mile.

The Inspectors put out another edition of their circulars. Mostly they turned to other duties—to mail-fraud cases, mailbox robberies, the old routine. The next two months produced nothing except a couple of sterling examples of the letdowns of real police work as compared to the brisk decisive investigation of fiction.

Hunting patiently through high-school annuals in Joliet, Illinois, the Inspectors learned the real name of Ray's wife Edith. They went to her home. Edith was there. Ray had brought her home, telling her, "I don't want you with me. You're getting too damned well-known." Edith was there, but so was the FBI, which had some kind of charge against her for possessing a stolen weapon. The Inspectors thought her more important for possessing a machine-gunning husband they needed. They would have let her alone, to lead them to Ray.

Actually, the brothers had separated. After leaving Edith in Joliet, Ray drove to Texas, with no purpose except to keep moving. As for Floyd, his sunny optimism was fraying fast. He began to run.

Leaving Chicago in December, he began to drive, aimlessly but hard. Helen was with him. She was becoming a little famous herself. She had been a waitress. The editors of a restaurant magazine had printed her picture—watch for this girl. And Floyd's picture seemed to be everywhere.

It wasn't. The Inspectors had distributed one million three hundred thousand circulars. But there were still tourist homes, even, which didn't know of Helen's habit of locking the glove compartment when she left the car or that the luggage would include a long case, covered in imitation leather, containing one Thompson submachine gun with box and drum.

Even so, a great many people seemed to look twice at Floyd. And which of his friends wouldn't turn him in for two thousand dollars?

He headed for Texas; he turned back toward the Midwest. It was his habit to drive one thousand miles at a stretch. In the spring he began hiding the car in the woods, under branches. He must have been an oddly citified figure to meet in the brush. He knew the obligations of position, and dressed as a gunman should. He favored a black double-breasted overcoat, a black hat, a quiet-color double-breasted suit. The only touch of flash he allowed himself was the .45 he carried in his right overcoat pocket—nickel-plated, with a pearl handle.

Ironically, in this final, skittering flight of his, nobody was chasing him. At no time that winter were the Inspectors on his heels. They ground out their circulars and waited for a lead. Floyd himself supplied it. In February he grew to hate automobiles, which he thought could betray him. He began buying cheap used models, driving them as little as three or four days. Sheriffs here and there reported a whole trail of abandoned cars. The Inspectors reached for their hats.

In March, a customer failed to call for a car parked in a garage at Springfield, Illinois. The garageman identified him as Floyd. The Inspectors went out like fanatic bill peddlers. They papered Central Illinois with their circulars. City carriers and rural carriers gave one to every tourist home, garage, used-car lot, café, saloon, gas station, dentist and barber.

It was the full distribution this time, the full publicity treatment.

On March fifteenth the Inspectors began doing this in Bloomington, Illinois, and suburban Normal, which adjoins it. Sometime that afternoon the mailman handed some of this literature to the landlady of a tourist home in Normal. She had some regular roomers, usually salesmen on small budgets, along with the transients. A group of the regulars spent the dinner hour discussing the circulars and snapshots.

"Boy!" said a book salesman. "How would you like to have four thousand dollars walk in here?"

As if on cue, the doorbell rang. A well-dressed man in his thirties asked about a room for the night. With him was his wife, considerably younger. Nobody thought anything about it. The salesman looked on idly as the last piece of luggage vanished up the stairs. It was a sample case apparently, long, covered with imitation leather.

The salesman's eyes bulged and he reached for the circular. The man in the picture was a hick. But did the man upstairs look like his successful city cousin? Was the girl about five feet six, weighing maybe a hundred and seven pounds, with big brown eyes?

"It's them," the salesman declared. The landlady, somewhat unhappily, agreed. They were not sure enough to call the police. Maybe if they got another look in the morning.

March can be cold or bland in Central Illinois, and next morning it was cold. In Bloomington the four Inspectors working the area set out to cover the hotels. In Normal, Floyd got one of those small bad breaks which until now had all gone to the Inspectors. His car wouldn't start.

The book salesman, a bold little wight, offered to push the stranger's car to a filling station. Meanwhile the landlady would call the police. Floyd said grumpily he'd be glad for the help. But now the salesman's car wouldn't start, he said.

It was perhaps ten minutes before the two cars rolled into the gas station. The salesman backed out again, fast.

The well-dressed traveler in the black overcoat got out. So did the brown-haired girl who didn't look tough. Her husband opened the hood. Four cars raced into the station from two directions, as if this were the finish line of some kind of race. It was. When Floyd looked up he was surrounded by police and deputies. The sheriff was on hand, and so were at least four men who looked like members of the Normal Rotary Club. Except that one had Helen's purse, in which she carried a trim little .25 automatic, and another had a large .45 low in Floyd's back.

That left Ray. He lasted only nine days longer.

"Fellow I locked up for being drunk," said the sheriff at Ellaville, Georgia, "threatens to turn the Bruce boys loose on me. He's just a country boy, but rough. Tells a real wild story. Crazy enough to be true."

The Bruce brothers, according to the drunk, intended to set up in a backroad cabin between Ellaville and Montezuma to rob banks. Fanciful as it was, it checked with other tips that Ray had begun "running like a rabbit" after Floyd's capture, but was heading toward his home state of Georgia.

Ray was sighted near Ellaville on March twenty-third. Now, after so many tantalizing misses, the Inspectors were in full control of this game. Inspector Rudolph Greer had been there, off and on, since March first, waiting for Ray. Two days later, Greer, the sheriff and two highway patrolmen put two cars across a country road. Ray was in a tenant farmer's house. But so were the farmer, his wife and four children. Ray was cut off from the machine gun, which was in his car. But he had the hunting rifle and his pistols. He could fire. For the police, it would be like shooting into a schoolroom.

In this impasse, Greer and the sheriff decided they might

as well ask the impossible. "Tell the man to come out!" they called. "The woods are full of police officers!"

Inside, Ray trained the deer rifle on Greer. The farmer's wife tugged his arm sharply. "You ain't going to kill nobody in my house," she said.

For fifteen minutes nothing happened, which surprised no one outside. Then the family filed out, followed by Ray, his hands up. "My guns are inside!" he called. Greer doubted it; he could see the .38 in Ray's right pants pocket. He and the sheriff approached with shotguns. Ray lowered his right hand a trifle. "Do that again," they told him, "and we'll shoot it off."

That fanciful tale the drunk told, Ray said, was true, though Floyd's capture had upset the plans.

The Bruce jury was out just thirty minutes.

The assortment of charges included transporting stolen currency and the theft of Registered Article 195. The sentence was fifty-seven years, to be served in Alcatraz.

It satisfied the Inspectors, who are not bloodthirsty but only determined that nobody shall rob the mail, whether of twenty-five thousand dollars or a three-cent stamp or somebody's post card from Yosemite. They marked Case 126086 D—"d" for "depredation"—closed. Out went new notices to all postmasters:

"The circulars in this case should now be removed."

I Remember John Dillinger

by MELVIN PURVIS

One of the men who helped build the present image of the Federal Bureau of Investigation was a young man from South Carolina, Melvin Purvis, not long out of college when he joined the Bureau. He was soon chosen by J. Edgar Hoover to be Agent-in-Charge of the Chicago Field Office during the early '30's. Thus, he was in the vanguard of the FBI's crusade against gangsterism. On the following pages is one of the most memorable chapters in FBI history —the head-on clash between society and the man who was possibly the most brazen outlaw in our history, John Dillinger.

JOHN DILLINGER was born in Mooresville, Indiana. His father was a farmer. His mother died when he was three. Shortly after that, the father moved to Indianapolis, where he operated a grocery store. When Dillinger was sixteen, he and his father moved back to Mooresville.

Four years later, he and another Mooresville boy, Ed Singleton, hatched a plan to rob an elderly storekeeper named Frank Morgan. They found it easy enough to rob the old man. Confronted with a gun, he handed over the store's receipts. Nevertheless, after getting the money, Dillinger hit him over the head with a lead pipe.

17

Both Singleton and Dillinger were recognized, and later identified by Morgan. Singleton entered a plea of "Guilty." Turning state's evidence, he received a lighter sentence than Dillinger, who was sentenced to serve ten-to-twenty years at the Pendleton, Indiana, Reformatory.

In the reformatory, Dillinger came in contact with more hardened and experienced criminals, and learned from them. After two unsuccessful attempts to escape, he was transferred to the Indiana State Penitentiary, at Michigan City. If Pendleton was his high school of crime, Michigan City was his university. Here he became fast friends with Russell Clark, John Hamilton, Charles Makley and Harry Pierpont, all serving long terms.

After nine years of imprisonment, all those responsible for sending Dillinger to jail were willing to sign a petition for his parole. Presented to the governor, it was signed, and Dillinger was freed on May 22, 1933.

When parole seemed in the offing for Dillinger, his pals— Clark, Hamilton, Makley and Pierpont—made plans for escape. On the morning of September 26, 1933, Pierpont and Clark informed John Stevens, superintendent of the prison shirt factory, that one of the guards wanted to see him. When Stevens arrived in the basement, he was seized by Hamilton, Makley, and six other convicts. A few minutes later, Assistant Warden Fred Evans accidentally walked in, and was also captured.

Using Evans and Stevens as hostages, the ten convicts started marching calmly toward the gate. Other guards noticed them, of course, but paid little attention because the two officials were walking naturally—thanks to the prisoners' concealed guns, which earlier had been smuggled into the penitentiary by Dillinger.

The escape went off without a hitch.

Once out, though, the escapees were faced with a problem. After a series of bank robberies in Indiana, Dillinger had just been apprehended in Dayton, Ohio, and transferred to the county jail at Lima.

Dillinger had helped them. Now, they decided to return the favor. On October 12, 1933, Makley, Clark, and Pierpont entered the office of Sheriff Jesse Sarber at Lima, and informed him they were officers who'd come to return prisoner Dillinger to Michigan City Penitentiary. The sheriff asked for their credentials. In answer, all three drew pistols. Sheriff Sarber was shot down before he could draw his own gun. Makley, Clark, and Pierpont got the keys to the cells from Sarber's pocket, found Dillinger, and left with him in command.

Now this new gang went into action.

They robbed banks at Greencastle, Indiana; Racine, Wisconsin; Chicago, Illinois; East Chicago, Indiana; New Castle, Ohio; Montpelier, Indiana; Farrell, Pennsylvania; and Bluffton, Ohio, to name only a few. It's impossible to determine the gang's exact number of robberies, and its incredible amount of loot. It likewise is impossible to determine definitely the number of people killed by the gang during those crimes.

It is definitely known, though, that Dillinger killed Policeman William P. O'Malley during the robbery of the First National Bank in East Chicago, Indiana, on January 15, 1934. Dillinger and John Hamilton, both carrying machine guns, were positively identified. It was also definitely determined that Hamilton killed William Shanley in a North Side garage in Chicago.

Dillinger headquartered in Chicago during November and December, 1933. On New Year's Day, he and six others held up a Chicago night club. Police arrived as they were escaping. In the ensuing battle, two policemen were killed.

Wanted by local police in many states, Dillinger and his gang fled Chicago. They regrouped late in January, 1934, meeting at the Congress Hotel, in Tucson, Arizona. Again they had to flee when the hotel went up in flames. Firemen entering their rooms saw guns and other articles of gang warfare. Later they identified the gangsters.

A few days later, police seized Russell Clark in a Tucson bungalow he'd just rented. That same day, Harry Pierpont was arrested by three Tucson policemen at a tourist camp. Within a week, Makley and Dillinger were also captured without fireworks.

Pierpont, Clark, and Makley, identified as the slayers of Sheriff Sarber, were turned over to Ohio authorities. Dillinger, identified as the killer of Officer O'Malley during the East Chicago bank robbery, was put in the custody of Indiana officials. They flew him from Tucson to Chicago, then brought him in manacles to the jail at Crown Point, Indiana.

A cordon of deputies, armed with machine guns and other weapons, was brought to Crown Point to make sure Dillinger didn't escape this time. The prosecutor at Lake County announced that Dillinger's trial for murder while committing a robbery would begin on February 13. Conviction carried the mandatory sentence of death. Dillinger's lawyers arranged for a postponement of the trial on technical legal grounds.

On March 3, 1934, I was in my office in Chicago when a *Chicago Tribune* reporter called me. He asked if I'd heard that John Dillinger had just escaped from Crown Point. I hadn't. I immediately called Mrs. Holley, the sheriff at that small Indiana town. She was "unavailable," but one of the deputies confirmed the report. I teletyped Director J. Edgar Hoover in Washington, then finally managed to get Mrs. Holley on the phone. I asked her for the license number of the car in which Dillinger escaped—a car belonging to her. She gave me the number. I promptly alerted all law officers in the area.

Shortly afterward, it turned out Mrs. Holley gave me the wrong license number.

There were many stories about how Dillinger escaped. Some said he bought his way out with cash. Others maintained he got away by holding his guards at the point of a wooden gun which they mistook for the real thing. How he escaped made little difference officially to the FBI. When the sheriff's stolen car was found across the Indiana state line at Peotone, Illinois, John Dillinger came under our authorized jurisdiction for the first time.

Now, the FBI organized its forces and began a manhunt. We made new contacts, using new underworld informants. Every spot Dillinger had ever been was covered or "planted."

> [To "plant" a place is to station a Special Agent in concealment, usually in a rented room or apartment overlooking the planted place, so that it may be kept under close, constant scrutiny.]

Many tips were received. Some were valid. Some were "spite" tips from people desiring to embarrass someone else —perhaps a neighbor against whom the person had a grudge. Some were from cranks who dreamed they'd seen Dillinger. Others came from fortunetellers who'd received a vision and a message. We had no way of determining from the glint in an informant's eye whether the tip was legitimate or not. Therefore, each had to be investigated. All told, we received more than a thousand such tips.

Then came April 22, 1934—a day to remember.

At about one o'clock that Sunday afternoon, the phone in my apartment rang. It was the United States Marshal in Chicago calling. He said a man named Voss, at Rhinelander, Wisconsin, desired to furnish important information. I called Mr. Voss.

"The man you want most is up here," he said.

"You mean Dillinger?" I asked.

At first, he didn't want to mention that name over the phone. Finally, he told me the gangster and some of his gang were at a resort called Little Bohemia. I asked the location of the nearest airport.

"Rhinelander," he said, "and that's fifty miles away."

I told him to wait at the airport, and to wear a handkerchief around his neck so I could identify him quickly and surely when we got there. Then, I called my office, and issued instructions to have every man report immediately. I also called Director Hoover in Washington. He sent word to the St. Paul Field Office to send additional men to help me. Within minutes, autos loaded with Special Agents started for Rhinelander from Chicago and St. Paul. The SAC in St. Paul chartered a plane. I chartered two, then called my office again and ordered trunks to be loaded with weapons, bulletproof vests, and tear gas equipment.

Now, only some four hours later, we were all here in this almost unknown speck on the map.

The Special Agents who'd flown in from St. Paul had already begun to obtain automobiles to take us to Little Bohemia. I located my telephone informant with the handkerchief tucked into his collar.

"Dillinger, five of his gang, and four women are at Little Bohemia," he told me. "They've been there since noon on Friday, and they're planning to pull out tomorrow morning."

Voss told me that Emil Wanatka, his brother-in-law, was the proprietor of Little Bohemia, and that Wanatka, his wife, their eight-year-old son, and two employees were being held in fear of their lives. Wanatka had placed a note in a package of cigarettes, and given the package to Voss. On the note was the information about Dillinger, and a request that Voss get in touch with the authorities.

From Voss' story, it appeared we'd have enough time to surround Little Bohemia properly before the following morning. One Agent was sent with Mr. Voss, with instructions to wait at the Voss home, about two miles from Little Bohemia. A friend who'd come to Rhinelander with Voss agreed to accompany us and point out the resort.

While we were still unloading the planes and making preliminary plans, Voss came rushing back onto the landing field, shouting my name. I quieted him, praying silently that Dillinger had no friends in the crowd.

"I just met my wife on the road," Voss told me excitedly. "She found out since I left the house that Dillinger has changed his plans. He's pulling out after dinner tonight."

By now, it was 6:30 and dark. Dillinger and his pals had probably already started to eat—and we had fifty miles to go through a bitter April night over bad, back-country roads. We didn't even have enough automobiles yet. I knew we couldn't possibly reach Little Bohemia in time to survey the territory and properly surround the place. We couldn't even wait for the Agents en route by car.

All we could do was try to get to Little Bohemia as soon as possible—and hope it was soon enough.

The town of Rhinelander was several miles from the flying field. Looking around desperately, I spotted a young man whose name turned out to be Isadore Tuchalsky. He was at the airport in a Ford coupe with his wife. I asked him to drive me into town. He did. When we got there, we learned it was impossible to rent five automobiles in Rhinelander on a Sunday. I tried to rent Tuchalsky's car. He refused, not knowing who we were, of course. When I told him, he insisted on lending us the car without charge. We then commandeered and rented four other cars.

We gathered in the darkness and made our hasty, last-minute plans. Six men were to follow me and attack the front door at Little Bohemia. The other ten were to split and move in from the sides. There was a lake behind the inn with no boats in it, so escape in that direction was impossible.

The roads to Little Bohemia were even worse than we expected, and the night became wretchedly cold. The cars were driven at a reasonable distance from each other to avoid suspicions. Before we'd gone half way, two of the cars broke down. The eight Agents in them were forced to stand on the running boards of the other three cars, hanging on for their lives. The cars still rolling were now heavily loaded with Agents, machine guns, rifles, shotguns, tear gas equipment, and, of course, the small arms each Agent carried.

Finally, our guide said we were two miles from Little Bohemia. I called a halt. All lights were extinguished. Agents were instructed not to smoke. Then we proceeded slowly through the crowded, unfamiliar timber and the frigid blackness.

Little Bohemia is located about 400 yards off the so-called highway, in the center of a wild hunting and fishing area. A single driveway leads to it from the road. The lodge, built of rustic logs, is surrounded on three sides by heavy forest, and at the rear by a lake. Among the trees on the right side is a group of small guest cottages.

We drove to the driveway entrance and parked two cars in a V to block the road. The Agents and I, swinging our chilled arms and rubbing our hands, got our weapons ready. Through the thick, bare limbs of the trees, we could see, at the far end of the driveway, the brightly lit front door of the roadhouse.

My men and I began to move toward our positions when disaster struck. Dogs began to bark loudly.

Immediately, five men appeared at the front of the lodge. Three hurried into a car parked there, the other two running back inside. I instructed every man to abandon all caution, and to proceed to his position as quickly as possible.

I yelled to the men in the car that we were Federal officers and ordered them to halt. They answered by trying to run through us. We fired. The car slowed down. As it did, one of the men jumped out and ran into the woods. Another tumbled out, wounded. The third slumped over the wheel as the car ran off the driveway into a tree. I crawled up to the car while other Agents covered me with machine guns. The driver was dead. The other two got back into the lodge.

In the meantime, the men going to the right of the inn were delayed by two barbed-wire fences. The men going to the left of the house were held up by a drainage ditch, invisible in the darkness. Those of us in front now moved up to a point at the edge of a clearing—and just outside the arc of light coming from a bright floodlight over the front door.

Gunfire began from the upper stories on the left side of the lodge. For a moment, I didn't notice the flash of fire from another sector. Then a bullet hit the ground a yard from my right foot. Two other bullets struck trees right behind me. The shots were coming from the vicinity of a small cabin on the right. I whirled around and squeezed the trigger of my machine gun. It jammed almost immediately. I threw it aside. With an automatic pistol, I returned the fire of a short, slender figure fleeing toward the woods. I was trading shots with Baby Face Nelson.

For a time, the noise was deafening. The Agents on the left side of the lodge, after scrambling out of the ditch, found themselves being fired on. Naturally, they answered. For what seemed an endless interval, there wasn't even a small pocket of quiet.

Then, abruptly, the firing from the roadhouse ceased. We didn't know it, of course, but Dillinger and the other hoodlums were scrambling out a rear second-story window, moving toward the right side of the lodge, and through the brush at the lakefront to freedom.

I shouted, commanding those in the house to come out. Finally, Mr. Wanatka and two waiters came through the front door with their hands up. Naturally very excited and frightened, they told me four men were still in the house.

The ominous silence lent color to the report that the gangsters were readying themselves for our attack. Since we had the place covered, I decided first to attend to the Agents wounded during the earlier firing before lobbing our tear gas shells through the lodge's windows. I sent Special Agents Jay Newman and Carter Baum to the nearest phone—at a country store owned by a man named Koerner—to get word to the Agents coming to Little Bohemia by car, and to call an ambulance from a nearby government camp.

Wanatka and the two waiters told us all they could about the layout inside the lodge, in case we had to fight a room-to-room battle. Then, as his excitement subsided, Wanatka began to suffer from the bitter cold. He left to go to a nearby friend's house for a coat. In a few minutes, he came running back, panting that "someone is holding up your men at Koerner's."

I sent two Agents to check. They returned with tragic news. Special Agent Carter Baum had been killed, and both Agent Jay Newman and local constable Carl Christenson had been severely wounded by one of the Dillinger gang.

We learned that Baum, Newman and Christenson, on arriving at Koerner's store, had seen a parked car with three men in it. Christenson told them it was Koerner's car. As the two Agents and the constable neared the store, a figure moved out from behind the parked car and started firing. It was Baby Face Nelson. After killing Agent Baum, and critically wounding the other two, Nelson leaped into the Agents' car and roared off into the night.

At the lodge, it soon became evident that all the other gangsters had escaped, for the sky was now getting light, and still no bullets came at our now exposed position. We moved in and searched the place. It was true. The raid had failed.

I called Director Hoover in Washington. He ordered me to leave a group of Agents in the area to investigate further, and to return with the others to our offices.

We knew, of course, that Baby Face Nelson and two other members of the gang had gotten away in the car stolen after the ambush at Koerner's store. We soon learned about Dillinger and the other pair of hoodlums. They made their way to Ed Mitchell's Rest Lake Resort, about two miles from Little Bohemia. There they ripped out the phone and forced a guest named Robert Johnson to drive them some thirty-five miles to Park Falls, Wisconsin, where they slugged him and took the car.

[Public dismay at the failure of the Little Bohemia raid was widespread. It even went so far as to include petitions from groups of citizens to Director Hoover which demanded that Purvis be ousted. Hoover ignored the petitions and the angry newspaper editorials crying for Purvis' scalp. The manhunt went on.]

Finally, on July 21, 1934, a hot Saturday afternoon, I got a phone call at the office from Sergeant Zarcovich, of the East Chicago, Indiana, Police Department. He and his superior, Captain O'Neill, wanted to meet me at a secret place. Zarcovich said they had "hot" information.

Special Agent Sam Cowley and I met them in a room at a downtown hotel. They told us a woman named Anna Sage had informed them that Dillinger had been visiting her house periodically with a woman named Polly Hamilton. The three of them, Anna Sage said, occasionally visited a neighborhood theatre.

They agreed to arrange for me to meet Anna Sage. Sergeant Zarcovich and I reached the designated spot—a dark street on the North Side of Chicago—and waited. Captain O'Neill and Agent Cowley were out of sight in a parked car down the street. Soon, Anna Sage appeared. She walked past our car and down the block, as if trying to make sure there was no trap. Then she returned, and on signal, got into our car. We drove a while and finally stopped at a secluded spot beside Lake Michigan.

There she told us the story of her acquaintance with John Dillinger. First, though, she told us about herself.

She'd come to America from her native Rumania. Now, for violation of an Indiana law, she was about to be deported. She had a great fear of being returned to Rumania, and wanted me to have the deportation proceedings called off in return for helping us capture Dillinger. I explained that I had no power to make that promise, but offered to recommend as strongly as I could that she be allowed to stay here if her information proved correct and useful.

She agreed.

Then she said that Dillinger usually didn't stay at her house very long. She told us that she, Polly Hamilton, and Dillinger usually went to the Marbro Theatre, on Chicago's West Side.

We promptly surveyed that theatre, making notes of every entrance, exit and fire escape. A map was drawn and shown to every Special Agent and other law enforcement officers. I set up a special "Dillinger Squad," with myself at the head of it.

The following morning, we all met at the Field Office, and made plans. We discussed every possibility. There was an air of confidence in the room. We knew we were ready for John Dillinger this time. We'd failed at Little Bohemia. We wouldn't miss at the Marbro Theatre.

We were still studying the layout of the Marbro at five o'clock that afternoon when the phone rang. A whispered voice came over the wire. It was Anna Sage.

"He's here," she said. "He just came. We're leaving in a

few minutes." I could feel my palms sweating. Then she added: "We're going to the Marbro—or the Biograph."

The Biograph! We hadn't even thought about that theatre, let alone surveyed it. Two Agents took off immediately to spot every entrance and exit, then to return to the office so we could choose vantage points.

Another Agent and I also went to the Biograph. Two others drove to the Marbro. We were to call the office every five minutes to check on whether Dillinger had been spotted at either movie. When he was, the Agents at the office and the ones at the wrong theatre would speed to already assigned positions.

I selected myself and four others as the first group to close in on Dillinger. If he escaped the five of us, the remaining Agents were to use their own judgment. They were stationed in pairs so as to set up a corridor through which this mad killer would have to run before he could escape again.

The other Agent and I sat in a car about sixty feet south of the entrance to the Biograph Theatre. He left the car every five minutes to call the office. Forty-five minutes passed. Dillinger hadn't been spotted at either theatre. We began to feel this might be another failure.

The small neighborhood movie began to fill rapidly. We kept watching without making any obvious movements that would frighten Dillinger away if he did show up. Suddenly, a man and two women walked past the car. Dillinger, Anna Sage, and another woman. The other Agent left the car and called the office.

After buying tickets, Dillinger and the women entered the theatre. He was wearing dark glasses, a straw sailor hat, gray trousers and no coat. The fact that he wore no coat was encouraging. It meant he couldn't be carrying many concealed weapons. It might've been simple for the two of us to take him as he was going into the theatre. To try that, though, meant gambling the lives of innocent bystanders on the sidewalk and in the lobby. We knew Dillinger's record, his utter ruthlessness, and his entire disregard for the lives of other people.

We let him enter. Then I worried about another problem. There were many women and children going in to see the show at the same time. That meant they'd be leaving when he did. And that, in turn, meant possible shooting in a crowd.

I bought a ticket to the movie, myself, and followed Dillinger into the theatre. I hoped to find three vacant seats behind him—if I could locate him in the darkness. My plan was to have two other Agents join me in those three seats. Then, on signal, one Agent could pin Dillinger's left arm, one his right, and the other his head.

The theatre was jammed, though, and I could find neither empty seats nor Dillinger. There was nothing to do now but wait outside, and cover every exit.

Soon, the other Agents and officers of the East Chicago Police Department arrived. I informed each man of the exact moment Dillinger entered the theatre, and the exact minute he'd come out if he and the women stayed for the entire show.

Two of the East Chicago policemen were stationed on the sidewalk, just north of the theatre lobby. Two Special Agents and I were on the south side. We five would close in on Dillinger when he came out. Every man was instructed to watch me. I was to light a cigar when I positively identified Dillinger. Then, a wave of my hand would be the signal for us to close in and capture him.

Our vigilance couldn't be relaxed for even a split second. Some innocent patron inside might arouse Dillinger's suspicions, and cause him to leave before the show was over. I bit off the end of the cigar and chewed it nervously for an hour. An hour and a half. Two hours. My throat was parched from the cigar, from fright, and from nervousness.

We were doing everything possible to avoid being noticed

by any of the patrons, or the staff of the theatre. Despite our efforts to appear to be just loiterers, the box office cashier spotted us, and feared we were planning to hold up the theatre. None of the staff knew who we were because we'd had no time to check on whether or not they were trustworthy enough to take into our confidence. The cashier called the manager. He in turn called the police.

I can't describe how I felt when, just about the time Dillinger was scheduled to come out, I saw a car pull up in front of the theatre—a car on which appeared the words "Police Department." One of the Agents immediately identified himself, and asked them to remove the car in a hurry. Fortunately, they did.

A minute or so later, a crowd began leaving the theatre. I stood with my cigar shaking in my mouth, a match in my hand ready to light it. My eyes ached from the strain. Finally, John Dillinger came out. On one side of him was Anna Sage; on the other, Polly Hamilton.

Dillinger was surrounded by women and children as the crowd moved out onto the sidewalk. Suddenly, he turned his head and looked right at me. Apparently, he didn't recognize me. I struck the match and lit my cigar.

Then, I waited for what seemed like an endless length of time, hoping against hope the crowd would disperse. As it reached the sidewalk, it did begin to separate. The number of patrons around Dillinger dwindled as he and the two women turned and walked up the street.

I looked toward the two East Chicago policemen, and gave the signal to join us in closing in. They didn't see my signal. They were busy talking to a pedestrian. I took a few steps to the middle of the sidewalk and repeated the signal. They still didn't see it. With extreme relief, I saw two Special Agents, who hadn't been designated as part of the five who were to close in, coming to our assistance.

They moved into position quickly. Dillinger was surrounded. I was about three feet to the left and a little behind him. I was very nervous. My voice was squeaky when I called out:

"Stick 'em up, John. You're surrounded."

Without turning, he drew his .38 automatic. He never got to fire it, though. Shot, he fell with his head in an alley beside the theatre. His gun was still in his right hand as he went down. I leaned over and took the gun. Then I called an ambulance. John Dillinger died on the way to the hospital.

The Oberleutnant

by RICHARD HARRISON

*In "The Oberleutnant," Richard Harrison uses his type
writer like a scalpel to lay open to public inspection the
arrogant contempt for democracy of one Prussian army
officer. In doing so, he also takes us behind the scenes of
one of the most important manhunts in history. Had J.
Edgar Hoover and his men failed on this World War II
assignment, the cause of the Free World might well have
been imperiled.*

Hans peter krug was born in Muchen, Saxony, the son
of an engineer. From his earliest years, he was an enthusi-
astic member of Hitler's various Nazi youth movements.

Finally, at the age of eighteen, he was allowed to enlist
in the German Air Force. By nineteen, he was an *Oberleutnant,* piloting a bomber. He was just past twenty when he
was shot down over London, and captured.

That was on August 28, 1940. Shortly afterwards, he was
shipped to Canada with a group of other Nazi war prisoners,
and placed in the Detention Camp at Bowmanville, Ontario.

On the afternoon of April 16, 1942, he and another captured Luftwaffe lieutenant, Erich Bohle, concealed themselves in a packing case intended for books being shipped
out of camp.

Within hours, the escape was discovered. An alarm went out. All border guards and officials, both Canadian and American, were notified. Bohle was recaptured within twenty-four hours, at Niagara Falls, on the Canadian side. He had, he said, no idea where Krug was.

At 7:30 on the morning of April 18, Mrs. Johanna Bertelman was just getting dressed. Her doorbell rang impatiently. She hesitated, puzzled. She was alone in the apartment at 259 Philip Avenue South, Detroit. Both her husband and her twenty-year-old daughter had already left for work. The impatient, imperative buzzing of the doorbell continued.

Mrs. Bertelman slipped on a dressing gown. Now slightly annoyed, she went to the front door, and opened it.

She found herself facing an unkempt, dirty-faced young man in soiled overalls. "You are Mrs. Bertelman?" he asked, in English, but with a broad German accent.

She nodded, mystified and a little frightened. She became more so when the strange, unprepossessing young man asked: "I may come inside, please?"

Mrs. Bertelman shook her head quickly. "No. Why should you? I don't know you. I don't know what you want. I'm very busy, and . . ."

"It is only that I wish to thank you in person for the sweater and scarf you knitted and sent to me," the young man interrupted.

For a startled moment, Mrs. Bertelman could think of nothing to say. It was true she'd been knitting socks, sweaters, scarves, and other things for the German war prisoners interned in Canada. After all, she was still a German citizen. Together with her husband and daughter, she'd come to the United States in 1929. Her husband, Richard Bertelman, took out citizenship papers, and was now a skilled employee at a Detroit defense plant. Mrs. Bertelman, though, was one of those who still retained strong emotional ties with the Fatherland.

Now, with dramatic suddenness, Johanna Bertelman found herself caught in a web. It was one thing to meet in secret with other women who belonged to the German Red Cross, and knit garments to be sent, with food parcels, to the Nazi prisoners of war in Canada.

It was quite another matter to be brought face-to-face with one of those prisoners.

Once inside, the young man pulled a small packet from his overalls. As he unwrapped it, and displayed a pair of epaulettes with the insignia of the Luftwaffe, he explained:

"You enclosed your name and address in the package with the sweater and scarf. As a loyal German, you can tell me to whom I can turn for help."

Mrs. Bertelman nodded. She knew just the man. Max Stephan, long the acknowledged leader of German-American affairs in Detroit. Stephan had come to this country in 1933. Two fingers of his left hand were permanently crippled as a result of wounds he had received while in the German Army during World War I.

In 1935, he fraudulently obtained American citizenship, and opened a tavern on East Jefferson Avenue. He called it the German Restaurant. A short, flabby man, he prospered in a modest way. Following Pearl Harbor, and the involvement of the United States in the war, Stephan called in a painter and tactfully had the word "German" blocked out. To prove his patriotism for his adopted country even more, he publicly bought some War Bonds.

He didn't, however, stop the top Bundists in the Detroit area from using his apartment over the restaurant for secret meetings.

Mrs. Bertelman called Stephan. He came quickly, but dealt very cautiously with the newcomer. He wasn't sure whether the young man was actually an escaped Nazi flyer or an underground agent cleverly coached by the American authorities. By this time, German Bundists across the coun-

try had learned—the hard way—that while the United States
Government was apparently allowing them to operate with-
out hindrance, the appearance was somewhat deceitful on
Uncle Sam's part.

Not only had undercover FBI Special Agents been planted
in various Bund organizations, but even some German-
Americans had joined the Bund and reported what they saw
and heard to the FBI.

As a result, Max Stephan was doubly wary.

"Both sides of the border are now heavily patrolled,"
Stephan challenged. "How is it you weren't stopped and
questioned?"

"I was," the young Nazi answered, "twice. Both times by
military police on the Canadian side."

"What did you do?"

As Krug answered, "We have friends in Canada," he dug
into the back pocket of his overalls, and pulled out a folded
envelope. Withdrawing two official-looking papers, he went
on, "Here are papers proving that I am Jean Ette, former
seaman on the liner *Normandie*, born in Strassburg. The
military police believed my story. The papers are very good
forgeries. Here. Look for yourself."

Stephan had one more question. "How did you get across
from Canada?"

"I left nothing to chance," Krug said briskly. "In the camp
library, I found an old copy of the *National Geographic*
Magazine with an article on the Great Lakes. It contained
an excellent map on Toronto and Windsor and the Detroit
River. I memorized it carefully. Last night, when I arrived
in Windsor, I went directly to the waterfront. I stole a row-
boat, and paddled to Belle Isle. I used the beacon on top
of the Penobscot Tower as a guide.

"When I got to Belle Isle, I walked across the bridge and
into the city here. Then, I came to see Mrs. Bertelman."

Stephan was satisfied. He supplied Krug with clothes and

money. Then, he took him to his restaurant and fed him. While Krug ate, Stephan asked about the Nazi's plans.

Krug had already worked out a program. First, he wished to go to Chicago, where he had another contact. Then, he intended making his way south, crossing into Mexico, and getting a ship to some neutral port in Europe, probably in Spain.

Why Stephan didn't let Krug depart immediately, and thus rid himself of a potential danger, has never satisfactorily been explained. For a long time, the Bundists had been ranting about the crass stupidity of the Americans, and the superiority of the pure Nordic Germans, and it's possible Stephan had come to believe his own propaganda.

Or it may have been that the arrogance of young Krug communicated itself to the older Stephan. At any rate, Max became carried away with the dangerous role he suddenly found himself playing. He was not by nature a brave man, or a stupid one. Yet only a man brave to the point of foolhardiness, or incredibly stupid, could have behaved as Max Stephan now did.

He persuaded Krug to prolong his stay in Detroit for another twenty-four hours.

In conversation, it developed this was Krug's twenty-second birthday. When Krug finished eating, Stephan took him on a personally conducted tour of the German-American colony.

First stop was the European Import Company, on Gratiot Avenue. The firm was headed by Theodore Donay, a naturalized American who'd been an officer in the German Army. He insisted on helping finance Krug's escape.

After that, Stephan took Krug on a round of the taverns and beer gardens that catered mostly to a German clientele. He introduced the young man as a friend from Milwaukee.

It was not until early the following morning—Sunday—that Stephan drove the young Nazi to the bus terminal, and bought a ticket for him to Chicago.

Before that Sunday was over, word of suspicion reached John S. Bugas, Agent-in-Charge of the Detroit FBI Field Office.

[The same John S. Bugas is now a Vice-President of Ford Motor Company, in charge of labor relations.]

Bugas had already received official notification from Canadian authorities about Krug's escape. He called the camp at Bowmanville, Ontario, and asked for photographs of the young Nazi. To save time, he sent an Agent to pick them up at Windsor.

By late that Sunday afternoon, copies were being run off in the photo studios used by the FBI. Then, Bugas sent Agents fanning out through the city, visiting likely taverns and beer gardens. Other Agents concentrated on interviewing ticket-sellers, porters, and attendants at various Detroit bus terminals, airports, and railroad stations.

In short order, Krug was identified by at least half a dozen people as Stephan's mysterious companion. By fast backtracking and innumerable interviews with neighbors, shopkeepers, acquaintances and even children playing in the street, Stephan and young Krug were traced by the Agents back to their first appearance together early Saturday morning—when they had left the apartment house in which Johanna Bertelman lived.

By eleven o'clock Sunday night, both Stephan and Johanna Bertelman had been taken into custody by the FBI. By midnight, both had confessed.

So far, so good.

Fast, efficient work had garnered two of the people who'd aided the escaped Nazi. Krug, however, was still free. There

was a special urgency to recapture him, over and above the
fact that he was an escaped POW.

The FBI never seriously thought Krug was a trained
espionage agent, or a saboteur. Even if he weren't, though,
he presented what might well have been a far more explosive
danger. He'd been aided in his escape by a top man in the
German-American Nazi groups. Every German-American
with similar pro-Hitler sympathies would be watching the
outcome intently; they would probably plan their activities
according to what happened to Max Stephan. Unless his
punishment was sharp and definitive, a vast number of
potential traitors would receive great encouragement.

John C. Lehr, U.S. District Attorney in Detroit, explained
the legal complexities to Bugas. Stephan expected to be
charged with harboring an escaped prisoner. That was a
misdemeanor. If found guilty, he'd receive a slap on the
wrist. Therefore, Lehr was recommending to U.S. Attorney
General J. Francis Biddle that Stephan be charged with
treason.

Therein lay the legal problem. To obtain a conviction for
treason, there would have to be corroborating testimony of
at least two witnesses to the alleged overt act. Without Krug,
that would be impossible.

The FBI went into all-out action. Half a million circulars
bearing Krug's photo and description were distributed
throughout the nation. From J. Edgar Hoover's office in
Washington went orders alerting every FBI Field Office.
Undercover operators in German-American communities
were contacted. So were Special Agents who had wormed
their way into various pro-Hitler societies.

By the time the FBI learned which bus Krug had taken,
the bus had already reached Chicago. The German American

colony in that city was checked. That turned up a number of leads. None produced results, though.

Trying to decide just where to concentrate the search, the FBI reasoned that Krug would try to get back to Germany. That meant boarding a ship bound for a neutral country in Europe. The embarkation point would have to be in Mexico.

There was a fairly large German colony in Mexico. Among them was a sizable group of Nazi sympathizers. In addition, the extensive border between Mexico and the United States is all but impossible to patrol and guard with absolute efficiency.

Krug had to be apprehended before he reached that border.

Follow-up orders went from Hoover's office to the Agents-in-Charge of Field Offices in Texas, Arizona, New Mexico, and California. Working with local police, Agents saw to it that circulars on Krug went to every hotel, every rooming house, to bus and railroad employees, and to the men on the Border Patrol.

It was blanket coverage of the entire Southwest—in its quiet way, the most intensive manhunt on record.

Around the clock, FBI Field Offices were flooded with tips. A man answering Krug's description was seen in a dozen different places, from San Diego to Houston.

At 10:30 PM, on Friday, May 1, Agent-in-Charge M.W. Acers, of the San Antonio, Texas, Field Office, got a telephone call. It came from a woman clerk at a small hotel on a side street near the Alamo—one of thousands of such hotels that had gotten a copy of the Krug circular.

The clerk was certain Krug was at the hotel. He'd checked in that afternoon. SAC Acers had already received similarly positive tips a dozen times that week. Within minutes, though, Agents were on their way, accompanied by detectives from the San Antonio Police Department.

They got a passkey from the helpful clerk, and went up-stairs. They hoped to take the occupant of the room by surprise and avoid bloodshed, if it turned out to be Krug.

In the room, they found themselves facing a young man protesting angrily at being awakened in such a way. He was asked to identify himself.

"Of course. Here are my papers. I'm Jean Ette."

He professed not to understand when one of the Agents suggested he might be escaped *Oberleutnant* Hans Peter Krug.

When the room was searched, a loaded .32 calibre revolver was found under a hat. A small handbag contained a quantity of canned food, two atlases, maps of the United States and Central America, and two boxes of ammunition for the .32 revolver.

He refused to offer any explanation for this rather peculiar luggage. It was decided to drive him to the FBI Field Office, for further questioning by Acers. On the short ride there, the professed "Jean Ette" was caught trying to swallow two small scraps of paper. He was prevented by force, and the paper recovered. When the scraps were later spread out at the Field Office, they were seen to contain names and addresses in Mexico City and Mérida, Yucatan.

At first, Krug continued to deny his true identity. Then, when Acers began to fingerprint him, he pulled back his hand, and angrily objected: "You must remember my position. I'm a German officer."

Well versed in the rights of prisoners of war, he now proceeded arrogantly to taunt Acers and the other Agents. "There is nothing you can do to me. You must return me to Canada. I have broken no laws in your country. It is the right of every prisoner-of-war to try to escape."

He refused to give any details of his travels after reaching Chicago. He showed no concern when informed that Stephan, Johanna Bertelman, and Theodore Donay had been arrested. Then, he was taken to Detroit. Eighteen witnesses there identified him as Stephan's "friend from Milwaukee." When they finished, Krug was taken through the Detroit River Tunnel, and handed over by Bugas to Canadian authorities.

In Detroit, a Federal Grand Jury indicted Max Stephan on twelve counts. Nationwide interest centered on the case. For one thing, Stephan became the first American in modern times to go on trial for treason.

The trial began on June 20, in Federal Court in Detroit. Presiding was Judge Arthur A. Tuttle. The jury was sworn in. Chief Assistant District Attorney John W. Babcock called the first witness for the Government.

A surprise witness.

Flanked by military guards, resplendent in full-dress blue uniform complete with all the insignia of a Nazi Luftwaffe officer, *Oberleutnant* Hans Peter Krug marched toward the witness stand.

In front of the bench, Krug stopped. He clicked his polished heels, and gave Judge Tuttle the Nazi salute. Even the Germans in the courtroom gasped at that display of arrogance.

Judge Tuttle carefully and slowly pointed out Krug's legal rights to him. As a POW, Krug was not obliged to take an oath before testifying, but merely to affirm his intention of telling the truth. For that matter, Judge Tuttle added, he didn't have to testify at all, unless he wished to do so of his own free will.

Krug nodded his understanding. He seemed to enjoy his obvious importance to both sides in this legal struggle. Stephan, it seems, intended to use as his defense the argument that he didn't know Krug's true identity when he met him at Mrs. Bertelman's, and that he had been taken in by the young Nazi. Such testimony would be difficult to attack, unless Krug could be made to contradict it.

When Krug told Judge Tuttle he was quite willing to testify, it was obvious that he had no intention of turning on his countryman.

Chief Assistant U.S. District Attorney Babcock recognized Krug's motives for what they were—the arrogant self-confidence of a young man anxious to parade his superiority before the American public, to relish to the last degree his hour in the national spotlight.

From that moment on, it was less a legal battle than a study in adroit psychology. Babcock played on the Nazi flyer's vanity, suggesting by his questions that during his two weeks' travel from Detroit down to Texas, he must have been engaged in ultrabrilliant espionage schemes. To such questions, Krug smiled, then answered:

"That is a military secret."

His manner of answering obviously implied that the questions might well be apt. Gradually, Babcock went from questions touching on military activities to seemingly less important ones. He outlined, detail by detail, Krug's activities from the moment he appeared at Mrs. Bertelman's apartment up to the time Stephan bought him his bus ticket to Chicago.

Krug verified every detail impatiently, waiting for Babcock to return to questions about the young Nazi's imaginary daring espionage activities. In attempting to fence with Babcock, Krug had, of course, fallen into the psychological trap set for him by the shrewd prosecutor. After Krug's admissions in the witness chair, the testimony of the others was anticlimactic.

Just four days after the trial started, the jury retired to consider a verdict. It took them an hour and 23 minutes to reach one.

The verdict was guilty.

Stephan was ordered to be hanged. President Roosevelt later commuted the death sentence to life imprisonment.

Whether Stephan lived or died was not the vital thing. The FBI had already accomplished the important, long-range objective. German sympathizers in the United States had been given warning.

It was a warning they did not forget.

A Nice, Busy Little Bank
That Ought to Be Robbed

by EVAN McLEOD WYLIE

For many reasons, fictional comedies involving crime are not often written. And a true comic crime is as rare as a clearance sale at Fort Knox. Yet Evan McLeod Wylie has found one, a classic among comedies of errors.

ALTHOUGH BANK ROBBING has traditionally been regarded as the most exacting of all crimes, to be attempted only by fiendishly clever operators, or gangs of hardened, desperate thugs, the field has recently become overrun by slap-happy amateurs.

Many are so bumbling and lackadaisical they'd seem more at home in a Damon Runyon story than in a bank holding a gun.

For sheer, outrageous success in the face of fantastic ineptitude, however, no robbery could possibly equal the one brought off by the three men who held up a drive-in bank in Port Chester, New York.

Through circumstances mostly beyond his control, Arthur Pais played the most prominent role. He is a short, balding individual who exudes good humor. From World War II until shortly before he became a bank robber, he was a law-abiding, topflight mechanic in a big garage in New Rochelle, New York, ten miles from Port Chester. The men who still work there recall him as a jovial, generous-natured fellow who loved to make friends. His home life was exemplary. He lived with his widowed mother, but spent most of his time romancing a neighborhood girl named Ida.

He indulged a love for animals by bringing home stray cats, giving puppies to all his friends, and owning a cocker spaniel. Also, to quote him, "I was interested in a particular end of horses—the betting end."

When a huge trotting track opened in nearby Yonkers, New York, Artie began to spend his evenings "at the trots." He also began to bet heavily—and to lose the same way. Presently, he left the big New Rochelle garage to open his own gas station a few miles away in Larchmont. The new enterprise quickly reflected the personality and interests of its proprietor. Puppies tussled in the window. A radio blared track results. The station became a hangout for local bookmakers and followers of the races.

Soon, Artie had two new friends. One was Angelo P. John, a tall, thin, darkly handsome individual who'd recently flunked the New York State written examination for horse trainer. Rather moody, his manner ranged from petulance to gloomy silence.

The other new friend was Frank Mateo, owner of a bedraggled yellow taxi in which he transported horseplayers to the track. While he charged for that service, Frankie's main interest was accepting wagers on the horses from his passengers. This practice is, of course, against the law, but Frankie's disregard for legal authority was well established. During World War II, he'd been first a draft dodger, then a Navy deserter. Later, he'd been arrested for lifting jewelry from a parcel truck. Because of his taste in cars, he was nicknamed Frankie Convertible.

Artie's gas station soon failed. He put what money he had left into Angie's business—dispensing sandwiches and coffee to construction workers from the back of a station wagon. That business also failed. Artie and Angie were facing a financial crisis.

Shortly after that, two bandits held up a small branch of the County Trust Company, in Mount Vernon, a few miles from New Rochelle. They tied up four bank employees, and spent half an hour in the bank before escaping with $97,000. They left no clues save a vivid impression on the bank employees of the amiable relaxed manner of the short, rotund bandit who held the gun—"He acted as if he owned the bank, and was very friendly"—and the brow-mopping nervousness of his stringbean partner.

The police were utterly baffled.

Artie and Angie promptly used their proceeds to become owners of a racing stable. With $7,000 in crisp bills, they purchased a hapless gelding named Battleover, whose grandfather was Man O'War, and shipped him to Florida for the winter racing season. Angie, having meanwhile retaken and passed the examination, became Battleover's trainer.

In his first race for the new partners, the horse threw his jockey. Then he went lame for several weeks. Refusing to become discouraged, Artie relaxed by sending a stream of optimistic postcards to Ida, still laboring away as a stenographer in snowbound Manhattan. Each card assured her the racing business would soon make marriage possible.

At that point, Artie and Angie had an unexpected visitor—Frankie Convertible.

Instead of congratulating Angie and Artie on their exploit, Frankie ungraciously demanded to be cut in on the loot. The ensuing discussion, which Artie recalls as "not pleasant," was brief. Frankie was given $7,000 to keep his mouth shut. He took the money and returned to New York.

By the time winter was over, and the horse vans rumbled

north with the spring, Angie and Artie's feed bills, track fees, veterinarians, jockeys, exercise boys, and "cooling-off" boys had consumed most of the Mount Vernon money. Battleover had not won a single race, and if he was sorry, he wasn't showing any signs of it. He was developing a bad temper, and several times planted his heels solidly in the seat of Artie's pants.

Most disgusted of all with Artie's equine enterprise was his girl Ida. She refused to have anything to do with the track, and was, in fact, seething because of what happened when she let Artie use her car one morning while his was in the repair shop. That evening, she was surprised to find herself charged with illegal possession of a revolver. The gun had been found by a policeman searching the car's trunk after Artie had absent-mindedly parked illegally.

Apologetically, Artie admitted the gun was his. A Florida racetrack friend had given it to him, he told Ida, and hastened to clear her name by going to court and paying a $100 fine.

When winter again approached, Artie and Angie sent Battleover to an elegant horse farm near New Rochelle for a rest cure. They visited him daily. So did Frankie Convertible, who astonished the horsemen by arriving in his battered taxi to renew old acquaintance.

To refinance their bankrupt stable, Artie and Angie decided to knock over another bank. This time, Frankie Convertible was to be an active partner. Leisurely, they began looking for a suitable target.

One afternoon, they stopped in nearby Port Chester for hamburgers. As they got back into their car, they noticed an attractive, one-story, tapestry-brick building with white columns and a white picket fence. It was the Irving Avenue branch of the bank which had already provided such bounty

—the County Trust Company. Artie, Angie, and Frankie sat staring at it with rapt attention.

"It seems," Artie said, "like a nice, busy little bank that should be robbed."

Angie followed up on the spur-of-the-moment decision by depositing some of the money he'd stolen from the bank's Mount Vernon branch. This gave him reason to drift in and out, and gain a clearer picture of the internal workings.

Very shortly, the trio's interest centered on Mary Kostolos, a gentle widow who'd been a teller with County Trust for twenty-eight years. She was, they noted, the last to leave at night, and the first to arrive in the morning, using a key to unlock the front door. A few days later, they drove to the railroad station in Larchmont and stole a green sedan belonging to a commuter. This would be the getaway car. Frankie Convertible volunteered to equip it with stolen license plates.

In that stolen green car, they now proceeded to trail Mary Kostolos around Port Chester, observing her off-duty habits. Their preparations continued at a leisurely, casual pace, from both preference and necessity. For one thing, their horse barn conferences were constantly being interrupted by grooms with buckets and pitchforks. Then, too, Angie was often late to the meetings because he'd been detained at home to boil bottle nipples and mix formula for a new baby. And Artie, too, had troubles. He'd developed a painful lump in the region where Battleover had kicked him. The irksome ailment bedeviled Artie so much he finally confided to Ida that he was sure he had cancer.

In practical, feminine fashion, she insisted he see her doctor. The physician diagnosed it as a nonmalignant cyst. Arrangements were made a few days before the planned bank job for a surgeon to remove the cyst at the hospital on the following Monday.

Thursday evening, the three conspirators met, and drove

both Artie's car and the green sedan to a supermarket parking lot a few blocks from the bank. Using the stolen green car, they drove to Mary Kostolos' house, and parked, waiting for her to return from her habitual Thursday night shopping. At 10:15, she drove up, turned into her garage, switched out her headlights, and reached for her parcels. In a flash, two men—one from each side—were with her in the front seat.

The two were Artie and Frankie.

Artie, behind the wheel, shot the car backward into the street, and drove rapidly up the block. Angie followed in the green sedan. Admonishing Mrs. Kostolos to be quiet, Artie told her politely:

"You're going to be all right, lady. All we want is the money down at your bank."

"But I can't get that money," she cried.

"Don't try to fool us," Artie answered. "We know you've got a key to that bank. You're going to open the vault for us, just like you do every morning."

"I've never opened a vault in my life," cried Mary. "I swear to you I don't know the combination. It's always opened by someone from the main office, at 8 o'clock in the morning."

A strangled gasp gave hint of the impact of this news on Frankie Convertible. Artie seemed less perturbed. With Angie still following in the green car, he continued to cruise around Port Chester for awhile before stopping in a side street. Then, leaving Frankie to guard the petrified Mrs. Kostolos, he strolled back to inform Angie of the 8 AM vault opening.

Angie took the news even harder than Frankie. Vivid memories of the nervous strain of the Mount Vernon robbery came flooding back to him. Forcefully, he replied that he'd decided the less he had to do with this particular bank robbery the better. Wishing Artie the best of luck, he drove the green car home, moped around the kitchen mixing baby formula, and finally went to bed.

For the next two hours, while Port Chester slept, Mary Kostolos was driven up one street and down another by Artie, while Frankie Convertible, crouching uncommunicatively in the back seat, got jumpier by the minute.

Toward 1 AM, Artie boldly drove up to the bank. Bright lights and juke box music still emanated from the bar and grill across the street.

"We'll have to wait for the drunks to go home," Artie observed, still as cheerful as ever, as they drove off. Presently, Mary declared she thought she was going to faint. "We'll find you a nice rest room," Artie replied. He drove until they came to a gas station closed for the night. Artie opened the door to the ladies room, and bowed Mrs. Kostolos inside.

This was too much for Frankie Convertible. Bank robbery, at least as conducted by Artie, was wearing him to a frazzle. "You can take all kinds of chances for this much dough," he cried, waving his arms, "but this is ridiculous." He told Artie he'd decided, like Angie, to go home.

Artie pleaded with Frankie not to leave him at such a critical point. Mrs. Kostolos drifted out of the rest room and got back into her car, but Frankie would not go on. He repeated to Artie that he'd had all he could stand.

In hurt silence, Artie drove Frankie to White Plains, dropped him, and returned to Port Chester with Mrs. Kostolos. At that point, he says, even his spirits had lowered, and he was almost ready to abandon the whole project. As they passed the bank, though, he noticed the bar and grill was finally closed. Irving Avenue was dark and deserted. He drew up to the curb, about thirty feet from the bank, then escorted Mrs. Kostolos to the front door. She opened it with her key.

Inside, there was, of course, nothing to steal. All the cash was locked in the small, but sturdy, vault. Fetching a customer's chair from the manager's office, Artie led Mrs.

Kostolos into the anteroom of a lavatory in a corner of the lobby, propped open its door, and helped her into the chair.

The time now was about 4 AM.

For nearly all of the next few hours, Mrs. Kostolos remained huddled in the chair, weeping quietly. Occasionally, she glimpsed Artie's bulky swarthy figure in blue-green jacket, slacks, floppy gray hat, and large horn-rimmed spectacles as he scrutinized the street through a slim crack in the blinds. She didn't know how many other accomplices might be waiting outside the bank. Likewise, she had no idea whether their plans called for killing her there, or carrying her off as a hostage.

What she had no way of suspecting, of course, was that Artie didn't know, either.

Thanks to the defection of his two ex-partners, Artie had no idea how he was going to get out of the bank safely. It was with blinking astonishment, therefore, that peeking through the blind shortly after 7 AM, Artie saw the green getaway car cruising slowly by the bank. Then, like a rescue ship passing up a castaway, it disappeared up the block. Angie and Frankie, it seems, had decided to return to Port Chester, if only to keep track of Artie's progress. Obviously, neither felt the need to assist him.

Toward 7:30 AM, Artie approached Mrs. Kostolos. "I want you to walk around the lobby, and do what you always do first thing in the morning. And don't try to give anybody any signals, or you'll be sorry." He stepped back out of sight of the windows as Mary tottered around weakly, lighting lamps. At 7:40 AM, she admitted a young teller named Ernest Marino. Artie quickly escorted both back to the lavatory. He'd just finished binding them with white plastic clothesline when Purdy Ungemack, assistant treasurer of County Trust in Port Chester, pulled into a parking space across the street. According to a rotating system, it was his turn to stop by the drive-in branch and open the vault.

"As I stepped inside the bank," Ungemack remembers, "this man came out of the washroom pointing the gun, and saying:

" 'All right, let's lock up that door.' "

Ungemack glimpsed Marino tied up in the washroom, and, hearing Mary Kostolos' sobs, presumed her to be guarded by one or more other men. He backed away from Artie, who said:

"Now get over there and open that vault. And don't set off any alarms, or I'll blow your brains out."

The time was now 7:47—and at Police Headquarters, the vault alarm had just automatically disconnected. Obediently, Ungemack turned the dials and opened the vault's outer door. Artie reached in and scooped about $10,000 of ready cash for the tellers' drawers into a cardboard box.

"Open the inside door, too," he ordered.

"I can't," Ungemack replied tensely. "There's a safety timer on it. It won't release for fifteen minutes."

"We'll wait for it," Artie answered decisively.

It now became deathly quiet, save for the cheerful ticking of the vault timer, and Mary's muted crying. Outside the bank, though, a steady stream of commuters drove past the bank to the railroad station.

Unlike banks in most other parts of the country, this one opened for business at 8 AM. The police car detailed to guard the bank at its opening nosed around the corner. Its usual parking space was blocked by a delivery truck, and the lone policeman settled for a spot a little further down the block. Cutting the motor, he sat back in his seat and watched the bank's early customers gathering on its front step.

As the village 8 o'clock whistle blew, some of the customers began to rattle the front door impatiently. Mary Kostolos murmured:

"Oh, my God, something awful is going to happen now!"

Two more incredibly long minutes passed before the vault timer stopped ticking.

"Now?" asked Artie.

Ungemack nodded, then swung open the inner door. Exposed to view lay nearly $180,000 in cash. As the customers continued rattling the front door knob impatiently, Artie crammed as much cash as he could into his cardboard box. Then he crossed the lobby with casual, relaxed steps, obtained a large trash basket, filled it, and covered the money with paper towels from the lavatory.

Then he turned to Ungemack. "Pick up the box. We're going out to the car. Tell those people outside you'll be back in a minute."

Ungemack was certain someone among the customers, neighboring storekeepers, or police would see what was happening. He recalls thinking numbly: "Here we go. Here's where the shooting starts."

When Ungemack opened the door, though, the customers merely stepped aside. Ungemack found himself proceeding to the street with the box containing upwards of $100,000. Inside the empty bank, Mary Kostolos and Ernie Marino steeled themselves for the shouts and shots. They heard only a resounding silence.

Ungemack reached the sidewalk. Across the street, a shopkeeper waved him a cordial good morning. The police officer still sat in his car.

"Up to the blue car," Artie ordered, and Ungemack realized Mary's car was to be used for the getaway. Artie quickly tossed his wastebasket in the back seat. "Put that box in front," he told Ungemack. As soon as that order was obeyed, Artie remarked casually, "Well, thanks. So long now," ran around the front of the car, leaped into the driver's seat, pulled out into the traffic, and shot up the hill.

Ungemack dazedly looked around for the rest of the

robbers. Suddenly realizing there were none, he vainly scanned the street for the police car—now obscured by the delivery truck and other parked cars. Turning, he rushed back into the bank, and phoned police headquarters.

Artie drove Mary Kostolos' car speedily to the supermarket parking lot where he'd left his own car. As he hurriedly transferred the loot-filled box and wastebasket to his sedan, Frankie and Angie materialized beside him. They stared goggle-eyed at the haul.

"Artie," they said. "We're here to help you."

"I'm not interested," Artie answered peevishly. Then he got into the sedan and sped out of the lot.

Angie and Frankie suddenly perceived that Artie had left them with (a) Mary Kostolos' blue car, which would certainly be pounced upon by the police at any moment, and (b) the stolen green sedan. It was a moment for a quick decision. Angie made one. He got into his own car, which he'd brought along that morning, and drove off. He departed alone because Frankie had dropped the stolen green sedan's keys, and was so nervous he couldn't find them. With first Artie, then Angie gone, Frankie found the parking lot singularly unattractive. He ran into the street, hailed a passing taxi carrying two girls to the railroad station, and boarded a train for New York City.

Artie and the loot reached home unhindered. By 4 PM, though, he realized a fact of life—he'd have to negotiate with his faint-hearted ex-partners to establish the price of silence. By phone, he arranged a meeting. After angry bickering, Artie sulkily handed $35,000 to Frankie and $30,000 to Angie. Then he went back home to nurse his cyst—due to be operated on in about seventy-two hours.

Meanwhile, Port Chester was reacting violently. Carloads of heavily armed police had sped to the scene. A large force of FBI Agents showed up. Within a very short time, a wild traffic jam developed on Irving Avenue as reporters, photographers, and crowds of the curious milled around in front of the little bank.

Newspapers said the bandits were professionals who made a clean getaway in a "perfectly executed, movielike robbery."

An FBI Field Office was set up in the Port Chester Municipal Building, and a large scale manhunt was set in motion. A general teletype alarm alerted 70,000 police in thirteen states, as well as FBI Field Offices as far away as Alaska and Hawaii.

Port Chester, itself, was saturated with teams of Special Agents. By suppertime Friday—the evening of the day on which the robbery was committed—the Agents' searching yielded results. One man's story seemed particularly interesting. A few minutes after 8 AM, he'd noticed two strangers arguing in a corner of the supermarket parking lot. Though he knew nothing at that time of the robbery, this alert citizen (who prefers to remain anonymous) took the trouble to memorize the first four symbols on the license plate of the car in which one of the strangers drove away.

He recalled them as "WS 45."

The FBI men's check on an apparently abandoned green sedan in the supermarket parking lot established that it was a stolen car. A key case found nearby seemed to indicate the car had been abandoned in haste. Then, two girls were found who told the FBI Agents about a stranger popping into their taxi outside the supermarket, and riding with them to the railroad station.

There seemed good reason to learn more about all the ninety-nine automobile owners whose plates begin with WS 45. By 10 PM Saturday night, a team of Special Agents wearily went about checking number eighty—a man named Arthur Pais. Some of their weariness vanished when they ran across the fact that Pais had been fined $100 some months earlier for illegal ownership of a revolver found in the car of a Miss Ida Revere, of the Bronx.

Other Agents traced the key case found near the stolen, abandoned green sedan to a used car dealer in Mamaroneck. They interviewed him, and checked his records. By curious coincidence, he'd sold a car to one Arthur Pais the year before. He heard Pais had driven it to Florida.

Soon, Agents in Miami were reporting that an Arthur Pais had raced horses in Miami the previous winter—in partnership with one Angelo P. Jonn, of 121 North Broadway, White Plains, New York.

This was a tasty morsel of news, since still other Special Agents had found that the stolen license plates on the abandoned green sedan had been removed from a car parked just two doors from Angie's address.

On Monday, an FBI artist added the large spectacles and floppy gray hat worn by the bank bandit to the rogues' gallery photo for which Artie had posed at the time of the pistol incident. The retouched picture was shown to Mrs. Kostolos, Ernest Marino, Purdy Ungemack, and the man who'd noted "WS 45" at the parking lot.

Their unanimous reaction was: "Why, that's him!"

Still, the FBI made no arrests, lest the loot—$188,784.51, which made it one of the largest bank robberies in United States history—be lost or destroyed. Another delaying factor was the discovery that Artie wasn't at home.

At this point in the investigation, Ida Revere was being treated as a possible major suspect, because of the gun found in her car. She became probably the most closely observed office worker in Manhattan, under round-the-clock surveillance.

In White Plains, Angie's apartment was discreetly but effectively surrounded. Agents crouched in cellars. Others observed his movements from the windows of neighboring apartments. Still more teams of Agents checked at the horse farms. Miami Agents hopefully set traps for Artie in Florida, and Pinkerton men cooperated by looking for him at racetracks and stable areas across the nation.

The silent, never-slackening watch continued throughout Monday night and all day Tuesday. That evening, Agents again maintained surveillance on Ida Revere as she returned home from work. After supper, they followed when she drove to a hospital. They tagged along, as closely as they dared without revealing themselves, as Ida went up to a second-floor semiprivate room.

There was Artie, now minus his cyst.

Still hoping to find some lead to the stolen money before revealing themselves, the FBI waited until the next day to confront Artie. He seemed astonished. "You're crazy," he protested. The Agents asked for Artie's permission to search his home.

"Go ahead. Search it," he answered generously.

The Agents knew immediately, of course, that the money wasn't in Artie's apartment. With characteristic thoroughness, though, they went over and rummaged anyway. One Agent looked in the back of a bureau, and found an old garage bill. The garage was located on Tremont Avenue, in the Bronx. Finishing at the apartment, the Agents went to the garage. They found Artie's car, opened the trunk, and found themselves staring at a sea of loose banknotes.

Artie confessed. Angie and Frankie were arrested, and all but $2,500 of the bank money recovered. Ida Revere was, of course, completely exonerated. The Agents accepted her declaration that if she'd ever known what Artie was up to, she'd have "crowned him, but good."

Although briefly he'd been one of the most spectacularly successful bank robbers in American history, Artie remained an unaffected, friendly fellow. At the conclusion of their trial, the judge sentenced Angie and Frankie—who'd been sullenly uncooperative—to twenty-five and twenty-two and a half years, respectively. To Artie, who cooperated amicably, he gave only eighteen years, with this comment: "I have a feeling deep inside of me, Pais, that somehow or other you are going to keep out of trouble from now on."

So far, at least, he certainly has.

Rendezvous with Murder, Inc.

by WALTER WINCHELL

*You may not remember a man called "Lepke." He ruled
an incredible criminal organization—Murder Incorporated.
As a sort of sideline, it undertook industrial sabotage projects. But its main activity was the sale of a service—protection. Both management and labor in New York City's rich
trucking, fur, garment, and other industries paid to avoid
trouble. Now and again Lepke ran across a businessman
who refused to deal with him. Lepke would give him one
warning. If the man refused again, Lepke had him killed.*

*Arrested in 1936, Lepke jumped bail and disappeared.
Potential witnesses against him met mysterious deaths. By
1939, Lepke was wanted for more than eighty murders.
New York City offered a reward of $25,000 for him, dead
or alive. Then, for almost the only time in its history, the
FBI likewise offered a cash reward—$25,000.*

*Special squads of Federal, state and city police hunted
for him twenty-four hours a day. They couldn't find him.
Then, the most famous newspaperman of them all stunned
the nation with this story.*

NEW YORK, August 25—The surrender of Public Enemy
Lepke Buchalter to the Government last night took place
while scores of pedestrians ambled by, and two police radio
cars waited for the lights to change near 28th Street and
Fifth Avenue.

The time was precisely 10:17 PM, and the search for the Most Wanted fugitive in the nation was over.

The surrender was negotiated by this reporter, whom G-Man John Edgar Hoover authorized to guarantee "safe delivery."

After a series of telephone talks with persons unknown, and with the head of the FBI, Lepke appeared to drop out of the sky, without even a parachute. The time was 10:15. The scene was Madison Square, between 23rd and 24th Streets, where we had halted our car as per instructions.

The following two minutes were consumed traveling slowly north on Fourth Avenue, and west on 27th Street to Fifth Avenue, where the traffic lights were red—and to the next corner where Mr. Hoover waited alone, unarmed and without handcuffs, in a Government limousine. Hoover was disguised in dark sunglasses to keep him from being recognized by passersby.

The presence of two New York police cruisers, attached to the 14th Precinct, so near the surrender scene startled Hoover as well as Lepke. The G-Man later admitted he feared a "leak."

Lepke, who was calmer than this chauffeur, was on the verge of rushing out of our machine into Hoover's arms. The police cruisers, ironically, were the first observed by this reporter in two hours of motoring to complete the surrender.

Not until the final seconds was there a sign of uniformed law. But it was too late. The long arm of the Government had reached out and claimed another enemy. The Federal Bureau of Investigation and the City of New York had saved $50,000—the total reward offered.

While pausing alongside one police car at the 27th Street intersection for the lights, Lepke, who was wearing spectacles as part of his disguise, threw them to the corner pavement. They crashed noisily. Two passersby, middle-aged men with graying temples, stopped and looked up at a building.

Apparently they thought a window had broken above. They never realized that the man for whom every cop in the land was searching was within touching distance.

After parking our car behind a machine which was parked behind Hoover's, we shut off the ignition and escorted Lepke into Hoover's car.

"Mr. Hoover," we said, "this is Lepke."

"How do you do?" said Mr. Hoover affably.

"Glad to meet you," said Lepke. "Let's go."

"To the Federal Building at Foley Square," Hoover commanded his chauffeur.

Lepke was a little excited. He seemed anxious to talk—to talk to anybody new—after being in the shadows for over two years with so many hunted men.

"You did the smart thing by coming in, Lepke," comforted Hoover.

"I'm beginning to wonder if I did," Lepke answered. "I would like to see my wife and kids, please."

Mr. Hoover arranged for them to visit him shortly after Lepke was booked, fingerprinted, and Kodaked. He had $1,700 on him. He gave $1,100 to the boy and $600 to the jailer—for "expenses."

When the Government car reached 14th Street, we got out and went to the first phone to notify our editor, who groaned:

"A fine thing! With a World War starting!"

The negotiations which led to Lepke's surrender began in this manner. On Saturday night, August 5, a voice on the phone said:

"Don't ask me who I am. I have something important to tell you. Lepke wants to come in. But he's heard so many different stories about what will happen to him. He can't trust anybody, he says. If he could find someone he can trust, he will give himself up to that person. The talk around town is that Lepke would be shot while supposedly escaping."

"Does he trust me?" we inquired.

"Do you really mean that?" said the voice anxiously.

"Sure," we assured. "I'll tell John Edgar Hoover about it, and I'm sure he will see to it that Lepke receives his Constitutional rights, and nobody will cross him."

"OK. Put it on the air tomorrow night if you can get that promise," and then he disconnected.

We wrote a brief radio paragraph which was addressed to Lepke, "if you are listening now," which said we would try to get him assurance of a safe delivery. The next afternoon, Sunday, we phoned Mr. Hoover and read him the paragraph.

"You are authorized to state," said Hoover, "that the FBI will guarantee it."

Hoover and his Assistant Director, Clyde Tolson, came to the studio and witnessed our microphoning. They remained for the repeat broadcast to the Coast an hour later—in case another phone call came in.

For two nights, voices contacted us by phone, and said:

"You're doing very well. You'll hear more later. If he agrees to come in, he will do it through you. But he may change his mind. Good-bye."

And then all the dickering abruptly stopped—until last Tuesday night. Then a person we had never seen before, or since, approached us at 53rd Street and Fifth Avenue, and said:

"Where can you be reached on a pay station phone in an hour?"

We went to the nearest phone booth, where the stranger marked down the number and instructed:

"This is about Lepke. This time it's important. Please be here in an hour."

He hastened away, hailing a passing cab, and taxied north.

When we so reported to Mr. Hoover, after what seemed to him like too much stalling, he was exasperated. For the first time in our seven years of knowing him, he barked at us:

"This is a lot of bunk, Walter. You are being made a fool of, and so are we. If you contact those people again, tell them the time limit is up! I will instruct my Agents to shoot Lepke on sight."

Promptly an hour later, right on the button, that pay station phone tinkled. We didn't give the voice a chance to talk. "I just spoke to Hoover," we said breathlessly. "He's fed up. If Lepke doesn't surrender by four PM tomorrow, Hoover says no consideration of any kind will ever be given him. For every day he stays away, it may mean an extra two years added to his sentence."

The voice interrupted. "He's coming in, but you simply have to wait until he can arrange things. He's willing to come in, but it can't be tomorrow. Maybe the next night. Where can you be reached tomorrow night at six?"

We gave him another phone number. He said he'd call— and the call came. But it didn't seem to be the same voice. This time the instructions included:

"Drive up to Proctor's Theatre in Yonkers."

How sure could we be that the "meet" was for the surrender of Lepke. We weren't sure at all. But we hoped to convince the G-Men that we weren't being made any "goatbetween"! And so we motored up to Yonkers, and before we reached Proctor's Theatre, a car loaded with strangers—faces we don't recall ever seeing before—slowly drew alongside. We heard a voice say: "That's him."

One of the men got out, holding his handkerchief to his face as though he intended to blow into it. He got into our car, sat alongside, and kept the kerchief to his face throughout the brief conversation.

"Go to the drugstore on the corner of 19th Street and Eighth Avenue," he instructed. "There are some phone booths there. Get in one, and appear busy. About nine PM, somebody will come up to you, and tell you where to notify the G-Men to meet you."

At 8:55 PM, we were in that drugstore. We ordered a Coke. The boy behind the counter looked at us as though we seemed familiar. Perhaps we imagined it. At any rate, we didn't get a chance to appear busy in the phone booth. A face met ours as we turned to look through the open door. The stranger jerked his head as though to telegraph "Come here." We joined him outside, and walked to our car slowly.

"Go back in there, and tell Hoover to be at 28th Street on Fifth Avenue between 10:10 and 10:20," he instructed.

We did so.

When we returned to the car, the man was at the wheel. He drove slowly, to kill time, for more than an hour. Up and down Eighth Avenue, Ninth, Tenth, in and out of the side streets, down to 14th, back to 23rd, and east to Madison Square, where he stopped the car, and said:

"Just wait here—and good luck."

And so saying, he left hurriedly. We took the wheel, turned our eyes left, and noticed many people across the street lounging around. It was very humid. Our clothes were dripping. The butterflies started to romp inside of us.

Suddenly, a figure approached our car in haste. Out of the nowhere, it seems. He opened the door, got in, and said:

"Hello. Thanks very much."

We released the brake, and stepped on the gas. "We'll be with Mr. Hoover in a minute or two," we said. "He's waiting in his car at 28th Street."

"Yes, I know," said Lepke. "I just passed him."

Gold Bricks on Signal Hill

by ALAN HYND

Every once in a while somebody tells a story about a confidence man selling a sucker the Brooklyn Bridge. There are other stories about suckers buying gold bricks. Nobody, of course, believes that anyone has actually been fool enough to pay over cash for a spurious title to the Brooklyn Bridge. As a matter of fact, though, there are numerous instances of just such transactions on record. And, also as a matter of cold fact, there are on record cases in which supposedly intelligent people have purchased bricks that they thought to be gold. What is probably one of the most incredible gold-brick cases on record was a by-product of the blue-sky days and, as such, was typical of the unusual investigations handled by the Giant Killers.

IN THE YEAR 1929, the placid life of Mrs. Dora Roberts, a fabulously wealthy widow of Big Spring, Texas, was destined to undergo a decided change, with the appearance of a stout and ruddy-faced confidence man whom we shall call Tanner. Mrs. Roberts, a most devout and charitable lady in her sixty-ninth year, had, in a comparatively short space of time, come into several million dollars, when oil had been discovered on her twenty-three-thousand-acre ranch. The story of the widow's good fortune had spread the length and the breadth of Texas, and among those who had become fascinated by the tale was Mr. Tanner.

Tanner—a Texan with an uncertain background, who had tried his hand at various enterprises without marked success—posed as an authority on oil drilling when he presented himself to Mrs. Roberts. He explained that he had heard rumors to the effect that a large and nationally-known oil company which was developing the petroleum on her property was not, by any means, making the most of the possibilities. Tanner thereupon proposed that Mrs. Roberts permit him to make further explorations for oil, she to finance the work and he to supervise the drilling.

It so happened that Mrs. Roberts was a shrewd business woman. Despite the fact that she had been in financial straits just a few years previously, prior to the strike on her property, she had adjusted herself admirably to her sudden wealth. She had invested, with considerable acumen, in acreage and real estate and had, among other things, acquired a controlling interest in the First National Bank of Big Spring and become the institution's president.

Mrs. Roberts thought over Tanner's proposition and decided that things were well enough as they were. She came to have a liking for the visitor, however (he was, needless to say, a charming man), and she was pleased to point out to him several points of interest on her property. One such spot was a promontory known as Signal Hill.

"There's quite a legend to Signal Hill," Mrs. Roberts explained. The widow said that, according to the legend, wealthy Spaniards who had lived in the vicinity of Signal Hill back in 1835 had buried immense treasures there when they had fled into Mexico during the war in which Texas had won its independence from the country south of the border. "The legend has it," Mrs. Roberts concluded, "that the Spaniards never got the chance to return to Signal Hill and that the buried treasure is still there—right on my property."

Mr. Tanner, with several interesting ideas turning over in his mind, inquired of Mrs. Roberts whether she knew any details about the type of treasure that the Spaniards had buried. "Yes," said the woman, "according to the legend, they buried gold and silver in the form of bars."

Three years passed. During all that time Tanner couldn't get the legend of Signal Hill entirely out of his mind. One day in 1932 he was telling the story to his uncle—a man to whom we shall give the pleasant name of Eden—a tall, pious-looking person in his late fifties. Eden, like his nephew, was ever on the alert for easy money, and he was quick to see in the Signal Hill legend the open sesame to a fortune. "Why," Eden said to Tanner, "all we have to do is to plant some buried treasure in that hill and you and I are made for the rest of our lives."

Eden inquired of his nephew as to the characteristics of the widow, the better to find a common ground upon which to enter into her confidence. When he learned that the woman was exceedingly charitable and devout, he said, "That settles it. I'll pose as a minister."

Tanner and Eden, both of whom lived more than three hundred miles from Big Spring, made a visit to the ranch of Mrs. Roberts in 1932, almost three years to the day from the time Tanner had first entered the woman's life. Tanner introduced Eden as the Reverend Doctor J. B. Bryant, an American minister who had devoted all of his adult years to missionary work in Mexico. "Doctor Bryant," Tanner explained to Mrs. Roberts, "is in possession of some very interesting information about the legend of the buried treasure on Signal Hill."

"Really," said Mrs. Roberts. "And just what is your information, Doctor?"

The man who was masquerading as a minister (he wore a clerical collar and a frayed black suit) disclosed that, while on his rounds as a missionary in Mexico, he had become acquainted with some Mexicans who were the rightful owners of maps which had come down to them from the Spaniards who had buried the treasure on Signal Hill almost a hundred years before. The maps, the Reverend Doctor Bryant went on, disclosed the precise locations of the buried gold and silver bars.

Mrs. Roberts was skeptical at first, but the Reverend Doctor Bryant was a man who inspired confidence. He suggested that Mrs. Roberts and Tanner join him in a prayer —a prayer in which he asked God to direct him to the buried treasure in order that he and Mrs. Roberts would come into gold with which to benefit the more unfortunate members of humankind, both in the United States and in Mexico. Eden prayed so fervently that Mrs. Roberts became thoroughly sold on him then and there, and when the prayer had come to an end she asked, "What is the first thing that has to be done to locate some of this buried treasure, Doctor?"

The impostor coughed and mentioned that a mere sixteen hundred dollars stood between them and a couple of gold bricks worth many times that amount. The Mexican heirs, according to Eden, were selling the maps at a small fraction of the value of the corresponding treasure. Mrs. Roberts withdrew sixteen hundred dollars from the bank and turned it over to the two scoundrels. Three days later she received a long-distance call from Mexico. The Reverend Doctor Bryant was on the wire. "I just wanted to tell you," he said, "that I am negotiating for the first map and will arrive in Big Spring in about a week."

While Eden, or Bryant, had actually gone to Mexico solely for the purpose of putting through an authentic-sounding person-to-person long-distance call to Mrs. Roberts, his co-conspirator, Tanner, had gone to the highly-reputable Acme Brass Foundry Company in San Antonio and had the company make up two roughly cast bars of brass about the size of ordinary building bricks. Tanner expressly ordered the bars made up in a crude manner so that they would appear to have been made a long time previously and by inexperienced men. After obtaining the bars, Tanner subjected them to a heat-and-chemical process to age them artificially.

The night before the two crooks were to appear at the Roberts ranch house they secretly visited Signal Hill and worked almost until dawn making a tunnel in the side of one part of the hill. When the tunnel was completed the two bronze bricks were shoved to the far end of the opening and then the tunnel was filled in. Thus, the ground immediately *over* the point where the bricks were deposited was firm and undisturbed, so that when digging for the treasure began the operation would be carried on through solid, undisturbed earth, thus circumventing suspicion that might arise if the treasure were found in ground that had recently been disturbed.

Shortly before noon on the last day of September, 1932, when the two rascals made their formal call on Mrs. Roberts, they found an unexpected fly in the ointment in the form of the old lady's son-in-law—W. J. Garrett. Garrett, like the oil widow, was nobody's fool and, while he knew that buried treasure on Signal Hill was within the realm of possibility, the actual discovery of the treasure was something that he had to see with his own eyes. Tanner and the

other impostor quickly adjusted themselves to the presence
of Mr. Garrett and, in fact, announced that they would be
very happy to have him watch the proceedings. The Reverend Doctor Bryant withdrew from a briefcase a large map
—an artificially-aged piece of parchment—which, he said, he
had purchased in Mexico for the sixteen hundred dollars
that Mrs. Roberts had furnished.

The two swindlers and the old lady and her son-in-law
drove from the ranch house to Signal Hill, and Tanner and
Eden put on an impressive show as they consulted the directions on the fraudulent parchment and struck off so many
paces to the north, so many paces to the west, then a few
paces to the southeast and finally arrived over the spot
where the two brass bricks were planted. "If I have read
this map correctly," said the Reverend Doctor Bryant,
"there should be two gold bricks right under where I am
standing."

Both Mrs. Roberts and her son-in-law thoroughly examined the ground on which the pious-looking one stood.
They assured themselves that the spot had not been disturbed in any way for a long, long time. Then digging began. The man posing as a minister swung a pick and Tanner
used a shovel. The quartet grew more excited as Tanner
and Eden went deeper and deeper—down some four feet.
When they got down five feet, Tanner put on a display of
discouragement. The second crook said, "Let us pray." After
a prayer, the digging continued, and when a depth of about
six feet was reached, Tanner shouted, "Here is something
shining!"

The first of the brass bricks manufactured in the San
Antonio foundry was lifted into the sunlight and the dirt
scraped from it. It looked for all the world like a genuine
gold brick, a century old. The second brick was found
shortly afterward. Everyone was jubilant except the crook
in ministerial garb. "This," he said, "is no time for joy. This

is a time to thank the Almighty." And so the impostor, for the second time that morning, closed his eyes and began to pray. It was a most touching and wonderful scene.

Mrs. Roberts was all for converting the gold into cash immediately. It was Tanner who cautioned against such a course. "We had better lay the gold away right here on your ranch," he said, "because if it ever gets out that we have begun to find the buried treasure here, the curious will flock to Signal Hill and your life won't be your own." Both Mrs. Roberts and her son-in-law saw the wisdom of the suggestion and agreed to hoard the gold until such time as there was a sufficient quantity of it to make a trip to the nearest mint—in New Orleans—practical. In the meantime, it was agreed, Mrs. Roberts was to furnish the cash with which the Reverend Doctor Bryant would return to Mexico and purchase further maps.

In answer to a question propounded by Mrs. Roberts' son-in-law, the spurious minister estimated that it would take at least two years of almost constant work to locate all of the treasure buried in Signal Hill. There arose the question of dividing the proceeds from the treasure hunts which, the crooks estimated, would run into millions of dollars. "I want none of the money," said the man in black. "It belongs to the Lord." Tanner agreed to accept whatever Mrs. Roberts chose to give him, but made it clear that there was no hurry. "Let us wait," he said, "until we recover a sizable amount of the buried bricks."

For more than a year the treasure hunts continued. The Reverend Doctor Bryant was apparently virtually commuting between Big Spring and Mexico; actually he was now merely returning to his own home after receiving another bundle of cash from Mrs. Roberts and preparing another spurious map. By this time, the swindlers had introduced variety into their operations to the extent of planting some bars of silver. For some reason or other, it never occurred to either Mrs. Roberts or Garrett, her son-in-law, to have the gold bricks analyzed. Garrett, however, took it upon himself to have two of the silver ones assayed and, when the bricks were found to be .999 fine, any misgivings that either Garrett or his mother-in-law had had about Mrs. Roberts' fantastic good fortune were thoroughly dissipated.

By February, 1935—two years and five months after the Signal Hill operations had first begun—a total of seven thousand pounds of brass bricks were stored at the ranch of Widow Roberts. In addition, the crooks had purchased six thousand dollars' worth of silver bricks. Against the comparatively modest outlay of Tanner and Eden, they had taken in from Mrs. Roberts almost a quarter of a million dollars. Whereas the first map had cost the woman only sixteen hundred dollars, the prices of the maps had gradually gone up to the point where they were now costing as high as fifteen thousand dollars each.

One afternoon, during the third year of the swindle operations, Mrs. Roberts received a visit from Garrett's wife —Docia Garrett, her daughter, who had just returned to Texas from a round-the-world trip. Among other things, Mrs. Garrett was very partial to a small movie camera, which she carried with her wherever she went. When she learned about the treasure hunts on Signal Hill she decided to make a film of the operations. She did not, however, say anything to anyone about her plans for making a movie, since the picture was to be in the nature of a surprise for her mother. And so one fine bright afternoon Mrs. Garrett concealed herself in some bushes on Signal Hill, only a few feet from where Tanner and the Reverend Doctor Bryant were busy digging while Mrs. Roberts looked on, and obtained about two hundred feet of film which she intended to entitle, "Treasure Hunt on Mama's Ranch." It so happened, however, that Mrs. Garrett neglected to have the film developed and stored it away among some miscellaneous effects prior to her departure for another extended trip abroad.

By the middle of 1935, Mrs. Roberts began to grow jittery about the amount of supposed gold bricks stored on her ranch. The value of the bricks, she had been led to believe, was in the neighborhood of three million dollars. The two crooks had been putting her off from time to time when she had suggested that the bricks be taken to the New Orleans mint, but now the old lady became so insistent that Tanner and Eden were obliged at least to go through the motions of agreeing with her lest their behavior excite suspicion. Accordingly, arrangements were made to transport the fortune from Big Spring to the mint at New Orleans.

For purposes of transportation, Mrs. Roberts purchased a covered Dodge truck, and Garrett and the two con men personally loaded the truck, over a period of days, with almost four tons of spurious bricks—supposedly worth about three million dollars, but actually worth a little less than four thousand. The arrangement was that the Reverend Doctor Bryant was to travel alone in the truck containing the bricks and that Garrett and Tanner were to follow him in a regular passenger vehicle. This was Bryant's idea. "Since I am a minister," he pointed out to Garrett and Mrs. Roberts, "nobody would think to hold me up on the highway, because ministers are usually poor."

A further arrangement was made whereby if the truck and the passenger car became separated and lost contact with one another during the journey to New Orleans, the Reverend Doctor Bryant and the other two men were to meet in the Rice Hotel in Houston—the first night's stop. The swindlers saw to it that they got caught in a traffic jam in San Antonio, late the first morning. As a result, neither Garrett nor Tanner laid eyes on the truck all the rest of that

day. When they arrived in Houston that night and registered at the Rice Hotel, they learned that the Reverend Doctor Bryant had not put in an appearance. Nor did he appear
all that night.

Early the next morning, Tanner rushed into Garrett's
room in a lather of excitement. "I just got a phone call from
a tourist camp operator back along the road at Richmond,"
he said to Garrett. "He says there is a man there named
Bryant who is badly hurt and who told him to call me right
away."

When Garrett and Tanner reached the tourist camp they
found the man in ministerial garb the victim of a terrific
beating. His body was covered with lacerations and bruises,
his eyes were blackened and his head was cut. "What happened?" asked Tanner.

The Reverend Doctor Bryant was hardly in any condition
to talk. As nearly as Garrett could make out, the man had
been held up by two highwaymen who had followed him
in a sedan and forced his truck into a ditch along a desolate
stretch of highway. Actually, of course, the two men in the
sedan had been hired by both Tanner and Eden to stage
the holdup and make off with the truck, so that the spurious bricks would never reach the mint, there to be detected.
The hired highwaymen, however, had displayed a little too
much enthusiasm for their work and had given the phony
minister such a thorough going over that they had really
put him in pretty bad shape.

Eden spent some time in a Houston hospital, and when he
recovered he and Tanner returned to Big Spring to talk
things over with Mrs. Roberts and Garrett. Strangely
enough, there was not the slightest suspicion on the part of
Mrs. Roberts or her son-in-law about either Tanner or the
man in clerical garb. The question of notifying the police
about the hijacking was, naturally, brought up by both
Mrs. Roberts and her son-in-law. Tanner counseled against

notifying the authorities about the crime because, as he put it, the United States Government would probably deal very harshly with anyone who had been in possession of three million dollars in gold and lost it while the gold was being transported to a mint. In other words, Tanner sold the widow on the idea that she had not lost her own property, but government property—an idea that was not so far-fetched as it might seem on the surface, for all gold had previously been called in by Uncle Sam and, had the bricks been real, as Mrs. Roberts thought them to be, she would have been open at least to a technical charge of hoarding the precious metal.

Within a few months after the staged hijacking, Tanner and Eden were ready to go to work on Mrs. Roberts again. They sold her on the theory that, since she had lost considerable in actual money laid out, it was only sound monetary practice to get that money back by means of purchasing more maps. The Reverend Doctor Bryant, now fully recovered, went off to Mexico again and returned with the story that he could purchase, for fifty thousand dollars in cash, one of the best maps available—a map that would be the key to the recovery of at least a million dollars in bullion.

Mrs. Roberts suddenly grew cautious. Fifty thousand dollars, she said, was too much to pay for one map. The phony minister returned to Mexico, called Mrs. Roberts on the long-distance phone and said that he had gotten the price down to forty thousand dollars. The widow thought that was still too high. After further supposed negotiations with the owner of the map, the price was marked down to thirty-two thousand five-hundred dollars, which was agreeable to Mrs. Roberts. The money was paid and the map was produced and a huge supply of gold bricks were found—the same spurious bricks that had been part of the hijacked cargo en route to the mint. After the fake holdup the bricks had been taken to a small ranch that Eden owned and there secreted until needed.

Apparently the latest treasure to be dug up was worth approximately one million dollars. Mrs. Roberts, desirous of recouping the loss she had sustained in the hijacking, was anxious that the latest batch of treasure be transported as quickly as possible to the New Orleans mint. It was Tanner who managed to stymie this move with a statement to the effect that he had heard that Uncle Sam was getting really tough with gold hoarders—and, he hastened to add, Mrs. Roberts was technically a gold hoarder. "But leave everything to me," Tanner concluded. "I'll attend to the technicalities so that you won't get into trouble, Mrs. Roberts." By this time—along toward the beginning of 1936—Mrs. Roberts had been clipped for almost a third of a million dollars.

Now Tanner, of all people, tossed a monkey wrench into the swindle machinery by getting drunk in a saloon in his home town in Texas. He began to boast, while in his cups, that he had just cleaned up a fortune by selling brass bricks for gold bricks. Inasmuch as Tanner had long been a character who was far from admirable, he had many enemies, and one of his enemies happened to be in the saloon when he did his boasting. As a result, a tip eventually reached the ears of Customs Patrol Inspector A. B. Cummings, a crack sleuth of long experience along the Texas-Mexican border —a garbled tip to the effect that Tanner was engaged in smuggling. As it happened, Inspector Cummings had from time to time in the past suspected Tanner of running contraband over the border, but he had never been able to pin anything on him.

Inspector Cummings and other Customs men spent considerable time shadowing Tanner, in addition to digging into his recent background. But they found no evidence of customs violations. They did find, however, that Tanner had apparently recently come into considerable wealth, for in a period of twelve months he had purchased no less than ten new automobiles for a wild-driving blood relative who wrecked the cars, one after the other. Moreover, Tanner had built himself a magnificent new home which was one of the show places of the vicinity. Cummings, despite the fact that he could get no evidence of crime on Tanner, decided to have a talk with the man. Tanner presented a picture of outraged innocence. "As God is my judge," he said, no doubt having picked up a spurious religious attitude from his co-conspirator, "I have committed no crime of any kind."

As time passed, Tanner, rolling in wealth, continued to indulge his pronounced taste for alcoholic beverages. He became swaggering, arrogant and abusive, and traveled the saloon circuit near his home with two surly Mexican bodyguards. He made enemies almost as fast as his Mexican bodyguards could count them. And he continued to boast— to boast about what a clever man he was, and how the Federal authorities had been on his trail but had been unable to get the goods on him.

More time passed. Occasionally, either Tanner or the Reverend Doctor Bryant would pay a visit to the Roberts ranch at Big Spring. Mrs. Roberts and Garrett, her son-in-law, had such implicit faith in the men that it still did not occur to either of them to suspect that everything wasn't exactly as the two swindlers pictured it to be. True, Mrs. Roberts had been stalled for a long time now in any attempt to dispose of the gold bricks that had been unearthed in 1935. But the crooks had had a likely story all the way along. They had thoroughly frightened the widow into believing that she would get into serious trouble if it became known that she had hoarded so much gold for such a length of time in violation of a Government law against gold hoarding. "But don't worry," Tanner assured Mrs. Roberts. "Gold is as good as cash any day in the week. Eventually we will find a way out of the difficulty."

In the meantime, Secret Service Agents and Intelligence Unit Agents, their ears to the ground, had begun to hear stories to the effect that Tanner had made a killing. A Secret Service investigation disclosed that Tanner had not run afoul of any regulation within the jurisdiction of that service. But when Elmer L. Irey, Chief of the Intelligence Unit, heard about the financial killing that Tanner was supposed to have made, he assigned Agent James R. Adams to run the story to the ground.

Agent Adams made it his business to contact enemies of Tanner. From these people he learned that Tanner had, over a period of years, beginning in 1932, made regular trips to Big Spring. Adams took a trip to Big Spring and talked with residents there and was not long in learning that a man answering the description of Tanner—together with another, older man—had frequently called at the ranch of Widow Roberts. When the Intelligence Unit Agent sought out Mrs. Roberts for an interview she seemed most uncooperative. It was only after considerable persuasion on the part of Adams that the old lady, who was now well into her seventies but clear of mind, told the story of the gold bricks and the silver bricks.

Agent Adams could hardly believe his ears. He had a talk with Garrett, a highly reputable man, and it was only after Garrett had gone over the entire swindle operation, step by step, that Agent Adams saw how devilishly clever the whole scheme had been. It so happened that Garrett had kept careful note of every expenditure that his mother-in-law had made. He had likewise kept just as careful a note of every brick that had been dug up from Signal Hill.

It took the Federal investigators only a short time to locate the place of origin of the brass bricks—the Acme Brass Foundry in San Antonio. The employee in the foundry, who of course had no idea of the purpose for which the brass castings were to be used, identified Tanner as the purchaser of the bricks. He also mentioned the fact that Tanner had on one occasion been accompanied by a tall, pious-looking man some twenty years his senior. This individual, Adams suspected, had been the Reverend Doctor Bryant who, of course, had been thoroughly described to him by both Mrs. Roberts and her son-in-law.

The only difficulty was that a thorough probe into all known associates of Tanner, both past and present, had failed to disclose anyone named J. B. Bryant. City directories and telephone books within a radius of three hundred miles of Tanner's home in Texas were carefully scrutinized for some trace of a J. B. Bryant, but to no avail. Telephone company records were subpoenaed—particularly records relating to calls that had been made from Mexico to the Roberts ranch—and the aid of the Mexican Police was also enlisted, but the Reverend Doctor Bryant remained a phantom so far as the investigators were concerned.

Chief Irey, directing the investigation from Washington, had Tanner's income-tax returns for the years of the swindle —1933, 1934 and 1935—looked up, and found that the man had paid no tax at all during the three years in question. Tanner was thereupon indicted for criminal evasion of income taxes. When he was arrested he was asked who his confederate had been. He refused to talk. An examination of Tanner's bank accounts and safety deposit boxes disclosed that during the years of 1933, 1934 and 1935 he had taken in approximately one hundred fifty thousand dollars, or exactly half of the total proceeds from the Roberts swindle. It was quite clear, then, that the Reverend Doctor Bryant, whoever he was, had split the Roberts swindle-take with Tanner on a fifty-fifty basis.

When Agent Adams and other Intelligence Unit investigators continued to probe the background of Tanner, they discovered that the man had an uncle named Eden. Very few people who knew both Tanner and Eden had ever seen the two men together. Nevertheless, Eden resembled, at least in a general way, the physical description of the Reverend Doctor Bryant as furnished by Mrs. Roberts and her son-in-law and by the employee of the San Antonio foundry who had seen the man in clerical garb on one occasion. A quiet investigation was forthwith begun into various bank accounts that Eden maintained, but no trace of the one hundred fifty thousand dollars that he was suspected of having gotten was found. Nevertheless, the Intelligence Unit felt that it had the right man.

There were, however, serious hurdles for the investigators to overcome, particularly relating to Eden. The statute of limitations had expired, so far as state prosecution for a swindle was concerned; and Mrs. Roberts still remained uncooperative, at least when it came to her going into court and testifying against either of the men when they were tried for criminal evasion of the income-tax laws. Moreover, Tanner himself absolutely refused to implicate Eden. All of which meant that perhaps a smart attorney might have convinced a jury that Eden had not really been the mysterious Doctor Bryant.

Then Agent Adams heard the story about the movie of the treasure hunt that Mrs. Roberts' daughter—Mrs. Garrett—had taken. The film had long since been developed and assembled under the title of "Treasure Hunt on Mama's Ranch." Agent Adams took the reels to the home of a friend who owned a projection machine and had them run off. There could be no question now as to the identity of the Reverend Doctor Bryant. Without realizing it, Eden had, years before, looked directly into the lens of the secreted movie camera. And that cooked his goose. When the film was run off for him, he abandoned his elaborate act of claiming that he was a victim of mistaken identity, told the investigators the whole story, and led them to the safety deposit boxes where, under assumed names, he had cached his half of the swindle loot.

On the last day of January, 1940, Eden and Tanner pleaded guilty to criminal evasion of income taxes when arraigned in the United States Court at Austin. The swindlers were sentenced to penitentiary terms and heavily fined and penalized.

Crime of the Century

by J. EDGAR HOOVER

Titles don't always fit stories perfectly. J. Edgar Hoover's does, however, for this crime affected the life of every person on earth. What makes this story important reading for every American is not only the dramatic recital of the crime but the fascinating insight into the mind of the man who committed it.

O N A JANUARY AFTERNOON in 1944, two men—one an American citizen, the other a British subject—came face-to-face for the first time at a street corner on New York City's lower East Side, and the history of the world began to change.

One man carried a pair of gloves and a book with a green binding. The other held a tennis ball in his left hand. By gloves, book, and ball, they were identifying each other in a clandestine meeting, planned months before across the Atlantic Ocean by their masters in espionage.

The two strangers took a cab to a restaurant on lower Third Avenue. Over the luncheon table, the shorter, chubbier one gave his name merely as "Raymond." Never, in all their subsequent meetings, would he disclose his real name—Harry Gold.

83

The other man—thin, sallow-complexioned, with stooping shoulders, balding head, and weak brown eyes behind thick lenses—was less secretive. He introduced himself as Dr. Klaus Fuchs.

Fuchs, in New York as a member of a British mission, told Gold he was collaborating with the Manhattan Engineer District in attempting to harness the energy produced by nuclear fission for use in military weapons.

Gold could scarcely speak. Not a profound scientist—as Fuchs was—Harry Gold was enough of a chemist to realize the appalling nature of an atomic energy project.

After that first meeting, Gold took a train back to Philadelphia, where he was employed in the laboratories of the Pennsylvania Sugar Company. Leaning back in his seat, he brooded in a kind of ecstasy on the Jekyll-Hyde existence he was living.

At home, he lived a quiet life with his mother and father. How did he get started as a traitor?

One must realize first of all that Harry Gold considered himself an idealist, which made him feel above the law, justifying means by ends. This moral confusion Gold showed in his high school days. Once, while helping a teacher grade examination papers, he stayed up all night making illicit erasures and corrections so not a single student would fail.

In Harry Gold's ideal life, "everybody should pass—they're entitled to it."

This country had treated him well since he'd been brought here, a three-year-old child of an immigrant family, in July, 1914. His father, a cabinetmaker, wanted Harry to learn as much as he could. After attending public schools, Harry went to the University of Pennsylvania, and to Drexel Institute, where he specialized in chemistry. Then, he got a job with the Pennsylvania Sugar Company.

Some time later, Harry Gold came under the influence of a man who was to alter the course of his life. Laid off by

Pennsylvania Sugar, he was referred by a friend to a singular character in Jersey City, whom we shall call Troy Niles. Niles helped Gold find employment in a Jersey City laboratory, and took him under his wing.

Away from home for the first time, and captivated by Niles, Gold entered a world of new ideas. He learned of his new friend's participation in atheist clubs and forums, his studies of Marx and Lenin, and how he'd become a member of the Communist Party.

Gold spent long evenings with his friend, hearing zealots talk politics, economics, and the Soviets. Niles was an eccentric individual who liked to coil a pet blacksnake around his neck, and who pitched marbles to a crow trained to catch them in flight.

When, a few months later, Harry Gold was rehired by Pennsylvania Sugar Company, he continued to see Niles regularly.

Gold did not quickly accept communism. He was not politically minded, and the talk about dialectical materialism bored him. In a legal sense, Harry Gold never was a member of the Communist Party. He became a Soviet agent through association with Red friends and misguided idealism for the "underdog."

"Russia," Niles told him one day in the middle 1930's, "is a downtrodden country where millions of honest men and women starve because they don't have enough to eat."

That statement hurt Harry Gold. It evoked his feeling that all people should have a fair chance—"everybody should pass." How, then, could a man help?

Niles was ready with an immediate suggestion. He had a friend at the Amtorg Trading Corporation, a Russian agency. As far as he could, Niles was helping his friend—and Russia— by passing along any technical information he picked up. Maybe Gold would like to help, too—by passing along industrial processes from the Pennsylvania Sugar Company?

Harry Gold was very thoughtful. Perhaps some chemical processes, secretly abstracted from his employers, might aid in the swifter industrialization of Russia, and thus help feed the wretched, starving millions.

Soon after that, on a bitter night in the winter of 1935–36, Niles and Gold stood together outside Penn Station, in New York City. Suddenly, a young, square-chinned man approached. He twitched his right shoulder as he passed. Niles at once fell into step, and Gold followed.

"This is Paul Smith," Niles said. Then Niles turned into a side street, and disappeared in the evening crowd. Harry Gold was alone with his first Soviet superior in espionage.

In clear, slightly clipped words, "Smith" came straight to the point.

"We're interested in solvents. There's a process involving the manufacture of absolute ethyl alcohol on which we know your chief chemist is working. You know anything about it?"

"A little. Not much."

"Look things over," Smith commanded, his tone conveying that he was boss. "And bring me a written biographical sketch of yourself at our next meeting. Make it detailed. And you are not to see Niles again."

Then, after arranging a later meeting, Smith turned without a parting word, and was lost in traffic.

From then on, Harry Gold stole secret industrial processes and formulas from the Pennsylvania Sugar Company and its subsidiary, the Franco-American Chemical Works. He prepared reports, often with sketches and diagrams, and passed them to intermediaries on New York street corners.

The inner ego of Harry Gold was getting a strange "lift" from this activity. Accustomed to a drab, dreary existence in a chemical laboratory, he felt that at last he was being "useful."

Within the space of a few months during late 1937 and early 1938, Gold received two new espionage bosses. The first was "Steve Swartz," a virtual giant, about six-feet two-inches tall, and weighing about two hundred twenty pounds. The Russians soon realized their mistake. The giant, gangly Steve walking down the street with little, five-foot six-inch Harry Gold would be likely to attract attention.

"Fred" was Steve's successor. He taught Gold to take extreme precautions in making contacts. He offered suggestions on how to determine whether he was being followed: stop and tie a shoelace, or walk up a deserted side street. And if Gold had a piece of paper he wanted to destroy? Tear it into very small pieces, and drop each piece in a different block.

The Soviets never sent Gold to a formal school for espionage. But hint by hint, instruction by instruction, he became skilled in the intricacies of underground intrigue.

The Russians obviously were grooming him for more important assignments.

Fred kept urging Gold to produce more information. Gold replied that Pennsylvania Sugar had been drained dry—there weren't any more secrets to steal.

"Then get a different job," Fred instructed, and specifically suggested the Philadelphia Navy Yard.

Harry stalled about changing jobs. Actually, he told Fred, he was planning to return to school for further chemistry studies. In September, 1938, he enrolled at Xavier University, in Cincinnati.

While the Russians would have preferred that he attend a technical institute, such as MIT, nevertheless a degree in chemistry would better equip him for espionage in the field of science. The Russians were quite willing to help financially, and during the next two years furnished Gold about $600 toward his education.

Harry graduated with chemistry honors, tenth in a class

of eighty-three. His lowest grade, prophetically, was in a course called "Principles of Ethics."

When he returned to Philadelphia, and to a better job at the Pennsylvania Sugar Company, the Soviet ring found new things for him to do.

From 1940 to 1943, he became more and more deeply involved, as the tempo and importance of his undercover activities increased.

By early 1944, he'd proved his dependability and trustworthiness as a contact man. "Sam," then his Soviet boss, told Harry he was to undertake a supremely important assignment. The new task was so critical, Sam said, that Gold must drop all other work, and concentrate exclusively on his new instructions.

This was the time when, with a pair of gloves and a book, Gold first met the pale stranger with the tennis ball, Dr. Klaus Fuchs. He was now entering the climax of his career as an espionage agent.

Six or seven times during the next six months—until June 1944—Gold and Fuchs met in New York. Sometimes the meetings were lengthy. Once they spent an hour and a half strolling along the paths of Central Park. Another time, they tramped a long portion of the Grand Concourse, in the Bronx.

They never engaged in idle conversation or small talk. Time was too precious to both, their encounters too dangerous. Every word spoken by Fuchs was addressed solely to the Russians, through Harry Gold.

When Fuchs knew he'd have written information to pass, he'd prepare Gold at a previous meeting, laying plans for a rapid transfer from himself to Gold, and from Gold to "John," Gold's latest Soviet supervisor. For these transfers, the meetings were short. On one occasion in March, 1944, for example, they were together less than a minute. Meeting on Madison Avenue, they took a few steps together, then turned west into a side street. There, Fuchs passed the papers to Gold, and slipped away.

Gold then turned down Fifth Avenue, and within fifteen minutes, handed the data to his Soviet partner in exactly the same manner.

The precautions Gold took en route to his meetings with Fuchs were elaborate. Frequently, he'd use various means of transportation—subway, bus, taxi, all going in a direction away from the meeting place. Only when assured he wasn't being followed would he proceed to his destination.

And then, suddenly and without warning, Dr. Fuchs disappeared.

This was in July, 1944. A meeting had been scheduled near the Brooklyn Museum of Art. Fuchs didn't appear. Nor did he show up at a scheduled alternate meeting on Central Park West. The bewildered Gold hastily reported the absences to John, who became alarmed.

"He left town," was all that could be learned from the janitor of Fuchs' apartment house at 128 West 77th Street, in New York.

From the biographical data on Dr. Fuchs in the possession of the Russians, John dug out the name of the scientist's sister, who lived in Cambridge, Massachusetts.

Gold was dispatched to question her. Mrs. Kristel Heineman knew only that her brother had been transferred to some place in the Southwest. She expected he might be home for a Christmas visit, however. Gold gave her an envelope containing a New York telephone number, requesting her to give it to her brother on his next visit.

What had happened, of course, was that Dr. Fuchs had been whisked off to Los Alamos. He and Gold re-established contact in Cambridge when Fuchs visited the Heinemans, shortly after Christmas.

Fuchs' manner now was tense and precise. Only with the greatest difficulty had he been able to wangle time off to make this trip. Henceforth, Gold—still known only as "Raymond" to Dr. Fuchs—would have to come to New Mexico if further information was to be delivered.

Arrangements were made to meet again on the first Saturday in June, 1945, at 4 PM on the Castillo Street Bridge, in Santa Fe, New Mexico.

Before they parted that winter afternoon, Dr. Fuchs turned over to Gold a bulky envelope crammed with all the data he could copy or filch—reports on progress-to-date in the Los Alamos experiment. By now, Fuchs had free access at Los Alamos to volumes of top-secret material, to the research results of first-rank colleagues.

On the appointed June day, Gold arrived in Santa Fe an hour and a half before the four o'clock appointment. Like a casual tourist, he entered a museum and obtained a city map. Now, he wouldn't have to ask directions to the Castillo Street Bridge. He aimed at leaving not a single clue.

A minute or two after four o'clock, a dilapidated old car with Fuchs at the wheel came chugging down Alameda Street. Work was going well at Los Alamos, Fuchs reported, but he reiterated a forecast he'd made once before—the atomic bomb process wouldn't be completed in time for use against the Japanese.

Their next meeting in Santa Fe was set for three months later. Then, just before the two men parted, Fuchs gave Gold a packet of vital information. It was standard practice for the incriminating parcel to be withheld until the last minute. If the two men were accosted together, Fuchs and not Gold would have the information on his person—and Fuchs had a right to it.

Several days later, the stolen material was in John's hands.

The final transfer of atomic bomb information—data on the completed process—was made on September 19, 1945, a little more than a month after two A-bombs had been dropped on Japan.

At 6 PM, Gold was waiting outside a church on the outskirts of Santa Fe. Dr. Fuchs appeared quite late, this time. He was driving the rattling old car. Fuchs was like a changed man, human for once, even jovial. The long months of work on the atomic project had ended in success.

He drove the old car to a nearby bluff overlooking the blinking lights of the city, just blinking on through the haze of dusk. He told Gold how awe-stricken he'd felt as he watched the first atom test explosion, at Alamogordo, New Mexico. It astounded him that atomic weapons had been completed in time for use in the Japanese war. He conceded that he'd grossly underestimated the industrial potential of the United States.

They talked a while longer. Then, as night came down, Fuchs started the motor and headed toward Santa Fe. Just as the car neared the downtown center, the scientist pulled from his pocket the last envelope of information. A moment later, he stopped the car. Gold slipped out and started walking toward the bus station.

The two men were never to see each other again.

Long afterward, the Federal Bureau of Investigation learned that the basic secrets of nuclear fission had been stolen. It was the responsibility of the FBI to find the guilty men. To this end, we immediately mobilized every resource known to us.

Investigation at home and abroad led us to conclude that the inside man was most probably a trusted member of a foreign scientific group. Day by day, as our researches continued, the finger of suspicion pointed more and more directly at a shy, brilliant young physicist and mathematician, Klaus Fuchs.

By this time, Fuchs had returned to England, where he was stationed at Harwell, the British atomic research plant.

Data developed by the FBI about Dr. Fuchs was promptly given to English authorities, and under the direction of the very competent Sir Percy Sillitoe, British security officials took up the investigation.

By January, 1950, Fuchs was identified beyond all reasonable doubt as the principal culprit. After prolonged interviews, he confessed. With his confession, however, we realized that our real search had just begun. For Fuchs, while indicting himself, implicated no one else by name.

He disclosed that while in the United States, he had dealt with only one Soviet agent. The man's name? Fuchs had never known it. The man appeared to know chemistry and engineering, but was not a nuclear physicist. Fuchs thought he was probably not an employee of an atomic-energy installation.

What did the man look like? Well, he was from forty to forty-five years of age, possibly five-feet ten-inches tall, broad build, round face, most likely a first generation American. A description which might fit millions of men.

Where did he live? Dr. Fuchs had never known. Fuchs had carried a tennis ball to their first rendezvous, and met a man with a pair of gloves and a book with a green binding. How many times had he met this person? Several times in New York City, once in Cambridge, and twice in Santa Fe. When? The New York meetings were in 1944. The last contact, Fuchs believed, was in the fall of 1945.

That was about all he could tell.

A flimsy fabric from which to find the identity of a spy who remained at large in the United States.

In all the history of the FBI, there never was a more important problem than this one, never another case where we felt ourselves under such pressure. The unknown man simply had to be found. And the job was all the more difficult because of the necessity for absolute secrecy. Only a few top American officials shared with me the full details and widespread ramifications of the investigation.

At the start, the quest was utterly unlike the pursuit of a bank robber who has left fingerprints on a safe door. Unlike the investigation of a "hot car" ring, where photographs, detailed identifying descriptions, and long criminal records often facilitate the job.

In this manhunt, the wanted person could be almost any man in the United States.

Our starting place was Cambridge, because Fuchs had admitted meeting the agent there, and because it was the home of Fuchs' sister, Mrs. Heineman. Already we knew the scientist had visited her there. Did Mrs. Heineman know anything about the Soviet agent Fuchs had mentioned?

Well, Mrs. Heineman recalled a man about forty years old, stocky, and with dark-brown hair. He'd called at her home three times. On his first visit, he'd introduced himself as a friend of her brother's, and said he was a chemist. He said he'd worked with Dr. Fuchs and was anxious to see him—this was at the time Fuchs disappeared from New York.

She couldn't remember his name. No, he had no accent.

The second call occurred when Fuchs was visiting the Heinemans after Christmas. It was clear to the sister that the two men had met before, as they greeted each other in her living room. Though present in the room part of the time, she hadn't followed their conversation. When the visitor left, her brother told her nothing. The Heineman children liked him, however—he brought them candy.

Some time later—a few weeks or months—the unknown had again appeared at the Heineman house, and had stayed for lunch. Mrs. Heineman thought he might've mentioned a wife and two small children.

The shadow seemed to be taking on a semblance of form. A man of about forty, stocky, with dark-brown hair. A chemist. A friendly, genial man, who liked children. Probably married, with youngsters of his own. He talked without an accent.

Part of this, as you see, was right. And part of it was very wrong.

Robert Heineman, Kristel's husband, offered more details. He'd seen the stranger at the time of the third visit. He recalled the stranger mentioning Philadelphia. He was of the opinion the man had arrived in Boston by train.

Another avenue opened. A friend of the Heinemans, who'd been present during one of the visits, recalled that the man discussed vitamins. From this conversation, he obtained the impression that the stranger was a bacteriologist, connected in some way with a New York wholesale grocery company.

And then Mrs. Heineman recalled that on the third visit, the stranger had promised her son a chemistry set. The youngster, six at the time, was questioned by his father, but could remember nothing about the man. Nor could his little sister.

Suddenly, Mr. Heineman remembered another clue. He thought the stranger's first name might have been James, with his last name starting with the letters, let us say, "D-a-v." "James Dav . . ." was the best Mr. Heineman could recollect.

Was there a "James Dav . . ." in New York City, Santa Fe, or Philadelphia, possible residence locations of the shadow? As a starting point on this lead, the FBI undertook to sift its own files, a tedious and time-consuming process, but no possibility could be overlooked.

Soon, during this file check, one name stood out above all the others—an individual we'll call James Davidson, an engineer residing in New York City. He met the general physical and background requirements, and employment records showed he was absent from his job during Fuchs' visit in Cambridge.

Moreover, James Davidson could have been available at other meetings.

A group of photographs was flown to England and laid before Dr. Fuchs in Wormwood Scrubs Prison. These were photographs of many different individuals, each a possible suspect.

Dr. Fuchs rejected all except one—a picture of the man we call James Davidson.

He examined that photograph for a long while, his delicate fingers tapping the table, his forehead wrinkling in deep furrows. "There's something familiar about this man," he murmured. Then, he covered the forehead to simulate a hat, and added: "I cannot swear, but I'm pretty sure this is the man."

The interrogator requested the German scientist to try to visualize his American contact, just as he saw him at their first meeting in Manhattan, then look again at the photograph. Fuchs complied, staring long and hard. Then, he nodded and repeated: "I think it's the man."

Obviously, no investigation can be allowed to rest exclusively on evidence of this nature. There had to be corroboration. The charges were too serious for any possibility of error. The next people to be shown the pictures would be the Heinemans, in Cambridge.

If they, too, selected Davidson's photograph from the others, Fuchs' identification would be greatly strengthened.

The Heinemans looked carefully at the pictures, then shook their heads. No, they'd never seen any of these men before. Later, Robert Heineman was given an opportunity to observe the real James Davidson in person, a test far more accurate than a photograph. Now, he was even more positive. James Davidson had never visited his home.

Who was right—Fuchs, or his sister and brother-in-law?

For the very same reasons that Davidson couldn't be arrested on the basis of Fuchs' identification, he could not now be dismissed on the Heinemans' rejections. The investigation still had a long way to go.

Since Fuchs and the Heinemans seemed fairly certain that Fuchs' contact had been a chemist, the FBI instituted a systematic review of all Bureau cases in which chemists had been involved. In our Washington headquarters, and in each of our fifty-two Field Offices, we were looking for a chemist who would possess the other identifying factors.

Soon, we had numerous suspects. Some tallied in virtually all details, others in some of them, and a few in only one. Each was thoroughly considered, and more and more photos were shown to the Heinemans in Cambridge, then flown across the Atlantic for Dr. Fuchs to observe.

In some photos, the Heinemans saw familiar characteristics. Dr. Fuchs saw familiar points in others. Nowhere, though, among the fifteen-hundred-odd photographs did the Heinemans feel they saw the face of the man who'd called at their home. Thus far, only in Fuchs' tentative identification of James Davidson had any recognition been obtained.

By now, the FBI's investigation was many-pronged. Here are some of the forms it took:

Agents set out to talk with all the tenants who'd lived in the New York City apartment house on 77th Street when Fuchs was a resident. Naturally, the years had scattered many of them to distant places, but they were located and interviewed. Could any of them furnish any information?

No.

Former members of the British Mission, and former employees of the Manhattan Engineer Project were also interviewed. All remembered Fuchs as a brilliant scientist, not given to social mixing or chatty conversation—and they knew nothing important about his friends.

In Santa Fe, Special Agents made inquiries at bus, air-travel and railroad ticket offices. Hotel registrations were analyzed. No information appeared which seemed to tie in with any suspects.

Could the chemical laboratories in New York City offer any leads? As an indication of the scope of such an undertaking, seventy-five thousand licensing permits were issued to chemical firms by the City of New York in 1945 alone.

The principal result of these widespread inquiries was definitely to eliminate James Davidson as a suspect.

Meanwhile, we were coming closer to our man. As suspect after suspect was eliminated, the field narrowed from fifteen hundred possibilities to only about a score. And in this final handful, one suspect was beginning to stand out. He was around forty, brown-haired and stocky, and while not a first generation American, he'd come to the United States as a small child, and might easily be mistaken for a native. He was a chemist, he lived in Philadelphia, and he'd taken many trips to New York.

His name was Harry Gold.

However, there were points of discrepancy. Gold was single; the Heinemans thought the stranger was married and had children. Mr. Heineman believed the chemist's name had been "James Dav . . ."; this in no way sounded like "Harry Gold."

Nevertheless, for one important reason, we began to concentrate on this man. The reason—in 1947, the FBI had found it necessary, in a different Communist inquiry, to question him.

We knew that *some* chemist had worked with Dr. Fuchs. And Harry Gold was a chemist who seemed to fit the general pattern in many other particulars.

Our hopes were high as photos of Gold were flown across the Atlantic to Dr. Fuchs. The wan prisoner squinted at the

American's round face and bushy hair. Then he shook his head.

"No," he declared. Harry Gold was not his American confederate.

Was the great search back again at the starting point? Such heartbreaking setbacks aren't unusual in investigative work. To start all over on another approach, and try to construct success out of the rubble of defeat, is more or less routine.

We still weren't entirely convinced, though, that Gold was cleared. We decided to dig deeper for more data about Harry Gold. We'd talk to people who'd been associated with him in any way. Perhaps they'd be able to clarify the character and career of this Philadelphia chemist. The most minute clue might open untold avenues of investigation.

In this process, a provocative detail came to light. A former associate of a man named Abraham Brothman, for whom Gold had once worked, stated that he remembered a friend of Brothman's named Frank Keppler. He hadn't seen Keppler for a number of years, but he felt that Keppler might be a chemist.

Could he pick out Keppler from a group of pictures? Looking at a large number of photos, he pointed unhesitatingly at one.

"This is Frank Keppler."

He was indicating a picture of Harry Gold. Why had Gold used an alias in meeting an associate of Brothman? Something was peculiar. Larger than ever, in the Spring of 1950, Harry Gold loomed as our most likely candidate.

It was May 15, 1950, when two Special Agents of the FBI entered the Philadelphia General Hospital and asked for Harry Gold. At that time, he held the responsible position of chemist in charge of biological research at the hospital's heart station. The Special Agents explained they wanted to interview Gold. He was busy. Would the Agents kindly come back a little later? Yes, they would.

That evening, declaring he was glad to cooperate, Harry Gold consented to be interviewed. He'd been questioned before by the FBI. What did the Agents want to know now?

The discussion centered first on Gold's general background. Then a picture of Dr. Fuchs was shown to him. Gold frowned at it for a moment, then surprised the Agents by exclaiming:

"He's that English spy!"

It was a tense moment. The Agents spoke with meticulous care. Had Gold ever known Fuchs? Certainly not. Had he ever seen Fuchs? No. He recognized the picture because it had been published in the newspapers.

Gold readily gave details regarding his life and employment—facts the FBI already knew intimately. But where had he gone on vacations and special leaves in 1944 and 1945? Gold asserted he'd never in his life been west of the Mississippi River, nor had he made any trips to New England.

These were points of significance, because Fuchs' partner had undoubtedly been in both Cambridge and New Mexico. For a moment the Agents changed the subject.

How about Abraham Brothman? Yes, Gold said, they'd been good friends. He'd talked with the FBI about Brothman in 1947. He'd stopped working for him in 1948 because the business enterprise in which they were associated had fared badly. Gold wasn't being paid, so he quit. He liked his job in the Philadelphia General Hospital much better.

Next a vital question: Why had Gold used the alias of Frank Keppler when he was introduced to one of Brothman's associates?

Gold had a ready answer. While he was still employed at the Pennsylvania Sugar Company, he was conducting laboratory experiments for Brothman, and didn't want his Philadelphia boss to find out about this unethical practice. This defense, though, was weak, and by now, Gold's eyes looked troubled.

Then came another discrepancy. Why had Gold told Brothman's secretary that he was married, was the father of two children, and further, that his brother had been a paratrooper killed in action?

Gold denied ever making the statements.

Next, they showed him pictures of the Heinemans. Could he identify them? Positively not. Who were these people? He'd never seen them in his life.

Now, a still more delicate matter. Would Gold allow motion pictures to be taken of himself? Of course. Why not? Take as many as you want. The Agents took motion pictures of him. Much earlier, however, unknown to Gold, the FBI had already obtained motion pictures of him. Those secret films had already been flown to Dr. Fuchs.

Gold was interviewed on several occasions in the next few days. He was always most polite, and offered his cooperation. Unfortunately, he kept saying, he didn't have much to tell. His life was that of an ordinary citizen. He'd never been prominent, received a high salary, or worked in plants possessing confidential or restricted contracts.

Now, to prove beyond any doubt that he had nothing to conceal, he offered to allow the FBI to search his rooms. He readily signed a written consent.

The search of Gold's dwelling was conducted by two Special Agents in Gold's presence on the morning of May 22. The chemist suggested they start in the bedroom, where he kept most of his personal possessions, papers, books, and chemical journals.

The Agents proceeded methodically. Whenever an item of interest was found, Gold was ready to give an explanation. He was supremely confident. He had an answer for every question.

Suddenly an Agent dredged up from behind a bookcase

a yellow folder. It was marked "Santa Fe, The Capital City." This Chamber of Commerce brochure contained a detailed map of the city. Silently, Gold was shown the folder.

A startled gleam flashed through his eyes. His mouth fell open, and momentarily, he seemed to freeze. This was the map he'd obtained at the Stanta Fe Museum, so he could find his way to the bridge without asking directions.

The shock of seeing the folder was profound. It unmanned him, shattering the habitual, impregnable poise of an accomplished deceiver.

An Agent intoned: "You said you'd never been west of the Mississippi. Or have you?"

The question seemed to pound with resistless force upon the stunned mind of Harry Gold. There was a pause. Gold said nothing. Then the other Agent prodded:

"About this map, Mr. Gold. Would you like to tell the whole truth?"

Then, abruptly, Gold blurted out:

"I . . . I'm the man to whom Klaus Fuchs gave his information."

With those words, the mysterious shadow we'd been seeking became a living, breathing prisoner. And, quite by coincidence, less than an hour after Gold's confession, a cable from London arrived at FBI headquarters in Washington. It said that Dr. Fuchs, after seeing the secretly taken movies, had identified Harry Gold as his American partner.

Standing in Federal Court in Philadelphia on December 9, 1950, Gold confessed his "terrible mistake" to Judge James P. McGranery.

"There is a puny inadequacy about any words telling how deep and horrible is my remorse," he declared. He thanked the Court for a fair trial, and commended the FBI and other agencies of the Department of Justice, and the prison authorities, for good treatment. "Most certainly," he asserted, "this could never have happened in the Soviet Union, or in any of the countries dominated by it."

And then the Judge pronounced the sentence:

"Thirty years."

The moon-faced prisoner nodded, and United States deputy marshals led him out of the courtroom.

Illicit Gold

by JOHN J. FLOHERTY

Smuggling—to reduce it to its simplest terms—can be compared to an outsized game of wits, the goal of the smugglers being an illegal traffic in goods of one kind or another. In this case the goods were shipments of gold and the obstacle course the United States-Canadian border. What the smugglers didn't take into account was that they were pitting themselves against Agents of the United States Treasury.

Some idea of the magnitude of the Treasury men's task may be gained from the fact that some fifty million people and billions of dollars in goods of all kinds pass under their close scrutiny every year. And yet I have been assured by experienced Customs men that the amount of contraband that slips through is negligible. There is a reason for such astonishing efficiency. Behind the nine thousand Customs officers who hold down the front line along our thousands of miles of border and seacoast are some two hundred picked men in the Customs Agency Service, every one of whom has been trained and tried in the art of the crime hunter.

These men are tops in their profession, chosen for their ability, their self-discipline and, above all, for their common sense. They work with the other law enforcement agencies of the Treasury, the Department of Justice and in fact with all accredited law enforcement agents. In the battle of wits that characterizes each case they handle, the smuggler is at a decided disadvantage. In fact the odds are so heavily against him, his chance of escape is little more than one in a hundred. If the smugglers only realized that an offense against Old Mother Treasury becomes a family affair in which some thirty thousand family members from six different departments take a hand, they would at least seek less dangerous fields in which to make easy money.

The futility of trying to outsmart the U. S. Treasury is well illustrated in the following case, taken from its records in Washington.

One sultry afternoon in 1941 a blue sedan, bearing New York license plates, pulled up at an attractive house on Grace Street in the residential section of Toronto, Canada. One of the two men in the car got out and in the most leisurely manner rang the doorbell. In a few moments the door was opened by a pallid young man with sharp features and a livid birthmark on his left cheek. The visitor entered —a stocky and forceful man with a foghorn voice—and said, or rather barked: "Why don't you bring the stuff to New York any more? It costs money to come all the way up here." His manner was churlish.

The young man replied apologetically, "Getting a passport is becoming tougher every day. It's easy for you to come here as a tourist."

"Where's the stuff?" the visitor asked gruffly.

The young man went to the cellar and returned presently with a small box. "Here it is," he said. "One bar and six buttons." The box contained a flat bar of gold and six large cookie-shaped disks of the precious metal. These disks are known to the smuggling fraternity as "buttons."

Without another word, the visitor drew out his wallet and

handed the young man eighty-five hundred dollars in Canadian money. Then he removed his coat and shirt, revealing a white canvas vest with numerous pockets into which he slipped the seven pieces of gold. He put on his shirt and coat, surveyed himself in a mirror that hung in the hall, and went to the door. He paused with his hand on the knob. "When you get more of the stuff," he growled, "give me a call in New York!" With that he hurried to the waiting car.

That same afternoon three men sat in serious conference around a table in the Toronto office of the Foreign Exchange Control Board, an organization set up by the Canadian Government to protect its wartime monetary system. They were Jonas Fell, head of the Board, Inspector Williams, and Constable McElhone of the Royal Canadian Mounties.

Their problem was "high-grading," the theft of gold ore from the mines. This illicit traffic had become a serious drain on the Dominion's national assets. One leak alone, through a single local outlet, showed a loss of nearly a million dollars annually.

The gold smugglers followed a simple plan. Each had a staff of "buyers" who purchased stolen ore from dishonest miners. Later the gold ore was pulverized and melted into bar or button form by means of a simple heater and common flux.

Investigation revealed that certain gold dealers and jewelry manufacturers were merely fences who sold the stolen gold to legitimate refineries.

The average commercial gold jewelry is rarely more than 12 carat or 50 per cent fine. Investigation showed that large quantities of high-grade gold not of the commercial type had been purchased from high-graders who had given fictitious names and addresses. These were soon rounded up and sent to prison. As a result, the Canadian refiners refused to buy any bar or button gold and so dried up the outlet for the illegal bullion. This should have put an end to the high-grading but it did not. Illegal gold still flowed out of the country.

With the Canadian outlets plugged up, it became obvious that the stolen ore was being smuggled across the border into the United States. Canadian officials Fell and McKee hurried to Washington. They called on Frank J. Wilson, Chief of the United States Secret Service, who assured them the fullest cooperation. The Canadians explained that in their effort to identify the high-graders they had placed a watch at the plant of a Toronto assayer. Assayers are licensed by the Mint to determine by analyses the standard of purity of gold, silver and other metals.

Among those obtaining assays were two brothers who had been suspected of high-grading for some time. They had been traced on several occasions to a house on Grace Street, Toronto.

"We have reason to believe," said Fell, "that this house is the headquarters of the conspirators, although we do not know that any gold has changed hands there."

"On what do you base your suspicion?" asked Chief Wilson.

Fell was thoughtful for a moment before he replied, "A youth with a livid birthmark has been seen several times at the house. We believe he is the contact man with the criminals in the United States. Our investigators—on several occasions while the young man was at the house—have seen two men arrive in a car bearing New York license plates and enter. When they left, our men trailed them to the Peace Bridge at Buffalo."

"Hm!" said Chief Wilson; that was all. In a matter of moments he was in communication with Elmer L. Irey, Chief Coordinator of the Treasury's law enforcement agencies, and within an hour the Treasury tentacles were reaching out, feeling and probing the haunts of the high-graders and gold smugglers. The Secret Service, the Customs Service and the Canadian investigators were lined up in a joint offensive. The big hunt was under way.

The next afternoon, Agent-in-Charge Manning at the Buffalo office of the Secret Service received a telephone call from Fell of the Canadian investigators, informing him that a blue Buick, license I B-7397, New York, was at that moment leaving the house on Grace Street, and in it were the two men who had recently been shadowed.

Manning phoned immediately to the Customs inspectors at the American end of the Peace Bridge. He described the car and requested that it be passed through with merely a routine examination. Then, hurrying to his waiting car with an alert assistant, he drove to the American end of the bridge and stopped within sight of the Customs inspection gate. Soon the blue Buick appeared. The Customs men merely asked the usual questions and, with a friendly wave, sent it on its way.

Manning was not far behind when the suspect car drove up to a gas station. He saw the driver enter the station and return a few minutes later with a briefcase and a traveling bag. The Customs Agent then trailed the car to an office building at Mohawk and Franklin Streets, Buffalo. Here the passenger in the shadowed car entered the building, his gait a little unsteady, as if he were carrying a load; yet the briefcase and bag seemed to be exceedingly light; indeed they might have been empty.

Half an hour later he returned. As he walked to the car, his gait was normal, but the two bags were evidently very heavy. During the next hour and a half, several stops were made by the suspect car. At the last stop, the Amherst Apartment House, the passenger entered while the driver took the Buick to a nearby garage and returned to the apartment building. The Agents kept the place under surveillance in the hope of identifying confederates.

A few evenings later, the two men in the blue Buick were observed making another visit to the house on Grace Street in Toronto. When they departed, they made a beeline for the Peace Bridge as usual. When they reached the Customs inspection gate, the driver got out and raised the cover of the trunk compartment for the usual examination, meantime cracking a joke with the Customs men whom he had come to know quite well. The joke turned sour before he had finished it. Customs men seemed to appear from nowhere. In a moment the car was surrounded. The terrified driver paled as he realized that this was no routine search. The passenger who had been lazily lounging in the rear of the car sat bolt upright, his bloated face now the color of a cod's belly, his pudgy hands trembling as he buttoned his coat more tightly around his paunch.

The rear door of the sedan was flung open. A mild-mannered man in blue uniform said almost politely, "Get out, please!" Customs men are noted for their courtly manners, even in a crisis.

With a grunt, or it might have been a sigh, the portly passenger eased himself from the cushions to the pavement. He tried to look unconcerned, as if it were all routine. As an Agent began to search him, however, his attitude changed suddenly. "Okay," he said, "I've got the stuff here!" Throwing open his coat, he unbuttoned his shirt, revealing the white canvas vest. The pockets bulged with high-grade gold, twenty-four pounds of it, with a value of ten thousand dollars.

The men were placed under arrest and taken to the Customs House for questioning. During the ordeal the Treasury men avoided intimidating methods. There were no loud voices, no third degrees or threats. The interrogation was carried on as if it were a conference between businessmen. Soon the driver was voluntarily telling all he knew of the conspiracy, which indeed was little. He had simply been hired to drive his prosperous passenger between Toronto and Buffalo on several occasions. While he certainly knew that those trips were not pleasure trips and that some valuable commodity was involved, he did not share in the profits. He was paid as one might pay a taxi-driver.

It did not take the passenger long to realize that he was enmeshed in a net from which there was no escape, so he made the best of it by admitting that he secured the gold in a house on Grace Street, Toronto, and that he had smuggled gold across the border on several other occasions. This contraband he gave to a relative who lived in the Amherst Apartment House for shipment by plane to New York City.

Search of his person disclosed the name, address, and telephone number of a relative named Bormann, who later fitted into the jigsaw puzzle which was now beginning to develop into a complete picture.

In the meantime word was flashed to the Canadian authorities of the arrest of the two suspects. Canadian Mounties raided the Grace Street house and confiscated scales, tongs, crucibles and other paraphernalia used by high-graders. Nearly nine thousand dollars in Canadian currency and a gold "button" valued at seventeen hundred dollars were discovered cunningly hidden in the basement ceiling. A notebook found in the living room contained, among other interesting data, Bormann's name, address, and telephone number. It contained also a telephone number which proved to be that of the president of a jewelry manufacturing concern.

The young man with the birthmark was the only occupant of the house when the Mounties appeared. He was arrested and promptly admitted that he had received the hidden

money from the passenger in the blue Buick. He also revealed that he had been instructed to call Bormann whenever he had gold to sell. He refused, however, to disclose
why the telephone number of the jewelry manufacturer was
entered in his notebook.

This was a circumstance that warranted at least an interview. Treasury Agents called on him at his place of business
in New York. He was suave and self-possessed. He scoffed
at the idea of Bormann being mixed up in gold smuggling.
Of the man with the birthmark, he knew nothing. He was
all in sympathy with the Agents and deplored the whole
business of high-grading. He prided himself on the fine reputation of his concern and volunteered to assist in any way
he could.

Taking him at his word, the Agents asked if they might
look through his books. He paled slightly. His disarming
smile hardened into a malevolent grin.

"The books? Oh yes, the books!" he said in a rasping voice.
"You see, our books met with an accident."

"What kind of an accident?" asked one of the agents.

"Sulphuric acid," he replied tensely, "a carboy of acid was
broken and the contents destroyed our records completely.
Too bad!" he added. "Too bad!"

A canvass of the Canadian banks and foreign-exchange
dealers showed that numerous sales of Canadian currency
and bank drafts totaling more than a million dollars had been
made to three Americans. The description of one of these
men fitted Bormann perfectly. Bormann was picked up without delay, and taken to the New York Customs House where
a number of Treasury men were waiting. Bormann was
placed among them. An official of the Canadian Bank of
Commerce was ushered in. Lined up on one side of the room
were several men whom the official had never seen before.
Bormann was among them.

When asked if he recognized anyone in the group, he immediately pointed out Bormann as the man who on several occasions had purchased currency at the Bank under the name of J. Roberts. Bormann angrily denied the accusation. Undaunted, however, the Treasury men pressed on. In Canada the authorities rounded up four of the smugglers, including the young man with the birthmark. Meantime, more and more evidence incriminating the jeweler came to light.

One cold morning in February the jewelry manufacturer and Bormann were taken into custody. Bormann was resigned, but the jewelry manufacturer set up quite a hullabaloo about his civil rights, his standing in the community, the integrity of his business. He also threatened vengeance on those law officers who had so ruthlessly dogged him. So great was his indignation, it seemed as if he were really the victim of circumstance. Yet, there was the evidence, cold and hard as ice. One of the Agents, a man of long experience, remarked, "That guy could make a fortune on the stage as the Number One actor of our time." As if to bear out the Agent's words, Bormann decided to confess. Then came a flood of confessions from the others, all but the jeweler. A network of intrigue and conspiracy involving many persons was disclosed. From the center of the web the jeweler directed the systematic robbery of two Governments to the tune of more than two and a half million dollars.

Justice moves swiftly when dealing with crime against the Treasury. The smugglers were indicted and tried in American and Canadian courts and sentenced to long terms in prison. The greedy jeweler, the mastermind of the ring, in spite of desperate efforts to beat the law, was sent to a federal prison, to remain there as a guest of the United States for a number of years.

Jimmy Hoffa vs. the FBI

by ROBERT F. KENNEDY

In "Jimmy Hoffa vs. the FBI," Robert F. Kennedy, United States Attorney General, younger brother of "a former newspaperman now in politics," relates the opening skirmish of a struggle still in progress, the outcome of which may determine the course of the nation's economic and political future.

THE MAN who first introduced me to Jimmy Hoffa was Eddie Cheyfitz, then a Teamsters' Union attorney. From the onset, Cheyfitz tried to steer our investigative attention away from Hoffa, and sought diligently to implant the thought that after a wild and reckless youth, during which he had perhaps committed some evil deeds, Hoffa had reformed.

Hoffa could be a strong force for good in the Teamsters' Union, Cheyfitz suggested. He urged me to sit down and talk with him. He wanted me to see what the man was really like, which I could do only by meeting him face to face.

Early in February, 1957, more out of curiosity than anything else, I finally agreed to have dinner with Mr. Hoffa and Mr. Cheyfitz at Cheyfitz' home. The date set was February 19.

A week before that, though, on the afternoon of February 13, 1957, a soft-spoken, mild-mannered, prematurely graying

112

man of about forty walked into the near state of bedlam that was our office, and handed his business card to my secretary. It read:

JOHN CYE CHEASTY, Attorney, New York

John Cye Cheasty had telephoned me from New York City the night before, after having talked to one of our staff there.

[At this time, Robert F. Kennedy was Chief Counsel for the United States Senate Select Committee on Improper Activities in the Labor or Management Field.]

On the telephone, Cheasty had told me:

"I have information that will make your hair stand on end."

In those days, there were few people I talked with who did not claim to have information that would make my hair stand on end, and I tried to see all of them. I invited Mr. Cheasty to Washington. About two o'clock the next afternoon, he was ushered into my private office. I was having a late lunch, and munched a sandwich as he sat down in the old black leather chair beside my desk and began to talk.

Within a few minutes, I had forgotten my lunch.

This is what he told me: James R. Hoffa had given him $1,000 in cash as a down payment to get a job as an investigator with our Committee. Hoffa wanted him to be a spy, and furnish secret information from our files. Cye Cheasty had taken the $1,000, and then come to me.

As he talked, he took money from his pocket—seven $100 bills and some loose cash—and laid it out on my desk. He had ticket slips to account for the money he'd spent on trips from New York to Detroit and back, and from New York to Washington.

Though perhaps I should not have been, considering what we already knew about Teamster officials, I was shocked by his story, and questioned him closely. We talked for more than an hour.

Cye Cheasty had been in the Navy, and had worked for the Secret Service. He was now doing legal and investigative work in New York. His practice was not extensive, but he kept busy. He said Hoffa had approached him through a common friend named Hyman Fischbach, a lawyer for whom Cheasty had done some legal work. A few days ago, Cheasty told me, Fischbach had called him, and invited him to join him in Washington on "business."

When they met, Mr. Fischbach explained that a client of his wanted a contact on the staff of the McClellan Committee. Did Cheasty know anyone on our staff? Could he get a job with us? Cheasty, as it happened, did have an acquaintance with Bob Dunne, one of our New York investigators.

Shaken by Fischbach's suggestion, and immediately on guard, he asked who the client was. Fischbach showed him a name in a book: James Hoffa, Detroit. He offered to telephone Hoffa and confirm the offer. Over the phone, Hoffa told Cheasty to come to Detroit to discuss arrangements.

Cheasty and Fischbach flew out at once. They were met at the airport, and taken directly to Hoffa's office. The Teamster leader gave Cheasty $1,000 in cash and agreed to pay him $2,000 a month if he got the job with us. The next morning, the two men flew back to New York. Cheasty immediately got in touch with Bob Dunne and outlined Hoffa's offer. His next step was to telephone me.

As he talked, I was continually conscious of the fact that here was a man to whom principle meant more than money. It would've been easy for him to accept the $1,000, and simply tell Mr. Hoffa he couldn't get the job. Since we needed experienced men, it would've been easy, perhaps, to use his contacts with the Committee in New York to get taken on with us, then to feed information to Hoffa for $2,000 a month.

Materially, he had nothing to gain by coming to me—and

everything to lose. When it became necessary to bring into the open the fact that Jimmy Hoffa had tried to "fix" a Committee investigator, Cye Cheasty, regardless of how noble his motives, would suffer. Men who will bribe or fix can be dangerous. Furthermore, clients do not like an investigator or lawyer who talks. Obviously, by talking to us, Cye Cheasty was jeopardizing his practice.

Yet, he was willing to take the risk.

Matter-of-factly, and without dramatics, he told me his reasons. He was proud of his service in the Navy and the Secret Service, and he thought Hoffa's offer to him was on a par with attempts by the Russians to get U.S. Government employees to turn over secret information. He was hurt that something in his relationship with Hyman Fischbach had led Fischbach to think Cye Cheasty would be even remotely interested. From the little he'd seen and knew of Jimmy Hoffa, Cheasty considered him an ugly influence and a threat to the country. He was determined to fight him.

Cye Cheasty was not a strong man physically. I later learned he suffered from a heart condition. And he was human. He'd been genuinely fond of Fischbach, and he was concerned because Fischbach's wife was pregnant. He didn't want to hurt either of them, and asked if there weren't some way to keep them out of the picture. Even before he finished the question, I could tell he realized there wasn't. This, for him, was the most difficult part.

He carefully put his initials on the money he'd received from Hoffa. Then, we walked together down the Senate Office Building Corridor to the office of Senator McClellan, to whom he repeated his story. We asked him [Cheasty] to return to the Committee offices to wait, while Senator McClellan called J. Edgar Hoover.

Mr. Hoover arrived within a few minutes and took complete control, arranging for a detailed interview of Cheasty that night by representatives of the Federal Bureau of Investigation.

Upon the recommendation of the Department of Justice, we decided that Cheasty should go along with the plan that Hoffa had proposed. Up to this point, what Hoffa and Fischbach had done was not a provable violation of the law. There was only Cheasty's word against theirs. More evidence was needed. The next step, then, was to see if Hoffa would, in fact, urge Cheasty to obtain documents and information from the files of the Committee.

Cheasty agreed to cooperate.

In addition to the mental strain, and the threat to his career, this meant a personal financial sacrifice for him. For the present, at least, he would have to give up his practice, where he was making considerably more than the $5,000 a year the Committee could pay him. We were legally limited to that amount because he was receiving a Navy disability pension.

From time to time, I've heard people question Cheasty's motives. Some have said: "Oh, he just wanted a job."

This is not a sensible conclusion. Aside from the fact that he came to work for our Committee at what certainly was hardly an attractive salary for any attorney, he also gladly gave up the $24,000 a year in cash that Hoffa was ready, able, and more than willing to pay. If Cye Cheasty was "just looking for a job," Jimmy Hoffa was offering him a good one. To my mind, he was a thoroughly unselfish man who was seeking only to do what was right and honorable.

On February 14—St. Valentine's Day—after being sworn in as an Assistant Counsel for the McClellan Committee, Cye Cheasty returned at once to New York to see if Jimmy Hoffa or Hyman Fischbach would make further advances. The calls came. Cheasty told them he had the job. From that point on, he was under the direction of the FBI, which guided his movements as he maintained constant contact with both Hoffa and Fischbach.

Hoffa wanted information. I furnished Cheasty with material which he passed on directly to Hoffa. Hoffa gave him $2,000 more, which Cheasty turned over to the FBI Agents. Always we were careful to furnish information Cheasty would normally come by if he were a Committee investigator. Never, of course, was it information that would jeopardize the work of the Committee.

That is how John Cye Cheasty came to work for the McClellan Committee—though I subsequently heard several other stories circulated. The simple truth was and is that Cye Cheasty is an honest man—and Jimmy Hoffa had failed to recognize that there is such a person.

When Cheasty came to me on February 13, I was tempted to break the dinner engagement for February 19. I felt if I did, though, it might seem peculiar, and arouse suspicion of Cheasty.

The day of the dinner, Cheasty was in Washington, and in contact with Hoffa. Early in the day, I supplied Cheasty with the names of four witnesses we planned to subpoena for our first hearing. Using the prearranged name of Eddie Smith, he telephoned the number Hoffa had given him. The number was listed to the office Cheyfitz shared with his law associate, Edward Bennett Williams. Hoffa took the call and arranged to meet Cheasty late that afternoon at the corner of 17th and I Streets.

It was snowing when Cheasty set out for the rendezvous. FBI Agents equipped with hidden cameras kept both men under close surveillance. At their street-corner meeting, Cheasty handed Hoffa the four names I'd given him. Hoffa told Cheasty he was acquainted with three of the four. Then, Cheyfitz came along in a car, picked up Hoffa, and they drove off together to Cheyfitz' house to meet me for dinner.

Cheasty made his contact immediately with the FBI. Then, he called me at my office to say he'd delivered the information to Hoffa. Because I'd been waiting for his call, I was a few minutes late arriving at Cheyfitz' house.

Both Cheyfitz and Hoffa met me at the door—Hoffa with a strong, firm handshake. Immediately, I was struck by how short he is—only five feet five and a half. We walked into the living room of Cheyfitz' elaborately decorated house, but chatted only a few minutes before going in to dinner.

The three of us were alone. Hoffa, I was to discover, can be personable, polite, and friendly. But that evening, though friendly enough, he maintained one steady theme in his conversation throughout dinner and for the rest of the evening.

"I do to others what they do to me—only worse," he said.

"Maybe I should've worn my bulletproof vest," I suggested.

From that first meeting, it seemed to me he wanted to impress upon me that Jimmy Hoffa is a tough, rugged man.

We discussed employers he'd encountered during his career. When they crossed him, he said, he destroyed them. He told me of the fights he'd been in. Always, he had won. We discussed his difficulties with law enforcement agencies. He pointed out that, mostly, they'd been unsuccessful in prosecuting him. We discussed the UAW-Kohler strike. He said if he'd been in Walter Reuther's position, he'd have won that strike shortly after it started.

When the talk turned to the future work of the Committee, Cheyfitz and Hoffa let me know they knew the name of a Portland, Oregon, Teamster official who'd be subpoenaed before our Committee. It was one of the four names I'd given to Cheasty. With some grimness, I admit, I gave no indication I knew where Hoffa acquired his information.

Around 9:30 PM, my wife telephoned. The snow that had

been falling in the afternoon when Cheasty met Hoffa was still coming down, and the roads were slick. A woman driver had skidded into a tree on our property. She was sitting in our living room, hysterical. I made my apologies, and left.

As I drove from Cheyfitz' house, I knew Hoffa must have spent the evening thinking he was playing a game in which he held all the cards—that with Cye Cheasty in his pocket, he was looking down my throat.

The next time I saw Jimmy Hoffa was three weeks later— on March 13, shortly after J. Edgar Hoover called my home late in the evening to tell me his men were ready to move in. I was out for a walk, but shortly after I returned to the house, a second call came from the FBI.

Hoffa had just been placed under arrest at the DuPont Plaza Hotel, with the Committee documents I'd given Cye Cheasty in his possession.

I went at once to the Federal District Courthouse on 3rd Street, and was waiting there in one of the courtrooms, in case I was needed, when the FBI Special Agents brought in Jimmy Hoffa. For a few minutes, we were alone in the room.

"I don't know any of your Agents," he said to me. I did not answer him, for the matter was now in the hands of the courts. There was an awkward silence, and then, somehow, we began talking about physical exercise. He'd read somewhere that I exercised a lot, and that I did push-ups. We had about exhausted this topic when Hoffa's lawyer, Edward Bennett Williams, arrived.

"What's this all about?" he demanded.

It was not my place to enlighten him, and I told him so. I was convinced the Federal Bureau of Investigation had given the Government an airtight case. Cye Cheasty was a good and honest man. He'd served his country with distinction. The evidence supporting his testimony—there were fast moving pictures of Hoffa receiving the documents, and paying off Cheasty—was solid.

I felt Jimmy Hoffa was finished.

So much has been written and said about this case that most people are aware the jury consisted of eight Negroes and four whites, that the Teamsters paid the expenses of former heavyweight champion Joe Louis to come from Detroit to Washington and appear in the courtroom for two days, and that he publicly embraced Mr. Hoffa.

It has been overlooked, however, that the judge, in a conference at the bench, took judicial notice of the make-up of the jury, pointing out that while the Government attorneys had selected jurors without racial discrimination, Mr. Williams, Hoffa's attorney, had used his challenges against white jurors only.

This circumstance, taken with the presence of Joe Louis, and other events that transpired during the trial, shows a definite effort to influence the judge and jury in ways other than through accepted legal channels.

Martha Jefferson, a Negro woman attorney, was brought from California to be at the trial. Another reputable Negro lawyer was employed for the same purpose. The law partner of the judge's brother was brought from Arkansas. Ed Williams, one of the nation's top criminal attorneys, hardly needed this legal assistance. And in the midst of the trial, Williams posed with Mrs. Jefferson for a picture that appeared in a full-page ad in the *Afro-American*, a Negro newspaper. The ad praised Jimmy Hoffa as a friend of the Negro race. (Later, our Committee heard testimony clearly indicating that Hoffa and his own Local 299, in Detroit, discriminated against Negroes.)

When it was reported in the press that the ad had been delivered to the doorstep of every juror, that was enough for

Judge Burnita Matthews. She locked up the jury to prevent further improper influences.

Then, while cross-examining Cheasty, Williams tried to establish that Cheasty had once investigated the National Association for the Advancement of Colored People. By the time Government attorneys objected, the jury had heard Williams, and it was too late. Cheasty testified that it was completely untrue.

Such methods seem extreme, and an insult to the court, to the judge, to the legal system, to the jury, and to the Negro race. But it is Mr. Hoffa's philosophy that every man has his price whether it is money, pressure, or prejudice, and he's willing to pay.

We later investigated the background of those jurors. It was apparent the Government had been as careless in accepting the jury panel as the defense lawyers had been careful in selecting it. One juror, for example, had a police record of 14 convictions, mostly for drunkenness. Another had nine convictions. Most of the charges against them involved common drunkenness and disorderly conduct. Some of the cases had been settled in fortfeiture of bonds in lieu of pleas of guilt. Some of the offenses had actually occurred during the trial, before the jury was locked up by Judge Matthews. The son of another juror had been sentenced on a twenty-month-to-five-year jail sentence, and was in jail on a narcotics charge at the time of the trial. Still another juror had been released from his Government job after refusing to take a lie detector test on the question of whether he was a homosexual.

Such people are not prohibited from jury service. But they certainly are persons the Government might find antagonistic to the aims of law enforcement in a criminal court.

Furthermore, the Government attorneys had not expected Jimmy Hoffa to testify. When he took the stand, they were unprepared to conduct an adequate cross-examination. The day before he testified, representatives from the United

States Attorney came to my office, asking what background material we had on Hoffa. We began to compile it, but of course there was no time for the attorney handling the case to assimilate such a mountain of information in such a short time.

As a result, while Hoffa testified with vigor and force, the cross-examination was unimpressive.

I was in the Senate caucus chamber questioning a witness from the Textile Workers' Union when I became conscious of a stir and a buzz throughout the room. Then a note was handed up to me. Cye Cheasty had telephoned from the courthouse.

Hoffa had been acquitted.

I read the note with utter disbelief. And yet it was not the first time he'd been acquitted. It would not be the last.

Mystery in New Mexico

by WILLIAM BRADFORD HUIE

The hardy pioneers who traveled by covered wagon learned humility in the sun-baked stretches of sand and wind-carved rock in the New Mexico-Arizona area they dubbed "The Badlands." It is a truly primitive area, undefiled by Man except for an occasional long, thin, straight, furtive thread of highway which, to one driving, seems an endless road leading nowhere. It is bitter country, a place for bitter crime. Writers of fiction have dreamed up countless bizarre mysteries with The Badlands as a setting. But no fiction is as morbidly absorbing as the grim, true, unsolved puzzle William Bradford Huie unfolds in "Mystery in New Mexico."

O N SUNDAY, MAY 19, 1935, two middle-aged couples left East St. Louis, Illinois, on a leisurely motor trip to the West Coast. They were Mr. and Mrs. George M. Lorius, of East St. Louis, and their friends, Mr. and Mrs. Albert A. Heberer, of DuQuoin, Illinois.

Lorius was a coal dealer. Heberer owned a barbershop. Both men were Masons, members of civic clubs, respected citizens. Neither had a known enemy. They were sober people, all about fifty.

They'd taken previous vacations together. They never

drove after dark. They never picked up hitchhikers. They stopped in hotels. They were not wealthy people, just reasonably prosperous.

They had perhaps $250 cash among them. Lorius had $400 in traveler's checks; Heberer, $100 worth. Lorius wore a diamond ring, and a Shriner's pin worth about $500. Mrs. Lorius wore a diamond ring of about the same value. They were traveling in the Lorius' 1929 Nash sedan.

On the first day, they covered three hundred fifty-two miles, stopping at Miami, Oklahoma. Next day, Monday, they drove three hundred sixty miles along Highway 66. That brought them to Sayre, Oklahoma. They mailed postcards from both places.

On Tuesday, they drove through Amarillo, Texas, then veered south on Highway 60. They spent the night at a small hotel in East Vaughn, New Mexico. In the morning, they headed for Albuquerque. According to a card mailed by Mrs. Heberer, they arrived there before noon on Wednesday.

That was the last word received from the party.

Apparently the four lunched in Albuquerque, then proceeded toward Boulder Dam. At their customary rate, they'd have driven either about two hundred sixty miles before dark, and reached Holbrook, Arizona, on Route 66, or, if they returned to Highway 60, they'd have driven two hundred thirty-five miles to Springerville, Arizona.

Six days later, the Lorius' car was picked up by police in Dallas, Texas.

An investigation was begun. The investigation was in two parts: (a) to find the man who'd driven the car to Dallas; (b) to find the Lorius party, or their bodies.

The story of the car was pieced together by FBI Special Agents who drove it from Dallas back to New Mexico. Along the way, they questioned hundreds of filling station and hotel operators. The car was seen in Albuquerque—in possession of the Lorius party—near noon on Wednesday, May 22. Around 6 AM next morning, it was seen turned on its side on the road 6.7 miles below Socorro, a town seventy-five miles south of Albuquerque.

As passers-by gathered to right the car, they had plenty of time to observe the nervous, thin-faced young man who said he'd dozed and run off the highway. He was between eighteen and twenty-three years old, about five-feet nine-inches tall, and weighed about one hundred thirty-five pounds. He had long, medium-brown hair, brown or hazel eyes, and a peaked face, with pointed nose. There was a small scar on his left cheek, and his left arm was heavily tattooed. He wore a blue shirt, gray trousers and gray vest, and his clothes were much too big for him.

He was probably wearing the clothes of Lorius or Heberer, both of whom were big men.

After passers-by righted the car, it was towed to a filling station in Socorro. There the car was serviced. Then, the nervous young man drove off toward El Paso, on Highway 85.

Everyone suspected something was wrong, but no one notified the police.

About 11 AM, the young man plowed into a bank as he rounded a curve forty miles south of Socorro, near Scotty's filling station. Two women, a Mrs. Burris and her daughter, Mrs. Cole, went out to help. They noticed the young man didn't know where the car's tools were. The two women flagged a truck, which pushed the Nash back onto the road.

The young man sped off without thanks.

The women suspected he was driving a stolen car. They, however, had no phone to notify police.

Around 6 PM, the young man registered at a rooming house in El Paso. He signed in as James Sullevan, East St. Louis, with a fountain pen containing green ink similar to that used by Lorius on his postcards. He insisted on a key not only to his room but also to the closet.

He had an unusual amount of baggage. All night, a girl in the next room heard him pacing the floor and tearing paper.

Next morning, "Sullevan" couldn't start the Nash. Two policemen in a prowl car pushed him to a garage. A mechanic put on a new fan belt. "Sullevan" paid with a $10 traveler's check. It was signed "George M. Lorius."

Later that morning, at Fort Hancock, Texas, the young man bought a cap, gas, and candy at the Gateway Camp. Inspector Bill Massey stopped him for questioning. He said he was George M. Lorius, of East St. Louis, and produced Lorius' Shriner credentials to prove it. He explained his nervousness by saying he'd been drunk in Juarez the night before.

Massey looked at him carefully, decided to arrest him, but then, on impulse, waved him on.

For that impulse, Inspector Massey has done years and years of penance. He's been reminded a hundred times that men don't usually become Shriners until middle age, that tattooed Shriners are rare. He views an average of 20 suspects a year, hoping to recognize his man again.

Between El Paso and Dallas, the young man the FBI calls "the unknown suspect alias Sullevan" forged 23 Lorius checks at filling stations. At Trent, Texas, a gas attendant crossed the street and showed one of the checks to a bank cashier while the forger waited.

The cashier said it was an obvious forgery. The two discussed having the driver arrested. They decided the local constable wouldn't arrest a man without a warrant.

The operator, therefore, returned and merely refused to cash the check. "Sullevan" pulled a large roll of bills from his pocket, paid for the gas in cash, and went his way.

In Dallas, on May 26, the young man bent a fender on a car owned by a department store manager. He paid the estimated $5 damage with a $20 Lorius check, the manager returning $15 in change.

That afternoon, the young man had the car washed. Then, he abandoned it. The FBI could find no fingerprints, no bloodstains, no bullet holes. When the car left East St. Louis, it had seat covers. Now, those covers were missing.

The speedometer, too, contained a clue. Lorius had had the oil changed the day before leaving home. The mileage had been recorded by the East St. Louis garage. Allowing for the Lorius driving, the speedometer showed two hundred fifty miles unaccounted for.

FBI Special Agents reasoned that this two hundred fifty miles must have been traveled in the eighteen hours between the time the Lorius party probably left Albuquerque and the time the car was discovered near Socorro.

This seemed to indicate Lorius had driven about two hundred twenty-five miles westward from Highway 85, along either Highway 60 or Route 66. Then the car had changed hands, and the young man had driven it one hundred twenty-five miles back, and onto Highway 85 at either Socorro or Las Lunas.

The search for the bodies was proceeding in routine manner until the Governor of Illinois offered a reward and implied that New Mexico was not safe for tourists.

Aroused, New Mexico's Governor Clyde Tingley called out his National Guard. He doubled the Illinois reward and assumed personal direction of the search. On June 20, at East Vaughn, he assembled the largest posse ever seen in the Southwest.

Tingley held to the hitchhiker theory. He insisted the Lorius party had relaxed their rule, and that somewhere along the road the nervous young man had managed to kill them all.

If this theory were true, then obviously the bodies had to be within a short distance of some road. The young man weighed about one hundred thirty-five pounds. Heberer weighed more than two hundred. Even if somehow the hitchhiker could manage to kill four adults, he couldn't carry the bodies very far. Therefore, the way to find the victims was to start at East Vaughn and search a strip two hundred yards wide along every possible road.

National Guardsmen began this task. They trudged across endless mesas. They dragged the Rio Grande River near several bridges. Then, because Lorius sold coal, someone suggested the party might have been lured to a deserted mine shaft.

Thereupon, every known shaft in the state of New Mexico was searched.

It was also reasoned that perhaps the only way one man could kill four adults would be to shove them en masse off a bluff. Planes began to explore every bluff area, searching for vultures. No bodies were found.

On June 29, there were two important developments. The big posse reached Quemado, one hundred eight miles west of Socorro on Highway 60; fifty-two miles east of Springerville, Arizona. A State Police officer drove the Lorius' car into Grandma Baca's filling station in Quemado. The operator, Richard Brice, identified it as a car he'd serviced about a month earlier. Brice gave an accurate description of the party.

He also said he'd directed them to a hotel in Springerville.

Then, young Brice remembered noticing a bolt missing from the Nash's luggage rack. The driver examined the rack, and decided to wait until he got to Springerville for repairs.

The officer went to the rack. The bolt was still missing.

The posse took heart at this information. They expected to find the bodies the next day. At midnight, however, the posse was on the way back to Albuquerque. Near that city, an even more startling discovery had been made.

Three miles east of Albuquerque, a cowboy found the charred remnants of a thermos bottle, two suitcase frames, a mechanical pencil, and a medicine bottle. The blackened label on the bottle was identified by a doctor in DuQuoin, Illinois, as cold medicine he'd given the Heberers.

Tingley took this find to be positive proof that the party had been murdered on Route 66, east of Albuquerque.

"Today, we've found the baggage," he told the press. "Tomorrow, we'll find the bodies."

During the next three days, the mesa between Albuquerque and the Sandia Mountains resembled a military maneuver area. Troopers rode at ten-yard intervals, scanning the ground for a grave, and watching the sky for vultures. They combed a strip fifteen miles wide and twenty miles long. For hundreds of yards around the spot where the baggage had been burned, infantrymen—many of them Apache and Navajo Indians—crawled on hands and knees.

They found nothing.

Then, Governor Tingley gave up. He dismissed his foot- and saddle-sore men, and announced that the fate of the Lorius party would have to be another of the great unsolved mysteries of the West.

Six years later, in 1941, the FBI assigned a veteran Special Agent, A. Raymond Gere, to the case. Gere knew the West, and had been with the Bureau since 1917. Retired in 1946, he lives in Sante Fe, and continues work on the case as a hobby.

When Gere began, he dismissed the hitchhiker theory. Four large adults and their baggage filled the car. The party, he insisted, were murdered by a man—or men—who came upon them in another automobile.

By analyzing the baggage remnants, Officer H.C. Martin, of the New Mexico State Police, had ascertained that the ashes had never been rained upon. A heavy rain had fallen at that spot, however, on June 19. Therefore, the baggage had not been burned until three weeks after the Lorius car was abandoned.

This indicated the baggage burning wasn't the work of the young man who'd driven the car to Dallas. He wouldn't risk returning to Albuquerque just to burn suitcases and bottles. The baggage had been burned, Gere figured, by an accomplice only after the case got "hot."

Where were Heberer's traveler's checks? The diamond rings? Lorius' wrist watch?

And only about half the baggage had been burned. Obviously, there had been a division of the loot.

Next, Gere went back to pick up the Quemado lead. Because Tingley had dismissed the Quemado evidence as unimportant, however, no record was kept of the location of the filling station or the name of the attendant. It took Special Agent Gere a full year to ascertain Brice's identity, and locate him in Arkansas.

Even after eight years, Brice and his wife impressed the FBI Agents with their detailed statements. Brice easily picked the picture of Lorius from a handful of photos. The Brice statements convinced Gere and the other Special Agents that the Lorius party had indeed reached Quemado, and had expected to reach Springerville before dark.

Gere studied the desolate and seldom-traveled terrain between Quemado and Springerville. The speedometer showed the Lorius' car probably hadn't been driven more than one hundred twenty-five miles west of Socorro. Therefore, he believed the murder had been committed within seventeen miles of Quemado. In this area, he found numerous gullies in which bodies could have been covered by two men working with nothing more than tire tools.

Then he began to reconstruct the crime.

This is the reconstruction on which the FBI bases its continuing investigation. The Lorius car reached the most likely area about 6 PM. For some reason, the car was stopped. Perhaps it was overheating, for it needed a new fan belt the following day. Another car, traveling east, approached.

The two thugs stopped, pretending to offer help. They took a look at the well-dressed party. Perhaps they saw the rings and baggage. Lorius and Heberer were outside the car, the two women inside. The thugs shot the men. The women, hysterical, leaped from the car. The thugs ran them down and killed them.

Then, perhaps under cover of darkness, the thugs began the grisly business of stripping the bodies, carrying them off the road, and burying them in gullies.

Sometime before midnight, the murderers completed their work, divided the loot, and proceeded east in separate cars. At Socorro, one went north toward Albuquerque. The other went south, and turned the Lorius car over on the road before 6 AM.

This reconstruction is consistent with all the known facts. It answers nearly all the questions. The big posse did not find the bodies because, ironically, the finding of the burned baggage stopped it only a few miles short of the most probable scene of the crime. Gere believes a search between Quemado and Springerville on June 30, 1935, would have unearthed the bodies, since newly disturbed soil would've been evident.

Now, after all these years, the finding of the skeletons depends on the chance unearthing of a human bone by an animal or a flash flood. If the bones could be found, they might contain bullets to help identify the murderers.

Each year, Gere reminds his friends in the FBI and other law-enforcement agencies that the thin-faced young "suspect alias Sullevan" is a year older, but that he probably still has the tattoos on his left arm and the scar under his left eye.

He undoubtedly is a confirmed criminal. A brutal crime like this isn't committed by a one-timer, Gere reasons. Already more than three hundred serious suspects have been questioned and cleared, or are still under investigation.

The murderer is now middle-aged, but unless he is dead (he could have been killed in the war), the FBI expects to get him.

One thing is sure. It'll never stop trying.

G. I. Burglars

by WILLIS GEORGE

Only the superintendent knew that the two men who came into the great glooming square-shouldered office building every night before midnight and then spent the next three or four hours working behind the locked door of a stuffy little room in the basement, were Naval Intelligence Agent Jack Larsen and Agent-in-Charge Willis George. The story of their activities is typical of a great deal of spying and counterspying that went on in the United States during the past world war.

WE WERE GOVERNMENT BURGLARS, Jack and I. But the employees on the night shift—it was a large office building in Chicago, and half a dozen men worked on the elevators and elsewhere all night—thought we were engineers testing a new air-raid detection device. This "cover" worked splendidly until one night a new boy on the elevators became suspicious.

"What are you fellows really up to?"

I put on my best Sunday face—hush hush, if a face can be that, and no end confidential.

"Well, you know how it is. A rich dame wants to get something on a guy, so—"

"Oh, a couple of divorce dicks!" he grunted, and promptly lost interest.

Building employees are frequently questioned by private detectives about the amorous adventures of various tenants, and to them a divorce case is old stuff. The men in this building were no exceptions. Beyond wondering who the "guy" might be and how much money the "rich dame" was spending, they thought little about our activities because they fell into a familiar pattern. And that was exactly the sort of cover we wanted; we could carry on unhampered by dangerous curiosity.

Each night we found the little basement room literally bulging with burlap sacks, all properly labeled. They contained scrap paper and other refuse collected by the building's cleaning staff from offices on the tenth and twelfth floors. We were interested only in the material from an elaborate suite on the twelfth floor, occupied by Stephen K. Ziggly, who had come to this country from a neutral European capital a few months before the United States entered the war. Everything that came from his office was examined under magnifying glasses, tested for invisible writing and, if necessary, photographed. Whatever could be identified as having been collected from Ziggly's own wastebasket was set aside for further study.

Ostensibly, Ziggly's business was banking and insurance, in both of which he had an international reputation. But American authorities suspected that he had other and more important business, that he had been sent to this country to organize and operate a Nazi spy ring. Unknown to him, Ziggly had been under investigation by American Agents in Europe for almost a year, and while nothing had been discovered that could be described as legal evidence, his activities had aroused suspicion. He maintained his own banking and insurance business in the neutral capital, but most of his connections were in Germany.

He had made two trips to Berlin, just before embarking for the United States, and he was known to have had very profitable business relations with high Nazi officials. He claimed Austria as his birthplace, but he was a naturalized citizen of the neutral country which had given him a passport. This and other papers were in perfect order when he arrived in New York; even if they hadn't been, a way would have been found to let him enter the United States. For the only way to trap him, if he should prove to be a Nazi agent, was to let him show his hand here. He spent a week in New York, living quietly in a good hotel and, as far as the authorities could learn, seeing no one except three or four businessmen to whom he presented letters of introduction. None of these men was involved in his later schemes. Then Ziggly went to Chicago, where he signed a five-year lease on offices in this building in the Loop.

Ziggly had insisted upon extensive alterations in his offices and the rearranging of the suite so that a visitor, to reach his private office, had to undergo the scrutiny of employees in four rooms. Soon after moving in, he complained to the building management that careless cleaning women had ruined a valuable document, and insisted upon employing his own cleaning staff. A little later he entered his office late one night and found the night watchman inspecting the premises. Although the watchman was only making his usual rounds, Ziggly became greatly upset, and soon thereafter installed new locks on all inner and outer doors of the suite. He put a particularly intricate lock on the door of his private office.

Although Ziggly's fussiness about his office had increased our suspicions, we let him pretty much alone for several weeks. We wanted him to make his American contacts, establish himself and get to work. We gave him a month; then *we* went to work. Nothing of importance developed immediately. His business affairs were apparently legitimate, and so were his conversations and correspondence. His social contacts were few and about what might have been expected of a man in his position. He talked and wrote little about the war; when he did, it was to express his detestation of war, and a horror of the instruments and machinery of war. In several conversations and letters he said that the war had so greatly affected him that he was unable even to look upon a gun or an airplane without a shudder of revulsion.

It was after surveillance, censorship and other methods had failed to produce any evidence of espionage that we decided to examine the scrap paper from Ziggly's office. For this, some preparation was necessary. The superintendent of the building, whose cooperation was essential, was investigated and found to be a good American citizen. I went to see him and told him outright that I was a Government man searching for spies.

"We suspect some of the tenants of your building," I said, "and we want to look over all the scrap paper taken from their offices."

"I'd like to help you," the superintendent said, "but all wastepaper is destroyed as soon as it is collected."

"We can fix that," I said.

I then gave the superintendent a list of some twenty tenants, among them Ziggly, but did not name him specifically. Several times during the next few days the superintendent told his cleaners, at my suggestion, that many complaints were being received of papers swept from desks into wastebaskets and so carried downstairs to be destroyed. A day or so after that, still at my suggestion, he told them that a new system of wastepaper disposal would be followed. Thereafter all scrap would be put in bags and sent to the basement, labeled with the office number from which it had been taken. It would be kept for two days, so that a search might be made if anything was reported lost. The superintendent himself, each night, sorted the bags and carried into the basement room the scrap collected from the offices on the list I had given him.

For three months we examined every scrap of paper taken from Ziggly's offices. And found nothing. But we learned a lot about him. For instance, he was an inveterate doodler. And, as the investigation progressed, we became more and more interested in the fact that most of Ziggly's doodling had to do with war, a habit greatly at variance with his often-expressed opinions. His doodles were nearly always neat little pictures of guns and ships, of airplanes and bombs; and occasionally there appeared among these figures a design which bore a striking likeness to a radar apparatus, and another which resembled a piece of laboratory equipment. Finally there came a night when we found, on a torn scrap of paper, half a dozen of the radar doodles and some words and fragments of words:

"Important—rad—meet—importa—arriv—"

Subsequently, we learned that this jumble of words reflected Ziggly's worry over the arrival of a German agent carrying information about American and British radar. At the time, the words seemed meaningless, except that it was obvious that they indicated the coming of someone whom it was important for Ziggly to meet. Who this person was, what his business with Ziggly was—these were facts it was up to us to find out; and it was not the kind of information we could be sure of finding in a wastebasket. So, a *surreptitious entry* was decided upon.

In some articles this operation is called burglary, but when it is performed for Uncle Sam—as it was in some two hundred instances in which I was personally implicated— it is usually called by a $64 word, or words. Not that the verbal camouflage protects the Government burglar if he is caught. He is on his own. He is without the law, and so without hope of support or recognition from the Government of a law-abiding country. Even if he is fatally wounded in the line of duty, he receives no Purple Heart.

To the building superintendent I explained that a search of Ziggly's offices was a thoroughly illegal procedure and a quite different matter from examination of scrap paper. I pointed out that if the entry was discovered, especially if no evidence was found, the Government would disclaim responsibility. The superintendent would face possible criminal prosecution, a suit at civil law, and loss of his job and reputation. He listened carefully. Finally, he said:

"Okay, I'll help you."

"Do you want money?" I asked.

"No! I've got two boys over there. Just make it look good."

"It'll look good," I promised.

Our team consisted of the following persons:

An Agent-in-Charge to organize and direct the operation;

A safe expert, able to open any safe by manipulation;

A lock expert, able to pick any lock within thirty minutes;

A camera expert;

A flaps-and-seals expert, able to open any type of wax or envelope seal and replace it within half an hour, and to do it so skillfully as to defy detection even by examination under violet ray;

An expert evaluator, able to run through documents and papers and to decide instantly what must be photographed;

Three security men to act as lookouts and guards;

Two radio operators.

Each man was provided with the equipment necessary for his particular job. As Agent-in-Charge I carried a revolver and blackjack; so did the three security men. Each of the others had a gas gun, pencil type. My first task, as we have already seen, was to obtain the cooperation of the superintendent. It would have been possible, though considerably more difficult, to search Ziggly's offices without the knowledge of either the owner or the superintendent. But since he already knew from our wastepaper activities that some of his tenants were under suspicion, I decided to continue to avail myself of his cooperation. The owner, who had previously been investigated, was also very helpful. He readily gave his consent to the entry. He insisted, however, that the searching party invent a reasonable excuse for entering the building. The old gags we had previously used on the elevator men were too thin. So I suggested that the group take the cover of engineers who were testing the sway of the building.

"All buildings," I explained, "develop cracks at stress points from swaying, and the possibility of air raids makes it plausible for you to want the stress points tested. Also, using this cover, we will be able to shut down or control the elevators, and so discourage traffic in the building during the search. We will tell your night staff that the vibration of the elevators would affect the delicate testing instruments."

"Okay," said the owner. "You're engineers."

Then my locksmith and I made a preliminary survey of Ziggly's premises. Very quietly—for we knew that if Ziggly were really a spy there would be traps—the lock expert picked the intricate lock on the outer door. He had the door open in less than fifteen minutes, and immediately sat down on the floor just outside the doorway and began making a key.

Working with a floor plan furnished by the owner of the building, I rapidly sketched in all of the partitions installed by Ziggly and noted the location of chairs, desks, file cabinets and other pieces of furniture. All this was done in complete silence. When it had been completed, I searched for traps. On a window sill behind Ziggly's desk I found a large suitcase from which a concealed wire ran to a base plug. I disconnected the plug and opened the suitcase. It contained a sound-recording device with an extremely sensitive switch. This switch was thrown automatically whenever a word was spoken in the room and the sound, picked up by microphones, was recorded silently on film.

A cellaret in a corner of Ziggly's private office, when opened, was found to contain a "burglar-proof" safe. The handle number of the safe was noted. Before leaving the office we made a careful check to be sure that everything had been restored to its original position. The polished floor, which bore the marks of our rubber heels, was repolished. A thin layer of dust which had covered the suitcase was replaced with our usual dust powder of talc and charcoal. On the way out, I investigated all possible escape routes in case of interruption, and chose a washroom a few doors from Ziggly's office for the camera work.

Meanwhile, the superintendent received a letter from the owner of the building, which he showed to his night staff. It advised them of the sway tests and directed them to assist. The owner ordered all elevators to be put under the control of the engineers, to reduce traffic in the building to a minimum. He also instructed the superintendent to check personally all tenants and visitors who entered during the tests.

Three days after the preliminary survey, about one o'clock in the morning, our group of eleven men drove up to the building in several cars and a large enclosed delivery truck on which was lettered, "The Northwest Engineering Company," with a street address and a telephone number. Incidentally, we had taken the precaution to hire a small office at the address given with the name of the company lettered on the door, and the telephone number was listed in the Chicago telephone directory. The place was used as a cover for several operations.

From the truck we unloaded a dozen boxes and suitcases, each stenciled with the name of the company, and containing not only the equipment necessary for searching Ziggly's offices but also instruments for measuring building sway. Nine of the men carried the boxes and cases into the building. Two remained hidden in the truck—a radio operator with a two-way radio set, and one of the security agents who could identify Ziggly's employees. From a concealed slot in the side of the truck, the security man had a good view of the entrance to the building.

I approached the superintendent in the lobby as a stranger, showed him the group's credentials, including identification cards and a copy of a contract for the tests signed by the owner of the building. I asked that elevator service be suspended until the tests had been completed. Two of the elevators were turned over to the "engineers," though they continued to be run by the regular operators, and the others were stopped. Carrying their equipment, the search team went upstairs, getting off at various floors and then walking up or down to the twelfth. Coats, hats and shoes were left in the elevator, and the operator was told that even the thud of heels on the floor caused enough vibration to affect the instruments.

One of our men, with the key made by the lock expert, went ahead to open Ziggly's door and make certain that the group was not walking into a trap. If he found himself in trouble, he would pretend to be a burglar and escape as best he could. But the way was clear, so he immediately entered the room, pulled down the shades, and turned on the lights. Then he disconnected the sound recorder which I had found during the preliminary survey. At his signal the rest of us entered Ziggly's offices, and each man went to work on his particular assignment. The radio operator established communication with the truck in the street, the cameraman set up his equipment in the washroom, and the lock expert picked the lock of an office across the hallway. This was to be used if flight became necessary.

It was well that the entry had been carefully planned, for some fifteen minutes after the work had started, the radio operator in the truck reported that one of Ziggly's employees had entered the building. Swiftly, but without haste, the men gathered up their equipment and retired to the room across the hall, and from there re-established radio communication with the truck. In less than ten minutes Ziggly's office had been vacated, with nothing there to show that it had ever been entered.

Meanwhile, the two men left in the lobby downstairs for just such a contingency were carrying out a prearranged plan of delay. One insisted that Ziggly's employee identify himself to the superintendent, and wasted more than five minutes telephoning empty offices, trying to find that official. The other security man went into a highly technical explanation of the sway tests, and told Ziggly's man there would be a delay because before he could be taken up in the elevator, the testing instruments would have to be disconnected. He asked the employee how long he expected to be in the building.

"The truth is I'm not going to work. I've got my girl in a bar around the corner, and I'm short of dough. I want to get a bottle of whisky out of my desk. I won't be but a minute."

So he was run up to the twelfth floor, and the elevator was held for him while he unlocked Ziggly's office and got his liquor. Then he left the building and was followed by one of our men until he had joined his girl in the bar. When the

security man reported by radio that all was clear, we resumed work in Ziggly's office. We didn't know until later
that Ziggly's employee, befuddled by a couple of hours of
steady drinking, telephoned Ziggly about four o'clock that
a lot of men were prowling around the building with queer-
looking instruments. All of which so alarmed Ziggly that he
started immediately for his office.

Meanwhile, Ziggly's "burglar-proof" safe bore a manufacturer's notice that if the combination were lost or forgotten
it couldn't be opened except with explosives. Nevertheless,
our expert opened it in a little less than twenty minutes by
manipulating the dial and tumblers.

As Ziggly's safe swung open, my eyes went at once to a
sealed package, the size and shape of which immediately
suggested a code book. On its paper wrapper I could read, in
the purple ink of an office stamp, "Received, 5:10 P.M.,——
——, 194—." The date was yesterday. Apparently the courier
delivering this package had arrived so near closing time that
Ziggly, knowing its contents, had thrust it unopened into
the safe. Tomorrow, he probably thought, would be as good
as today for studying it. I made a detailed sketch showing
the exact location of the sealed package, so that we could return it to its proper place and position, then took it from the
safe and turned it over to the flaps-and-seals expert who
had already laid out his paraphernalia.

His first step was to wrap the package in cellophane with
holes cut through it to correspond with the seals and
through which they were exposed. Then he mixed in a
small cup some of the impression paste used by dentists.
When this had reached a creamy consistency, he applied it
a little at a time to the exposed wax seals until small cones
about an inch high formed. In about ten minutes, when
these cones had become firm, he lifted them sharply from

the seals so as not to break the edges, removed any specks of the compound that remained on them, and then, using a heated pencil-point soldering iron, he cut through the seal along the edge of the wrapping paper. As the wrapping paper had been glued before the seals were applied, the expert next moistened the upper surface of the wrapper with a solution used by collectors to remove stamps from envelopes. He allowed time for this to soak through the paper and soften the gum paste beneath it. Then gently he raised the free edge of the wrapper.

At last we had the code book and rushed it to the waiting cameraman, who photographed each page and returned it to the flaps-and-seals expert, who was ready to rewrap it. Placing the code book squarely on the paper, aligning it with the original creases, he applied a little fresh gum and, using an electric iron, smoothed the paper and dried it. Then, using the matrixes which he had made with the dentist's compound, he placed them carefully on the broken seals, which had already been made soft with a very hot soldering iron, and pressed them firmly into place. When, after a few minutes, he lifted the matrixes, the original wax seals looked as they had originally and showed no indications that they had been tampered with in any way. The package was ready to go back to its resting place.

While this was going on, we had discovered in the safe what looked like a trap—a string laid in zigzag fashion atop a dust-covered tin box. Twenty minutes were required to sketch and measure the string and to make sure that it didn't lead to something else. Then the remaining contents of the safe were removed and all ledgers, papers, etc., were examined one-by-one by the evaluator. This procedure was followed with papers and documents taken from desks and filing cabinets.

Everything judged to be important by the evaluator, who knew four languages and used all of them before the search was completed, was sent to the washroom to be photographed. As soon as the picture had been taken, the article was put back where it had come from, and in exactly the same position. In the washroom the camera expert worked like the proverbial beaver. In a little less than four hours he made two thousand photographs of letters, codes, reports, and other material.

In the lobby of the building, for the benefit of the employees, we made a considerable show of packing away the instruments used in the sway tests, and in putting down elaborate calculations in notebooks. We were about halfway through this job when Ziggly rushed into the building, hurried past the Agents, and demanded that he be taken upstairs immediately. Confident that he would find no traces of our visit, we ignored him.

Fifteen or twenty minutes later, Ziggly appeared in the lobby, very jovial and smiling broadly; it was obvious that he had found all his traps in place and suspected nothing. He showed great interest in the sway-testing instruments spread out on the lobby floor, and seemed pleased when one of the "engineers" told him the building was safe. Presently he departed, whistling gaily.

It may have been the last time he so whistled, for two days later Government Agents went quietly into his office and, still quietly, led him away.

The Lindbergh Tragedy

by LEON G. TURROU

In 1927 Charles Lindbergh flew nonstop from New York to Paris, and into the hearts of the people of a dozen nations. When, less than five years later, he was outrageously victimized, the crime became the most widely publicized kidnapping in the history of modern journalism. Here, Leon G. Turrou, from his vantage point as a Special Agent, tells the intimate details of the investigation.

On the night of march 1, 1932, in Hopewell, New Jersey, a man came out of a little clump of woods just beyond a neat, whitewashed fieldstone house. It was a black, windy night. The man made a dark, awkward figure as he struggled under the weight of a long ladder. Reaching the house, he tilted the ladder against the wall and began to climb.

Finally, he reached the window. Raising it, he hoisted himself inside.

A dim yellow lamp glowed in the corner. From a white-enameled cot, he heard a little sigh. He walked to the cot and saw the baby. He bent over and lifted the child. It stirred in its sleep. For a moment, he thought it would wake. Quickly, he carried the child to the open window, dropped a slip of paper on the window sill, and started the descent.

Near the bottom of the ladder, a rung gave way. He

gasped as the child fell from his arms, and he felt himself sliding to the ground. Picking up the infant, he turned, ran across the lawn, and disappeared into the woods.

In the morning, he woke early and bought a newspaper. Topped by large headlines, the story was there. It was also on the front page of almost every paper in the world.

The kidnapped child was the infant, first-born son of Charles Augustus and Anne Morrow Lindbergh.

So strong was public indignation that President Herbert Hoover called FBI Director J. Edgar Hoover to the White House. The President ordered the FBI into the case. He knew kidnapping wasn't a Federal offense, but merely a violation of state laws concerning extortion, and though a strong advocate of States' Rights, President Hoover was convinced that in this instance, the prestige and honor of the nation as a whole was at stake.

An FBI "Lindbergh Squad" was formed in New York. I was a member of it, along with other Special Agents including Thomas H. Sisk, Wayne Merrick, William Seery, J.E. Seykora, A. Sandberg, and Harry Leslie.

We were to work with New York and New Jersey local and state police. In addition, we were not wanting for unofficial assistance. Overnight, a myriad of amateur sleuths sprang up throughout the country, offering free advice, clues and tips with persistent enthusiasm.

One morning, a call came in from a man who said we could find the Lindbergh baby on the third floor of a slum area tenement.

"I can hear him cryin' all day," the man said excitedly. "I don't think they're feedin' him."

A few of us got a car and raced through the crowded traffic. We ran up the flights of stairs. There, behind the door of Apartment No. 18, we could hear plaintive whimpering.

"Ma-ma," the soft voice seemed to be saying, over and over. "Ma-ma, Ma-ma . . ."

"Stay here," I told one of the other Agents. "If there's anyone inside with the kid, we want to surprise him. I'm going outside and up the fire escape."

I ran down the steps, through the alley, and into the back yard. I lifted myself onto the dangling end of the fire escape and began to climb. Finally, I reached the right window. I approached slowly. The crying was getting louder. I thought I could hear a note of urgency. I drew my gun and jumped into the flat. It seemed to be empty. I crossed the room I was in, carefully. I stopped at the door, set myself, then yanked it open.

There was no one in the bedroom but an old parrot. No sound. The crying had stopped. Suddenly, it started again.

"Ma-ma," the parrot was crying. "Ma-ma, Ma-ma . . ."

That incident was typical of the frustration which plagued us. Soon after that, a nearly hysterical woman called us. She swore she knew where the baby was. She gave us the address of a cottage on a lonely beach in Westport, Connecticut.

I asked her how she could be sure it was the Lindbergh child.

"I've seen him," she said. "I recognized him from the pictures in the papers. It's him. I give you my word. He's not sick. I think they're taking good care of him. Oh, for the love of God, please come and get him!"

She sounded so sincere, and so certain, that despite similar worthless calls, my hopes rose. Special Agent Wayne Merrick and I got the fastest sedan in the FBI garage and took off. We made the sixty rain-drenched miles to Westport in under an hour. We knocked at the cottage door. A man opened it. As I started to identify myself, Merrick interrupted.

"Leon. Look," he said, pointing into the room. "It's the kid, all right."

The child was propped up against the pillows of a crib. His face was just as had been described in police circulars all over the country—the same large head, blue eyes, and stubby nose.

"My God, we've got him!" I cried, bounding across the room.

The child gurgled as I picked it up. Merrick, the man who'd answered the door, and a woman were around me.

"Please, mister, what're you doing with our baby?"

"Your baby!" Merrick shouted. "Boy, you two've got a lot of talking to do in New York. We're FBI men, and . . ." He stopped as this time I interrupted him.

"Never mind, Wayne," I said. "It's a girl."

After finally identifying ourselves, and apologizing, we trudged painfully across the room, and left.

Naturally, all of us on the Lindbergh Squad took special pains to keep these blunderings out of reach of the reporters. The FBI was still struggling for recognition and respect, and couldn't afford the public's horselaughs. Our only excuse was J. Edgar Hoover's directive which applied to every case—each lead, no matter how incredible it might seem, must be fully investigated.

After several weeks of maddening, barren investigation, an elderly eccentric—Dr. John F. Condon—dropped onto the scene. Patriot, philosopher, recluse, pinchpenny, Dr. Condon had all the attributes for the strange role of intermediary he was to play.

Acting on his own, Dr. Condon had inserted an ad in the *Bronx Home News*, offering to act as go-between for the kidnapper. He used the pseudonym "Jafsie"—from his initials, J.F.C. The FBI was no less astonished than the Lindberghs and the nation when the kidnapper responded via a note delivered by a cab driver who then immediately drove off. Dr. Condon had the presence of mind to jot down the cab's license number. He phoned the FBI Field Office to give it to us.

"What was in the note?" I asked.

"None of your business," came the quick reply. "That's strictly between Colonel Lindbergh and myself."

He clamped down the receiver, and the nation's police machine ground to a halt, except for locating the driver of the taxi. He told us he was given the note by a man he described as slight of build, who spoke with a German accent.

Several succeeding notes between Dr. Condon and the kidnapper completed arrangements for the ransom payment. On the morning of April 2, 1932, Colonel Lindbergh appeared at the New York FBI Field Office. He told us he and Condon were to be at a certain plot of St. Raymond's Cemetery in the Bronx, at midnight.

E.J. Connelley, Special Agent-in-Charge of the New York office at that time, called Director Hoover in Washington. Hoover issued firm instructions to be passed along to every man on the Lindbergh Squad—under no circumstances should we interfere. Our first concern was to get the baby back alive. The kidnapper had warned that the presence of police in St. Raymond's Cemetery would mean disaster. Connelley passed those orders along to us.

That night, we waited nervously in Dr. Condon's home. He and Lindbergh had left with the money at 11. I felt like a strait-jacketed, starving man tantalized by a sumptuous feast he can look at but not taste.

At 1 AM, they came back. Only Dr. Condon was smiling. "There's nothing to worry about now," he was saying. "Everything'll be fine."

I turned and looked at Colonel Lindbergh. "And the baby?" I asked.

"He said the baby was all right," Lindbergh answered.

"He told us we could find it on a boat called the 'Nelly,' near Buzzards Bay. I'm taking a plane at once."

Lindbergh flew up to Buzzards Bay alone. He searched and questioned for five hours without success. We knew the kidnapper had duped us. The colonel, a stoic and reticent man, said nothing. Some of us on the Lindbergh Squad were furious. Dr. Condon merely shook his head.

"Now, I'll tell you," he said. "I'm really surprised, and that's the truth. I thought he was playing fair and square. Why shouldn't he? He's got the money, and we didn't touch him. Now I call that being dishonest!"

At last our hands were untied. We no longer had to tread softly. The kidnapper had $50,000 in ransom money. We'd made up the package of money. The $10 and $20 bills were gold certificates. They could be traced by the serial numbers. We had lists of every number. We also had huge maps at the FBI office—maps of every street and alley of New York's five boroughs—and colored pins to record each appearance of a ransom bill.

We were counting on the money to lead us to the kidnapper. We almost had to, with so little else to work on. We had only a vague description of him from the cab driver. We assumed, because of his accent, that he was probably of German origin. Our most definite lead was that he either lived or frequented the Bronx, because he'd answered Dr. Condon's ad in the *Bronx Home News,* a suburban newspaper whose circulation is limited to that borough.

Then, on May 12, the FBI and the world were shocked.

Early that morning, a Negro laborer working in the woods near the Lindbergh home in Hopewell found a tiny, decaying corpse under a pile of dry leaves. The New Jersey medical coroner found lacerations on the body, as if from a fall. He also found a small bullet hole through the baby's head.

Colonel Lindbergh was called in for positive verification,

at Trenton, New Jersey. Tall and slender, his boyish face expressionless in the cold light of the chamber, he walked unhesitatingly to the table. He turned back the sheet. There wasn't a sound in that room. Twenty of us were standing around, but we might as well have been statues.

Finally, Lindbergh replaced the sheet. "This is my son," he said softly. Then he turned and went out. His face was stony. Most of us had tears in our eyes.

We went back to work, doubly determined now to crack the case. After a year, though, the FBI had nothing to show— except a few pins stuck in a map. The gold certificates that did show up had been spent in bars, garages, and grocery stores. They centered mostly in Yorkville, the German section of New York.

Agents were assigned to cover the district block by block. Occasionally, one of us would report that bunches of fresh vegetables had been found discarded in garbage cans. Because those days were the depths of the Depression, nobody was throwing away good food. Whichever Agent found the vegetables would go from grocery to grocery, until he found one which had a ransom bill in the register.

Then, on March 14, 1933, came our big break. President Franklin D. Roosevelt clamped an embargo on gold. All gold certificates were called in by the Government. People throughout the country were filing into banks to redeem their gold-colored cash before the scheduled deadline.

We were jubilant. The kidnapper would have to put the rest of the ransom loot into circulation, or have it become worthless.

Every bank already had the FBI-prepared list of serial numbers. It also had a copy of Dr. Condon's sketchy description of the kidnapper. Now each bank was again alerted.

Some days later, a small, sallow-faced man walked into

the Federal Reserve Bank. He laid $2,980 on the teller's window.

"I want to change these gold certificates," he said.

It was near closing time of a hot, humid afternoon, and business that day had been heavy.

"All right," the teller said tersely, without looking up. "Sign your name here."

The name signed, "J.J. Faulkner." The teller counted the bills, pushed the corresponding amount of greenbacks across to the man, who mumbled thanks and strolled away.

Later, the teller discovered the bills were ransom certificates. "But it was too late," he told us remorsefully. "I'm really sorry. I feel like a heel."

I didn't feel any too well, myself. I had every New York City telephone directory from 1890 to 1933 piled up around my desk. I was supposed to go through them and trace every person with the name J.J. Faulkner, or anything close. It was an impossible job. By the time I got halfway through, I'd've been eligible to be pensioned out. Besides, only an absolute moron would have given anything but an alias.

Public clamor for solution of the case continued. Editors all over the country screamed for police scalps with the fervor of crazed Apaches. That didn't improve our morale. Nor did it help us to think the killer had been just beyond the reach of our fingertips for more than a year, almost taunting us with nose-thumbing bravura, daring us to lay our hands on him.

He had pulled the most novice, yet most sensational, crime in our history, and was practically pirouetting on our doorstep—but we kept just missing him.

No matter how we felt, though, we went on working. Banks reported hundreds of ransom bills. Each was investigated, each depositor located and questioned. Quite a few of the people remembered who'd given them the bills. None could supply any name, but they described the passer as well as they could. Eventually the picture of one man slowly came into focus. A composite pen and ink likeness was made.

Then came a fateful morning—Tuesday, September 18, 1934.

The 125th Street Branch of the Corn Exchange Bank & Trust Company called our office. Another $10 ransom bill had been received. Special Agent Thomas H. Sisk went to interview the teller. The bill had been part of the weekly deposits of a Bronx gasoline station. Sisk immediately drove to the station.

"Sure, I remember that bill," the attendant said. "I had a feeling maybe it was counterfeit. Last week, some sharpie passes off a phony ten-spot on me, and the boss says I got to make it good. That's a third of my salary. Okay, I said to myself. It ain't gonna happen again. I meant it. From then on, I said I was gonna take the license number of any guy that gives me bigger than a fin."

Sisk nodded. "And what about this bill?" he asked, trying not to appear excited. "Did you get this guy's number?"

"You bet your sweet life," the attendant snapped. "Once a sucker is enough. Look. I marked it right down on the bill."

Sisk looked. The number was there in the corner—small and lightly inscribed, but legible. Now Sisk reached into his pocket and took out the composite sketch.

"That's him!" the attendant snapped. "Sure. I remember him. He talked quiet. With a German accent."

Sisk rushed back to the office. We called the New York State Motor Vehicle Bureau. They checked the license number. Those license plates belonged to a 1929 Dodge. It was registered to a man in the Bronx. His name was Bruno Richard Hauptmann.

That afternoon, a momentous council of war was held.

The entire Lindbergh Squad was present. So were detectives from New York and New Jersey police departments. This was our first really conclusive lead. We were determined that every step would be planned with extreme care. We couldn't afford another "almost, but not quite." It was nightfall when we finished our conference.

A few of us went to Hauptmann's home at 1279 East 222nd Street, in the Bronx. It turned out to be a small, two-story frame bungalow. Secretly, we made a complete survey of the terrain. We decided not to arrest the German just then, but to try to catch him the next day in the act of passing one of the ransom bills.

At 8:55 AM, a short, sallow-faced man came out of the house. He went into the garage, backed out a 1929 Dodge, and drove slowly up the street. We followed in three waiting cars.

Under the Third Avenue "El," Hauptmann sensed he was being followed. He began to drive a zigzag path. Then, he tried to make a break for it, shooting past a red traffic light. Our lead car sped to his side, and forced him to the curb.

"What's the matter?" Hauptmann asked.

"Passed a signal, mister. Let's see your license."

He didn't seem troubled. He reached into his coat and took it out. The name was Bruno Richard Hauptmann. His picture on the license might have been our artist's composite portrait. And even there on the street, with my inexpert eye, I saw that the crude handwriting resembled the lettering of the ransom notes.

"Can we have a look at your wallet?"

He gave it to us slowly. In it was a $20 gold certificate. The serial number checked with our ransom list.

We hustled Hauptmann down to headquarters. If this was the curtain, we were determined not to muff it. At all costs, we wanted no word of what was happening to leak to the press. A premature revelation might ruin our chances of ferreting out evidence. It would also drive possible accomplices into hiding.

Somehow, Walter Winchell discovered the facts in time for the early morning editions of his column. Discreetly, he abstained from revealing them. It was a fine, perhaps heroic, certainly patriotic gesture. Unfortunately, the story broke the following afternoon for his competitors.

Hauptmann answered our questions slowly, contradicting himself, his sentences sometimes trailing off into near gibberish. I spoke to him in German, because his English was unintelligible. At first, he said he'd never been to New Jersey. Later, he begrudgingly admitted having worked in the state as a carpenter. He also admitted having entered the United States illegally, but denied what we subsequently proved—that he had a criminal record in Germany. As for the ransom bill found in his wallet, he said he'd gotten it in his change at a store.

One thing he steadfastly and persistently denied: that he had anything to do with the Lindbergh kidnapping. His obstinacy was formidable. He'd never yield even the most obvious point. His perspective of truth and falsehood was hopelessly twisted. We continued to puncture his story at every turn, but never would he confess.

Then, I asked him to copy a sentence from the newspaper. He stuck his tongue between his lips and began to struggle with the pencil like a third-grade schoolboy. He knew we wanted to get a sample of his handwriting to check against the ransom notes, and managed to disguise his style.

The FBI knew something Hauptmann didn't, however. If one writes long enough, his natural handwriting eventually will become evident through any attempted camouflage. I kept Hauptmann writing continuously for two hours, now and then interjecting a word from one of the ransom notes. He'd just finished a stretch with the *Congressional Record*, and was starting on *The Wall Street Journal*, when I could see that he was tiring badly. It's fatiguing for a man to work constantly adding unaccustomed curlicues to letters, or remembering to cross his t's differently than he usually does.

If he was tired, that made two of us. I'd done straight duty for thirty-six hours. After telling him he could rest, I collected his final half-hour's labors, put them in an envelope, and dispatched them to Washington by fast messenger.

At 8:30 the next morning, Charlie Appel, head of the FBI Laboratory, called. "Congratulations," he said, simply. "It checks."

I went to Dr. Condon's house and picked him up. While we were en route to the Greenwich Street Station, where Hauptmann was being held, I told him we had a suspect we wanted him to try to identify.

"Who?" he asked. "The kidnapper?"

"I don't know, Doctor. It may be."

"Don't worry, son," Dr. Condon said. "If he's the fellow I met, I'll know him. If I live a million years, I'll know him." Then he quizzically tilted his head toward me and whispered: "Now look here, describe this suspect you've got."

That surprised me. "I'm sorry, Doctor. I can't tell you that. The whole point of this is that you pick him out yourself."

"Why? Just tell me why? That's a fool notion," he protested.

When we got to the station, Hauptmann was in the lineup. Instead of trying to identify the suspect, Condon got into squabbles with Inspector Lyons, of the New York City Police, and others. Finally, in almost a tantrum, he stalked from the room. I followed him.

"I won't identify him for those insolent morons," he told me.

"But have you seen him before, Doctor?" I asked, referring to Hauptmann, whom Condon at one point had approached and questioned in German.

"No," he said, with finality. "He is not the man. But he looks like his brother!"

A few days later, after Hauptmann had been taken to the Bronx County Jail to await extradition to New Jersey, Dr. Condon reversed his statement. There, leveling a finger dramatically at the German, he accused him of being the extortionist with whom he had dealt. Whether the doctor's change of heart was prompted by senility or a simple allergy to New York City's policemen is anybody's guess.

At any rate, we all realized our job was far from done. The legal case against Hauptmann rested dubiously on an old man's querulousness, a $20 gold certificate, and a handwriting analysis. Not until the ransom money was found could we be satisfied.

Later that morning, another conference was held, attended by all the police agencies working on the case. Director Hoover and the entire FBI Lindbergh Squad were convinced the money was somewhere in the Hauptmann home. Colonel Schwartzkopf, head of the New Jersey State Police, vociferously denied this could be possible. The New Jersey police had searched the house thoroughly, he said, and found nothing. I ventured that Hauptmann's dull mentality probably wouldn't permit any other hiding place. Director Hoover agreed, and suggested that another search be made. Colonel Schwartzkopf reluctantly agreed.

Four of us were assigned.

In a concealed compartment in the south wall of the garage, two five-gallon gasoline cans were found. In the first, a hundred $10 gold certificates were wrapped in an old copy of the New York *Daily Mirror*. The second can contained eighty-three $10 gold certificates, wrapped in a page of the New York *Daily News*. The numbers of the bills checked with our ransom list.

The rules of evidence are such that the money would not have been legally admitted as evidence by the court unless a member of the household—in this case Mrs. Hauptmann—were present. We therefore replaced the cans, and called in Mrs. Hauptmann.

"Can you tell us if any money is hidden here?" I asked in German.

She shook her head. "Money? Money in this house? You're crazy. We're poor people. Where would we get money to hide? Please. Please, Herr Policeman, why are you holding Richard?"

We went through the motions of searching, and found the gold certificates for her. Mrs. Hauptmann, a plain, buxom German *hausfrau*, wrung her hands in peasant fashion.

"*O, mein Gott im Himmel!*" she exclaimed. "Richard had all that money in the house! And I had to pay rent and feed three mouths and take care of the baby on thirty dollars a week!"

She didn't have the intelligence or sophistication to be acting.

Presently, another cache of gold certificates was dug up from the garage floor. Another rolled-up wad of bills was found stuffed in holes drilled in a 2 x 4 panel hidden in the wall of the garage.

Returning to the station, I asked Hauptmann what had by this time become a routine question—"Is there any money hidden in your house?"

"I swear," he said, "there is no money there."

"What about the garage?" I asked. "Is there money hidden in the garage, Hauptmann?"

"No."

We brought out one of the gasoline cans.

"Oh," he said, "yes, I know about that. A man named Fisch gave it to me."

We asked him if there was any more money in the garage.

He said no. He admitted nothing until we showed him the rest of the ransom money we'd recovered. Then he insisted vehemently that all the money was given to him for safe-keeping by one Isador Fisch, a Jewish friend who had died a few months earlier in a German t.b. sanitarium. To give Hauptmann every benefit of American justice, the New Jersey State Police sent Supervisor Russell A. Snook to Germany to examine Fisch's personal papers.

Snook, a top investigator, could find no records to substantiate Hauptmann's last-minute, mystic tale of such incredible generosity. Tried at Flemington, New Jersey, Bruno Richard Hauptmann was found guilty by the jury, and died in the electric chair in Trenton, New Jersey, on April 3, 1936.

The Double-edged Sword

by CHARLES WIGHTON
and GUNTER PEIS

"The Double-edged Sword" is the story of a brilliant
counterespionage coup. That it was accomplished by an
organization as inexperienced in dealing with professional
perfidy as the FBI, was regarded by veteran foreign service
officers as little short of a miracle. You may recognize the
story of William G. Sebold as the basis for the screenplay
by John Monks, Jr., The House on 92nd Street—the first,
and to many the best, film ever made about the FBI.

DURING THE SUMMER OF 1939, Germany's top Nazis
knew, of course, that war was imminent. That brought to the
fore the serious problem of future communications with
Nazi spies in America.

The Nazis knew that, when war came, the British would
blockade the Atlantic. That meant continued courier service
by stewards of German ships stopping at one or another
U.S. port would be severely restricted, if not impossible.

Nicholas Fritz Ritter, one of the heads of the Abwehr—the
Nazi's military intelligence organization—was under considerable pressure from Berlin to organize a system of radio
links with the United States. At that point, he received a call
from the Abwehr officer at Munster, in Westphalia. The

Abwehr had just come across a German-American visiting his ill mother in the Fatherland who might be useful.

This German-American—William G. Sebold—was an engineer employed by Consolidated Aircraft Company, in San Diego, California. The Abwehr officer reported that Sebold had apparently gotten into some kind of passport difficulty.

The Abwehr officer on the phone told Ritter that he'd interviewed Sebold personally, and that the German-American had professed great admiration for the New Germany. In addition, he'd also hinted he might be willing to do something for the Third Reich on his return to the United States.

Ritter ordered the officer to bring Sebold to his office immediately.

"Dr. Ranken"—Ritter's "cover name"—was very impressed with Sebold, and decided to enlist him in the Abwehr as a radio operator. This obviously involved Sebold's remaining in Germany for training. The German-American told Ranken he'd have to go to the United States Consulate in Cologne, and have his passport put in order. When he returned from Cologne, he told the Abwehr that everything was in order.

Toward the end of 1939, Sebold was proficient in Morse code and in the operation of shortwave transmitters and receivers. Because of the danger that radio equipment might be detected by the FBI if he carried an Abwehr spy set in his luggage, Sebold was shown how to build the necessary equipment with parts easily obtained in New York.

As a reserve means of communication, he was instructed in point photography—the method by which a message a full page in length could be microphotographed and attached to a postcard or letter as nothing more than a typewritten period mark.

Sebold finished his training and left for the United States. He reached New York at the end of January, 1940. His instructions were to establish an engineering consultant's office in Manhattan as a cover for his Abwehr activities.

While building the shortwave transmitter, he was to maintain communication with his Nazi superiors through a steward aboard the U.S. liner *George Washington,* which was sailing from New York to ports in then still neutral Italy and Spain.

Sebold had originally been told to contact Frederic Joubert Duquesne, one of Germany's most trusted and valuable agents. The Abwehr felt that Duquesne was sufficiently experienced to deal with any difficulties that might arise from Sebold's inexperience in the field of espionage.

In addition to Duquesne, Sebold also contacted other Abwehr agents in the New York area, and delivered instructions from Germany that they were to use him as their radio link with Germany.

Shortly after Sebold arrived, he opened an office on 42nd Street, as per instructions, and installed a radio transmitter in a house he rented in Centerport, Long Island.

At that point, Admiral Canaris, head of Nazi intelligence, thought of Hermann Lang. Lang was the naturalized American who, while working as an inspector in the Long Island factory of C.I. Norden Company, had stolen what was then America's top military secret—the famed Norden bombsight.

Luftwaffe bombers equipped with the German version of the bombsight were making sorties over the British Isles. Canaris knew that sooner or later one of the bombers would be shot down and an intact bombsight would fall into the hands of the British. Canaris also knew that details of the bombsight having been captured would then reach Washington.

It was therefore urgent, from the Nazis' point of view, that Lang should leave the United States and return to Germany. A message to that effect was sent to Sebold. He was instructed to contact Lang, who still worked at the Norden plant.

On March 7, 1940, in response to Sebold's call, Lang came to the 42nd Street office. He sat down opposite Sebold, who had his back to a wall. Lang was oppressed by the intense light by which the room was illuminated, but thought little of it.

Sebold hinted that Lang should steal the Norden bombsight.

"Steal the Norden bombsight—steal it—what do you mean?" gasped Lang. "Why man, I've already given the bombsight to Germany!"

Before Sebold could say anything, Lang went on to add that as long ago as 1938, during a visit to Germany, he'd instructed German technicians on the best methods of constructing the bombsight.

Hurriedly, Sebold looked at a sheet of paper before him, and then said:

"You must excuse me. Yes. I see you have already given important information to Berlin. Well, if you hear of any new developments, let us know."

At that moment, there was a flash as though one of the electric bulbs had burst. Blinded by the flash, Lang wasn't sure what had happened. When he looked up, he saw that Sebold was smiling.

"Well, excuse me again, Herr Lang," Sebold said. "I must say you sure are a good soldier of *der Führer*."

"Yes," said Lang, as they shook hands. "I am a true follower of *der Führer*. I am an *Alte Kaempfer*"—one of the old fighters who had taken part in Hitler's famous march through Munich in 1923.

Lang then left. Sebold grinned again—for he was an FBI counterspy.

Everything Lang had said had been recorded by two Special Agents located in the adjoining office. The blinding flash had been from a camera whose lens was behind a one-way mirror in the wall facing Lang. The camera had filmed his entire interview with Sebold.

The FBI did nothing about Lang at the time, nor about the thirty other Nazi agents of the spy ring Sebold had penetrated. They merely kept each of them under strict surveillance.

Sebold's radio transmitter and receiver had been built and installed by FBI radio experts. Under the Bureau's supervision, Sebold maintained constant contact with the Abwehr and the members of the spy ring.

For good value, the FBI occasionally added authentic tidbits to the spies' messages—usually about technical projects which, after long investigation, had been found to be abortive. The effect was that German technicians, given the details by the Abwehr, spent many long months working on such useless projects.

The FBI preferred keeping its eyes on spies it knew. So long as the United States remained at peace, there was little point in rounding up the Abwehr ring. Better to let it function and alter what its members were reporting. Arresting the spies would mean they'd be replaced by others, who might not be detected until they had done some serious damage.

By the summer of 1941, though, the United States and Germany were so close to war that other considerations came into play. Finally, J. Edgar Hoover issued instructions to the FBI Field Office in New York.

Early on the morning of July 30, the great roundup began.

Lang, whose home was on 64th Street, in Manhattan, was arrested at a small bungalow he'd rented for the summer at a nearby beach community.

At his trial, Lang, defended by a distinguished New York attorney, G.W. Herz, claimed he'd acted under Nazi pressure. He told a melodramatic story of how, when he landed at Cuxhaven in 1938, he'd been accosted by a man from the

Gestapo. He was threatened, Lang said—if he didn't send the Nazis blueprints of the Norden bombsight, reprisals would be taken against his family in Germany.

His story collapsed when testimony was given by the two Special Agents who'd been in the office adjoining Sebold's.

The sensation of the trial, of course, was the appearance of Sebold himself—revealed in court for the first time as an FBI counterspy. He testified that after losing his passport in Germany, he'd been placed under arrest, and told he wouldn't get his passport back unless he agreed to work for the Abwehr. He did agree, and then was permitted to go to Cologne, where he reported everything to the U.S. Consul.

The Consul told him to go ahead and do everything the Abwehr asked, assuring him that "things would be taken care of" when he returned to the States.

Returning to the Abwehr in Hamburg, he went through the Nazi spy school. When he finished his course, he was given a thousand dollars in American currency and four microfilms which contained the names and addresses of agents he was to contact in New York. He hid the films in the case of his wrist watch and departed for America.

Landing in New York, he was met by two FBI Special Agents. He gave them the money and the microfilms. Using Abwehr funds, they set up the 42nd Street office for Sebold, and also one next door for themselves. They likewise used the Nazis' funds, which came to Sebold via Mexico, to rent the house at Centerport and to purchase the radio equipment.

Canaris, who read and spoke excellent English, followed the trial in detail from the reports in *The New York Times* and the *New York Herald Tribune*, which reached him via Lisbon. The trial in New York dragged on for three months, until just after the United States entered the war in December, 1941.

Lang, like all the rest of the spies, was found guilty and sentenced to a long term in Federal prison.

After the war ended, this entry was found in the captured diary of Canaris' top assistant, Erwin von Lahousen:

"As a result of these arrests by the American FBI, our entire network of Abwehr agents, built up in the United States with such great difficulty, has received its death blow."

That sentence was a great tribute to the FBI. Even more important, it was true. For the remainder of the war, the Germans were unable to establish a single effective professional spy ring in the United States—thanks to William Sebold and the FBI.

Death in Illinois

by IRVING CRUMP
and JOHN W. NEWTON

"Death in Illinois" is the story of a manhunt for a depraved, desperate, heavily armed killer. His real name was Lester Gillis. Never heard of him? Probably not. Ambitious to advance in crime, he realized—even in those days, when motivational research was virtually unknown— that a name is important, and that "Lester Gillis" didn't have much of a ring to it. On Madison Avenue today, they'd say it didn't have the impact to create a super-virile image. Gillis wouldn't have understood that language—all he knew, in his uneducated way, was that he needed a new name. You may be more familiar with the one he chose for himself—Baby Face Nelson.

B Y FEBRUARY 1931, Baby Face Nelson was establishing the credentials which would, in time, make him Public Enemy Number One.

Captured during the robbery of the Hillside State Bank, in Chicago, he was given a one-year-to-life sentence at Joliet State Penitentiary. Instead of sending him there at once, however, Illinois authorities shipped the young criminal to Wheaton to stand trial for the robbery of the Itasca State Bank.

168

Evidence against him at Wheaton was so conclusive that he was convicted and again sentenced to from one year to life at Joliet.

Handcuffed, Nelson was taken to the railroad station. "Get a good look," the guard said to the surly, savage prisoner as the train moved across the plains, "because you'll never see it again."

Nelson didn't reply.

At the end of the train ride, he obeyed the guard's command to hurry to the taxi waiting to take them from the station to the huge State Penitentiary. They had barely started when Nelson suddenly poked something into the guard's ribs.

"Know what this is?" he asked. "A gun. It's loaded, too. Now get these bracelets off me."

Amazed, the guard looked down at Nelson's manacled hands. He saw the revolver. How Nelson had gotten it was a mystery. He'd been searched before leaving the courthouse. Somewhere between Wheaton and Joliet—probably on the train—somebody slipped Baby Face the gun.

The guard knew one wrong move and Nelson would pull the trigger. He tried to parley. Nelson was in no mood for conversation.

"I'll give you three to get these off. One. Two . . ."

The guard unlocked the handcuffs. Nelson twisted his wrists free. Swiftly, he searched the guard and took his gun. Then he commanded the taxi driver to get them out into the open country.

Nelson ordered the cab driver to stop at a cemetery beyond the city limits. He told the driver and guard to get out. Then, flinging the handcuffs after them, he drove off.

Nelson, of course, knew about John Dillinger, designated at the time by J. Edgar Hoover as Public Enemy Number One. He didn't know Dillinger, though, but he wanted to work with him. Searching out the famed gangster, he quickly became a valuable member of John's mob.

It was his main duty to keep the gang supplied with arms and ammunition. It was a job he was obviously well fitted for, considering the amazing way he'd gotten a gun while being escorted to the Penitentiary.

In those days, Dillinger and his gang were moving fast to avoid the pursuing FBI. After one job, they went to a hideout at Little Bohemia Lake, near Mercer, Michigan. The G-Men traced them there. In the raging gun battle that followed, Special Agent Carter Baum was killed.

Baby Face Nelson was marked as the trigger man who fired the fatal shot. From then on, Nelson knew his safety depended on his ability to move fast on his own, and to find safe hiding places.

The FBI taps the underworld grapevine of information as readily as criminals do, because there are always Special Agents, disguised as criminals, working with various gangs. From that grapevine, the FBI heard a rumor that Nelson had quit the big cities and gone into the woods of upper Wisconsin.

Special Agents moved into the area. The search continued for weeks. It didn't yield much in the way of information. Then, word was picked up from trappers and Indians of a man who might be Nelson. He'd been seen in the vicinity of Dismal Swamps, up in Iron County.

The G-Men began to concentrate there.

While they were experts at trailing someone in a city, the Special Agents realized they weren't quite so proficient in open country work. To aid them, they enlisted the services of local trappers and Indians. A big posse was organized. It included woodsmen, Indians, Special Agents, plus local and Wisconsin State Police.

All heavily armed, they threw a cordon around the Dismal Swamps area. Then, they began to move in slowly toward a common center. They were confident they'd find Nelson. Indian scouts reported that signs of the strange man who'd come into that country a few weeks before were still in evidence all through the swamp.

Several Indians insisted that if given a chance to work inside the lines of the cordon, they could run Nelson to earth very quickly. This was such dangerous work, however, that the Special Agents felt only they, themselves, should take it on.

The search now began to produce results. A car Nelson was known to have been using was found abandoned at Squaw Lake. Two hours later, Sheriff Frank J. Erspamer, at Hurley, received reports of a strange man, dressed in city clothing, caked with mud, passing furtively through the woods.

Then the posse discovered the hut of an old Indian in the region of Lac du Flambeau. It contained evidence that Baby Face had lived there at least four days. That, however, was the end of progress.

Baby Face stole another car near Fifield, Wisconsin, and amazing as it seems, passed right through the tightly drawn line of guns to freedom. Once on the loose, he went back to join the remnants of the Dillinger gang, with plans for their next operations.

Now, the FBI had to wait for him to crop up again. This would've been quite soon, except that dissension broke out among the hoodlums. The squabbling interrupted plans for a pair of bank holdups Nelson had worked out. The banks were in the Iron Range section of Minnesota.

Under instructions from Nelson, Homer Van Meter was looking over the field in northern Minnesota, including the towns of Hibben, Virginia, and Eveleth. His job was to decide which two banks could be looted simultaneously by Nelson and his gang of ten.

Van Meter went to St. Paul on his own to look over the

bank situation there. A St. Paul policeman spotted him. After vainly calling for Van Meter's surrender, the policeman shot him dead.

Because of Nelson's escape from the Dismal Swamps area, it became a matter of pride as well as public safety with the FBI to capture Nelson. They stepped up the tempo of the manhunt. They barely missed Baby Face in several places, but arrested people who had harbored him, or aided him in any way.

Those arrests narrowed Nelson's path to freedom. He became fearful of everyone. He knew that as soon as he was spotted anywhere, his presence was revealed to the police. Life became a continuous game of hide-and-seek. He was always on the move. Always shifting from one hideout to another. Forever trying desperately to cover his trail.

The FBI seemed always to be just a step behind him. Finally, on November 27, Special Agents from the Chicago Field Office developed a lead that Nelson was in the neighborhood of Barrington, Illinois.

A squad of Special Agents went out in several cars to patrol all roads. In one car were Agents Samuel P. Cowley and Herman E. Hollis, two of the Bureau's crack men. They stopped a suspicious-looking car. They were about to search it when another car came in sight. It sped past them, ignoring their signals to stop.

Something about that second car interested the two Agents more than the car they'd stopped. They leaped into their own car, and went after it. Then began a wild race.

With the accelerator down to the floor boards, and their car careening at every curve, Cowley and Hollis began to overtake the fleeing vehicle. As they drew closer, the back window of the fugitive car was shoved out. The muzzle of a Tommy gun appeared. It spit fire. The two Agents now knew they'd been right. Nelson must be in that car.

In spite of the rain of bullets, Cowley and Hollis kept overhauling the other car. Hollis, of course, was doing some shooting of his own as Cowley fought the wheel to take every curve in the twisting country road. One of Hollis' bullets hit the gas tank of the gangster's car. A jet of gasoline spurted out. The driver of Nelson's car—a desperado named John Paul Jones—suddenly jammed on his brakes. The car went skidding off the road and into a ditch.

It was all so quick the G-Men's car went speeding past before it could stop with safety.

Meanwhile, Nelson and Jones leaped from the car. With Tommy guns and ammunition, they tried to get over a fence and into the nearby woods. They were too heavily loaded down. By this time, Cowley and Hollis were firing at them.

Nelson realized there was nothing to do but fight it out. Both gangsters leaped for the cover of their own car. The fierce battle was on—with each side firing Tommy guns at close range.

Soon, Cowley crumpled and fell forward into the road. Hollis, now alone, scurried across to a ditch. Crouching beside a telegraph pole, he continued to shoot it out with Nelson and his pal, plus a third person in the car—Nelson's wife, Helen. She'd been lying flat during most of the gun-fight, but now decided to take a hand.

Hollis was hit, but continued to fight. Then, a bullet caught him in the chest. He fell over, dead.

Baby Face Nelson had now killed three FBI Agents.

Eyewitnesses who'd gathered at a safe distance reported that the three fugitives transferred their weapons from their disabled car to the car of the G-Men. Then, they sped off down the road.

In the battle, Nelson had been hit several times and seriously wounded. In fact, his wife later said he scarcely entered the Special Agents' car, and started the motor, when he slumped over the wheel. She tried to revive him. Finding it hopeless, she stripped him of all identification and valuables, left his body beside the road in front of a cemetery, and drove off with Jones.

The Actor from San Francisco

by DON WHITEHEAD

*As almost every reader of crime news knows, Don White-
head is the author of* The FBI Story *and also of the more
recent* Journey Into Crime. *From his earlier book came the
successful motion picture of that name, starring Jimmy
Stewart. For years, Whitehead was a Washington correspondent for the Associated Press. Working for a press
association is to work every minute under the tremendous
pressure of a deadline. Don Whitehead's dream was to
leave the turmoil of Washington, to return to the serenely
beautiful countryside around Knoxville, Tennessee. The
success of his books made that dream come true, and he's
now writing a leisurely column for the* Knoxville News-
Sentinel. *A sparkling column. After all, in Washington,
Knoxville, or anywhere else, he's still Don Whitehead.*

THE HANDSOME HOME nestled in a fashionable section of
Fairfax, near San Francisco, was the residence of William
Liebscher, Jr.; thirty-nine, university-educated, well-man-
nered, and handsome. Liebscher was proud of his home with
its landscaped garden, and the balcony where you could
stand at dusk and look at the lights winking on across a prosperous community.

All of it was evidence of the achievement and success of

174

an automobile broker who had the respect of his neighbors.

Liebscher's first marriage had been a failure, but now he was happily married. He and his young wife, Jan, enjoyed doing things together, and Liebscher particularly enjoyed the nights of play-acting with the community's Little Theatre group. As an actor, Liebscher admitted to himself, he wasn't bad—not bad at all. He was aware that he made an impressive stage appearance with his broad shoulders and his height of six-feet-one.

Liebscher's business friends accepted him for what he appeared to be—an aggressive, home-loving, successful automobile broker. Once when he was dining with a friend at Fisherman's Wharf in San Francisco, the friend said:

"Bill, you're obviously doing all right. What do you think is the most important part of building a sound business?"

Liebscher replied without hesitation. "A good credit rating. You've got to have good credit. It means everything. You can't go places without credit. . . ."

"Okay, okay," the friend laughed. "Don't get so excited about it."

"I'm not excited," Liebscher said. "I'm just telling you."

Occasionally a shadow of foreboding passed across Liebscher's mind with the thought that someday he might lose the house on the hill—the shining, solid symbol of his standing in the community. The shadow came with the thought that *they* might be closing in, that he had, somewhere, somehow, made a mistake since that first job he had pulled off so easily on . . . when was it? . . . on February 3, 1956.

But Liebscher had pushed such thoughts out of his head on the sunny Friday morning of June 14, 1957, when he kissed his pretty wife good-bye. "I've got a busy day ahead, sweetie," he said. "I'll call you if I'm going to be late."

During the morning, Liebscher sold a couple of cars. Then, after a quick lunch, he headed his car for Fairfield, about fifty miles northeast of San Francisco. He drove into a parking lot just off the main street, shut off the ignition, and then looked around to be sure no one was near. Quickly, he took a makeup pencil and mirror from the glove compartment and skillfully drew a small mustache. He added crow's-feet to the corners of his eyes and deftly deepened the age lines around his mouth. Satisfied with what he saw in the mirror, he put on green-tinted glasses, changed hats, and reached under the front seat to pull out a realistic-looking plastic pistol. He shoved it into a gray sock until the barrel protruded from a hole cut in the toe. He transferred a money order from his wallet to his coat pocket, into which he also stuffed the pistol.

Liebscher, who had aged himself ten years in two minutes, stepped from his car and strolled toward the main street. He turned the corner and walked to the nearby First Western Bank.

The young woman teller at the window near the door reached up automatically for the money order being tendered by the towering man wearing dark glasses. But suddenly he turned the money order over, and in a glance, she saw printed on a small card:

"Be calm and I won't shoot. Give me your 20's, 10's, and 5's."

Then she saw the muzzle of a revolver pointing at her, sticking from a hole cut in a piece of material. Terrified, the woman handed over $2,555 in cash, and watched the robber walk from the bank before she recovered and screamed an alarm. But when a guard and officials rushed to the street, the mystery robber had disappeared.

Liebscher had simply walked from the bank, run quickly across the street, turned the corner and walked into the parking lot. Then, swiftly, he wiped away the makeup lines with a piece of tissue daubed with cleansing cream. He put the gun and sock back under the seat, and shoved the money beneath the floor mat into the compartment housing the car battery.

Then he drove from the lot and headed for Fairfax.

There was a tense minute outside Napa City when he was stopped at a police roadblock and questioned briefly about his business and destination. But the police waved him on after making a routine notation of his automobile registration and license. It was close, but he was sure they hadn't suspected him, and he heaved a breath of relief as he headed toward the home in the hills and his wife who was waiting—a wife who never dreamed that her husband was returning calmly from his thirteenth bank robbery in seventeen months.

"What kind of a day did you have?" she asked.

"Not bad, sweetie, not bad." He pulled her into his arms. "Business is getting better. What's for dinner?"

Monday morning, en route to work, he visited his bank and paid off $1,500 of the loan about which the bank had been nagging him lately.

He felt better after the visit to the bank. A man couldn't afford to get a bad credit rating, not if he was going to move ahead. He could see the time coming soon when he wouldn't owe anybody a dime—except for the mortgage on the house. And, hell, everybody had a mortgage. Some pretty sharp guys argued it wasn't smart to pay off a mortgage, not when you could charge off the mortgage interest against income taxes.

He felt better, too, when he read the Sunday and Monday morning papers, and saw that the Fairfield police didn't have a clue to the identity of the bank robber. Best of all, no one had seen the getaway car. He wasn't surprised by this news of a lack of clues. Before he started the bank robberies, he'd worked for a time as a bank teller. He noticed in the newspaper stories about robberies that witnesses usually gave a scrambled description of the robber, and hardly ever was anyone able to recall the license number or make of a getaway car. That's why he always used his own car on the jobs he pulled.

He remembered that in bull sessions with bank employees, they often discussed what they would do if suddenly faced by a robber pointing a pistol at them. Without exception the line had been:

"It's not my money, and the bank is insured. If they point a gun at me, I'll give them the money."

Liebscher was the only one who'd said that given a chance, he'd try to grab the robber and disarm him. But then most of the tellers were women, and the men weren't as big as he was, nor had they been boxers, as he'd been while in the Army Air Corps from 1941 to 1945.

Liebscher had reason to feel safe. His theory, that a simple robbery was the best system, had worked without a hitch thirteen times, and netted him $27,765 of untaxed income. The reactions of the bank tellers and witnesses had been precisely as he had expected they would be.

He felt so confident that on July 10, 1957—using the same technique as in the past—he walked into a branch of the American Trust Company in San Francisco, presented his demand card for the fourteenth time, backed by the toy pistol, and walked away with $700. But Liebscher would not have felt so smugly safe had he known how swiftly the circle was being closed by the police and the FBI.

For months, FBI Agents had studied photographs and backgrounds of scores of hoodlums and former bank robbers, and checked out their alibis. Stolen car reports were screened for any possible connection with the robberies. Witnesses were interviewed again and again for a better description of the robber whose *modus operandi* had become painfully familiar.

But even though banks were issued warnings after each robbery, the phantom bandit came back again and again, and then walked away with little left behind to single him out from millions of men in the San Francisco area.

But Liebscher had left telltale clues behind him that slowly began to accumulate, piece by piece, as they were supplied by local police. None alone was much help, but when put together in the FBI's central file, they became more and more important.

The first major clue was left behind by Liebscher when he robbed the Westlake Branch of the Bank of America at Daly City, near San Francisco, on July 18, 1956. At that time, he walked out with $1,750—but he failed to retrieve the money order used to camouflage the demand note. The money order was signed with a fictitious name, but it gave the FBI a sample of the robber's handwriting.

Bank employees, when asked to give their impression of the robber's profession, agreed generally that he probably was a salesman—and some even guessed that he was an automobile salesman. One witness, a young Chinese optometrist, came up with an unusual bit of information. He recalled seeing a man of the robber's description standing at a table near a teller who was robbed.

"This man wore glasses with Shuron frames and Calobar D lenses," the Chinese said. "They were prescription glasses, in my opinion, because the frames were too expensive for ordinary sunglasses."

"How can you be so positive?" he was asked.

The young optometrist grinned. "You may think it's odd, but even when I see an attractive young lady wearing glasses, I notice the glasses first—and then her legs."

The FBI sought to trace their man through professional

men who prescribed glasses in northern California. They came to a dead end, as they did with so many efforts which took hundreds of man hours of work. But every possibility had to be checked out.

A scrambled clue—but an important clue—turned up after Liebscher got $2,555 from the Bank of America at Napa City on May 10, 1957.

After reading about the robbery in the newspapers, a Vallejo, California, schoolteacher informed Napa City police he believed he'd seen the robber in his getaway car. This witness said he'd been driving through Napa City about the time of the robbery. He saw a well-dressed man run across the street and disappear around a corner near the bank.

"I thought something might be wrong," he said, "so I circled the block. I saw an automobile drive out of a parking lot, and as it passed me I got a glimpse of the driver, a big man."

When the teacher heard no sirens and saw no indication of unusual excitement in the street, he drove on toward his home in Vallejo, and forgot about the incident until he read news stories about the robbery.

Napa City police passed on this information to the FBI. Agents also talked to the teacher, and added these bits to the file: the suspect car was a tan sedan, and the teacher thought it looked like the pictures of the 1951 Packard which Agents showed him. The car carried a California plate, and the license numbers, as he remembered, were prefixed by the letters EPC.

The Department of Motor Vehicles at Sacramento supplied the FBI with all EPC Packard registrations in northern California. Agents located the owners, one by one, through successive ownerships and changes of address. They made sure none of these cars had been in the vicinity of Napa City on May 10. When this avenue produced no results, the search was expanded to all tan automobiles with an EPC license.

And then, unexpectedly, came the clue which pulled the pieces together. The Napa City police handed over to the FBI in San Francisco the list of vehicle registrations and license numbers jotted down by the officers who threw up the roadblock after the Fairfield robbery. From Sacramento, FBI Agents obtained physical descriptions of the registered owners of the cars. And Agents studying the list noted that one car which passed the roadblock was a 1953 tan Lincoln Capri carrying license CPC 874.

One Agent said: "You know, all this time we've been looking for the letters EPC. Maybe that teacher at Vallejo saw the letters CPC. That's close."

The driver's name, the Agents noted, was William Liebscher, Jr., whose business address was a used car lot in Fairfax. Also, Liebscher was a big man, and his description tallied with that of the robber—except for his age.

This thing looked hot. Liebscher's car was tan, and could've been mistaken for a Packard. The letters CPC were close to EPC. He was an automobile salesman—and he'd been in the vicinity of Fairfield at the time of the robbery.

A squad of Agents drove to Fairfax and compared the handwriting on the now dog-eared money order, used in the 1956 robbery, with the handwriting on automobile sales transactions known to have been written by Liebscher.

The writing appeared to be identical.

It was late in the afternoon when Liebscher came back to the used car lot where he conducted his business. When confronted by the FBI Agents, he hesitated only a moment before admitting his guilt. He confessed to all eighteen robberies, and he wasn't coy about it. He knew his little world of fraud and deceit had come tumbling down.

"I'm sorry, gentlemen," he said quietly, "for all the trouble

I've caused you." He explained how he'd gone deeper and deeper into debt because of his first marriage and some bad automobile deals—and how he tried to pay off his debts with the robberies to protect his credit rating.

Liebscher made one telephone call before he went to jail. He called home, and when his wife answered, he said:

"Sweetie, I won't be home for a long time . . . I'm in trouble . . . I'm with the FBI . . . I hate to tell you this, but I've been robbing banks for a year and a half—and they've got me."

In the big house on the hill in Fairfax, a stricken young wife said through her tears:

"It's strange. It's strange that you can live with a man for three years and not know . . . I must talk with him before I can believe anything."

On September 11, 1957, Liebscher was sentenced in U.S. Federal Court to fifteen years imprisonment.

And, incidentally, the glove compartment of his car yielded the green-tinted glasses. Just as the young Chinese optometrist said, they had Shuron frames and Calobar D lenses.

Round Trip to Nowhere

by QUENTIN REYNOLDS

*Our friendship with Quentin Reynolds dates back to our
tour of duty as sportswriters in New York, and to our tours
of duty at "Toots Shor's," a Manhattan pub operated by
the sentimental saloonkeeper whose light is a homing beacon for so many of us. "Quent" went on to become a foreign correspondent for* Collier's Magazine *during the early
'40's, and the world found out what his Manhattan friends
knew all along—this bear of a man is one of the most tal-
ented writers to come our way in a long, long time.*

ALVIN KARPIS didn't steal because he was hungry or
because he couldn't get a job. At the age of sixteen, in
Topeka, Kansas, he decided he'd never work for a living.

He started by breaking into candy and grocery stores, and
rifling the cash registers. One day, he broke into a jewelry
shop and got away with several valuable pieces of jewelry.
He tried to sell some of the stolen goods to a respectable
pawnbroker, who tipped off the police. As a result, Karpis
was caught, tried, and sentenced to ten years in the reformatory. He served two years, then escaped.

He went to Tulsa, Oklahoma, and in 1931, joined forces
with a criminal named Arthur "Doc" Barker. Assisting them
were Doc Barker's three brothers, and their mother, a fat,

183

pleasant-looking woman—and one of the trickiest, most evil criminals in the country. She trained all four of her sons to be hoodlums, highwaymen, kidnappers, and murderers.

It was to her headquarters at Tulsa that Doc brought Alvin Karpis. "Ma" Barker became his teacher. At that time, she had twenty hoodlums in her gang. She planned the robberies and the getaways. When a robbery was over, she hid those who took part in it. If any of the criminals were caught, she hired lawyers to defend them. If they escaped from prison, she sheltered them in a hideout in the Cookson Hills of Oklahoma.

In time, Alvin Karpis became such an important member of the gang that the others looked up to him as Ma's number two man. Karpis thought he could get away with anything. What he did after he and Doc Barker robbed a store in Missouri is proof of that.

The gangsters made their getaway in a DeSoto. The next day, they left the car in a garage, where it was recognized by a mechanic, who notified Sheriff R.C. Kelley, of White Plains, Missouri. When the Sheriff walked in to question Karpis and Barker, they fired, and killed him.

As a result, police throughout the country were on the hunt for them. They kept out of sight, though, in one of Ma's hideouts.

Then, Ma moved her gang to St. Paul, Minnesota. She and Karpis had decided that the simplest way to make big money was to kidnap a wealthy citizen.

Ma decided to kidnap Edward George Bremer, whose family was one of the wealthiest in St. Paul. The gang studied Bremer's movements carefully. Every morning, he drove his nine-year-old daughter to school. One day, a big black car followed him. Two blocks from the school, he stopped for a traffic light. Suddenly, a man appeared on the left side of the car. He stuck a gun against Bremer's ribs, and said:

"Move over."

The gunman opened the door and slid behind the wheel. Another member of the gang stepped into the car from the other side and hit Bremer on the head with a heavy instrument. He slumped to the floor, unconscious. Then, the gunmen drove off with him.

The next day, Walter Magee, a close friend of the Bremer family, received a ransom note, demanding $200,000. There was another note attached to this, in the handwriting of Edward Bremer. It said:

> I have named you as payoff man. You are responsible for my safety. I am responsible for the full amount of the money.
>
> (Signed) E.G. Bremer
> Deal only when signature is used.

Magee immediately notified the FBI. Back in Washington, J. Edgar Hoover held a conference with his chief assistants. The Bremer kidnapping appeared to them to be the work of the Ma Barker-Alvin Karpis gang. Mr. Hoover sent twenty extra Agents to St. Paul.

There, they learned that the Bremer family was ready to pay the ransom. Mr. Hoover, who had taken charge of the case, told the family to go ahead, for he has always insisted that the life of a kidnapping victim has to be protected.

By this time, the kidnappers knew the G-Men were in St. Paul. Another note, in Edward Bremer's handwriting, was delivered to Walter Magee. It read:

> Dear Walter:
> I am sorry to have called on you, but I felt you were the old standby. Tell the family I am all right. The people that have me know the police and G-Men are after them. Walter, please call them off, and work all alone. The people who have me are going to give you a new plan for the ransom money. Work according to their directions. Again I say, do it alone, no police, just you.
> Edward

When Mr. Hoover read this note, he said:

"We don't want to do anything that will make the kidnappers kill Edward Bremer. We'll wait till he's returned."

Now, Walter Magee received another note. He was to drive to Farmington, Minnesota, and proceed to the bus terminal in time for the departure of the bus that left at 9:25 each night. He was to follow this bus until he saw four red lights on the left side of the road. Just beyond the red lights, he was to turn off on the first road to the left, and continue until he saw the headlights of a car flash five times. Then he was to stop and put the two boxes containing the ransom money on the right side of the road.

Magee did everything the gang had ordered, then drove home. The next day, Bremer was released.

The FBI's first job was to find out where Bremer had been hidden. They questioned the victim. He could give little information, for he'd been blindfolded most of the time. Then, bit by bit, he recalled certain facts. At night, he said, his blindfold was taken off. For that reason, he was able to give a good description of the bedroom in which he'd been locked, and to describe the wallpaper in great detail.

Within twelve hours, the Special Agents had samples of all wallpaper sold in St. Paul during the preceding few years. Bremer was able to identify one specimen as the kind of wallpaper in the hideaway's bedroom.

More facts were needed. "Try to remember every sound you heard," the Special Agents prompted.

Bremer came up with the information that there were two dogs outside the hideaway. Although he'd never seen them, he'd heard them bark quite often. He also remembered that every day he heard children playing outside the house.

Two or three times a day, sounds had come from the next room. It seemed coal was being shoveled from a bin into a scuttle. Probably the sounds had come from a coal stove in the kitchen.

Now that the flow of recollections had started, Bremer found it easy to go on. He described the noise of the traffic outside the house. He said that quite often he'd heard brakes being applied either on buses or trucks. More than likely, the Agents reasoned, this meant the house was near a STOP sign.

He also said he could hear the sounds of trains which seemed fairly close. He didn't know, of course, whether the hideout was in St. Paul, in nearby Rochester, Minnesota, or in some smaller city.

With the help of Bremer's clues, the FBI Agents located the house in which he'd been held. It was empty. Meanwhile, the observant Bremer had given the Agents another valuable lead.

"After the gang had the ransom money, they put me into their car. I was blindfolded. We drove 'round and 'round. I guess they did that so I'd never be able to trace the hide-away. They stopped once when the driver said they needed gas. They didn't stop at a gas station, though. One of the men took three or four cans out of the trunk rack, and filled the tank from them. Then, I think they threw the cans away."

Mr. Hoover asked his Agents and the local police for a hundred miles around to look for empty gasoline cans along-side the road.

The next day, four were found at the side of a road, about fifty miles from St. Paul. They were flown to Washington, and hurried into the FBI Identification Division. One finger-print was found. Within a few minutes, Mr. Hoover received a call.

"The print is from the right index finger of Arthur 'Doc' Barker."

Meanwhile, other Special Agents had been searching for the red lights Walter Magee had seen on the left side of the road. They found four flashlights. Good investigative work revealed the flashlights had been sold by the Grand Silver store in St. Paul a week before. The salesgirl was able to describe the man who bought them.

One of the Special Agents showed the girl a dozen pictures of "Wanted" criminals. She looked at them, then pointed to the picture of Alvin Karpis.

"That's the man who bought the flashlights," she announced.

The FBI also knew something else. It had a list of the numbers of the ransom bills. Every bank in the Midwest had the same list.

Before long, some of the bills turned up in Chicago. Others turned up in Toledo and Cleveland. Then came an important break in the case. Late one night, the body of a criminal named Fred Goetz was found on the streets of Cicero, Illinois. Goetz, who'd been killed by a shotgun blast, was known to have been a member of the Ma Barker-Alvin Karpis gang.

Special Agents talked to people in the Cicero rooming house where Goetz had lived. One said the gangster had boasted that, together with Doc Barker and a man named Volney Davis, he'd picked up the $200,000 in ransom.

Further investigation revealed that Goetz had often visited a Dr. Joseph Moran, at a Chicago hotel. Dr. Moran specialized in treating gangsters. The Agents questioned hotel employees about others who'd visited Dr. Moran. From the descriptions, they were able to identify Harry Campbell, Oliver Berg, Russell Gibson, James Wilson, and William Harrison—all known to be members of Ma's mob.

Pictures of these men were sent all over the country, and the Chicago newspapers printed photographs of all known members of the gang.

The publicity was extremely valuable. Soon, the FBI began to receive tips from people who thought they recognized one or more of the mob. Each tip was followed up closely.

One finally brought results. G-Men were told some of the gang were living in an apartment on Pine Grove Avenue, in Chicago, and that others were at an apartment on Surf Street.

Both were surrounded by Special Agents.

They had no sooner taken their positions than Doc Barker walked out of the house with Mildred Kuhlman, one of the women who associated with the gang. Doc didn't have a chance to draw his gun. Both he and the woman were handcuffed and hurried off to the FBI Field Office to be questioned.

In the meantime, other Agents had closed in on the Pine Grove Avenue apartment. One of them commanded the occupants to surrender. Clare Gibson, wife of Russell Gibson, Ruth Heidt, and Bryan Bolton complied with the command.

Russell Gibson chose to fight it out. He fired a Browning automatic at the Agent guarding the door. The Agent returned the fire. Gibson fell, mortally wounded.

When the Agents searched the apartment, they found a small arsenal. There were automatic pistols, police revolvers, Browning automatic rifles, a 20-gauge shotgun, and a large amount of ammunition. In the apartment there was also a map of Florida, with a penciled circle around the town of Ocala.

The Agents learned Karpis and Fred Barker were hunting an alligator known as "Old Joe." Within two hours, a special squad of Agents was en route to Ocala.

They found that a man resembling Fred Barker and a woman resembling Ma were living in a cottage on Lake Weir. Early one morning, they surrounded the hideout.

The Agent-in-Charge called to the occupants to surrender. The only answer was a blast of machine-gun fire from the house. The G-Men fired back. Again, the Agent-in-Charge cried out for those inside to surrender.

The answer was the same.

Ten Agents now rained fire into the cottage. Suddenly, everything was quiet. They entered the house. Two bodies riddled with bullets lay on the floor—Ma Barker and her son, Fred.

Fourteen thousand dollars of the ransom money was found in the house.

Alvin Karpis and Harry Campbell, hiding in Miami, trembled when they saw the headlines. They had plenty of money, but what good was it when they were "Wanted by the FBI"?

They decided to drive to Atlantic City, New Jersey. Buying a secondhand car, they started north. The G-Men soon learned the license number of their car, and sent word to every police chief in the country.

One morning, a policeman in Atlantic City caught sight of the car in a garage. He told his chief, and the Atlantic City police moved into action. They learned the identities of the men who'd put the car in the garage, and traced them to their hotel. Karpis had registered as Carson; Campbell, as Cameron. The police knocked on the door of the hotel room where the men were staying.

The door opened, but Karpis and Campbell came out shooting. Then, they dashed down the stairs to the street. They ran to a garage and made off with a Pontiac sedan. Soon, they were speeding out of the city.

Now, the FBI had to start all over again.

Karpis and Campbell drove to Quakertown, Pennsylvania. There, they abandoned their stolen car and set about getting another. Soon, they saw a man getting out of his car. They went up to him. Pointing a gun, Karpis growled:

"Get back in the car, and drive where I tell you."

"I'm a doctor on a sick call," the man protested.

"Get back in there and drive," Karpis said.

The doctor, Horace H. Hunsicker, was forced into his car and made to drive all the way to Ohio. Then Karpis and Campbell let him go and continued on to Toledo. There they hid for several weeks before joining forces with a man named George Keady, called "Burrhead" because his hair stuck up like the needles on a porcupine.

Karpis now had dreams of organizing a new gang as big and powerful as the one Ma Barker had headed. He needed money, though, so he, Campbell, and Burrhead held up a U.S. Mail truck at Warren, Ohio. They escaped with $72,000 in loot. Karpis then took on other partners-in-crime—Sam Coker, Fred Hunter, and John Brock.

Now that he had a gang of his own, Karpis planned new crimes.

They robbed a train in Ohio, getting $34,000. When the FBI heard the details, they felt it had been done by Karpis and his new mob. Immediately after a big robbery, the FBI tries to find out how the criminals got away. As a matter of routine, they now checked all airports in that part of Ohio. At one, they located a pilot who'd flown three men to Hot Springs, Arkansas.

When the flier described his passengers, the Agents knew they were Karpis, Fred Hunter, and John Brock.

At once the FBI moved Agents to Hot Springs. Two of the trio had already gone, but it was learned that Karpis had done a lot of talking about deep-sea fishing. In the cottage where he'd stayed, Special Agents found pamphlets describing the fishing in Florida and other southern waters.

By this time, Karpis and his gang were in New Orleans. Alvin's own mother probably wouldn't have recognized him. Doc Moran had done plastic surgery on his face. Karpis' nose, broken in an early gang fight, had been straightened. Now, he brushed his hair straight back and wore glasses.

This fiendish killer, who hated the world, looked like a mild-mannered college professor.

The FBI covered many Florida and Louisiana fishing resorts. Their search narrowed to New Orleans. There, they found a fisherman who'd taken two men out a few times. The Agents knew what Karpis looked like, despite the plastic surgery. Railroad men who'd been on the train he robbed had given a good description of his new appearance.

One of the fisherman's passengers—the one he knew as "Mr. O'Hara"—seemed to answer Karpis' description. Agents went to every shop in New Orleans that sold fishing tackle. They found one shopkeeper who'd sold a rod and reel to a man who gave the name of O'Hara.

Eventually, they learned that Mr. O'Hara owned a car. One person remembered the number of the license plate. While Special Agents searched the city for the car, J. Edgar Hoover arrived in New Orleans to take active charge of the case.

And then one day, an Agent cruising in an FBI car spotted the license number they were all looking for. It was on a car parked in front of an apartment house at 3343 Canal Street. The Agent and his partner reported their find to the Director.

"Park a hundred yards away, and keep the car in sight," Mr. Hoover said. "We'll be there immediately."

As the Director and his assistant, Clyde Tolson, hurried to Canal Street, Mr. Hoover radioed orders. He wanted Karpis taken alive. The block on which the apartment house stood was to be surrounded. Other Agents were to take stations at the back of the house.

When he arrived, he waited until all of his men had taken their assigned positions. Hoover decided to approach the house from a southerly direction with Clyde Tolson. Two other Agents were to approach from the opposite direction.

The four would meet in front of the house, and go up to Apartment 1, on the first floor.

As the Director and Tolson approached in their car, two men came out of the house. At least twenty Agents spotted them as Alvin Karpis and Fred Hunter, but the men weren't aware of it, for there was no excitement, no shooting. The Agents were afraid gunfire might kill innocent bystanders.

Suddenly, the watching G-Men grew tense. A man leading an old white horse came slowly along the street. Rather than wait any longer and take chances, Hoover jumped out of his car and dashed for Karpis and Hunter.

Karpis literally froze in his tracks when he saw, coming toward him, the man he'd boasted he'd kill.

"You're both under arrest," the Director said. "Put up your hands."

Karpis' hands shot up. Fred Hunter looked startled. He turned his head quickly, all set to run. Then, he looked again at Hoover.

"Okay, okay. I surrender," he cried.

Not a shot had been fired. Passing automobiles didn't even slow down. Their drivers never knew two of the nation's most dangerous criminals were being led to an FBI car at the curb.

With the capture of Karpis, the Ma Barker-Alvin Karpis gang was completely broken. In all, twenty-six members of the mob were tried and sent to jail.

Six, including Karpis, were given life sentences.

The Lady with the Dolls

by KURT SINGER

*Dr. Kurt Singer has made more money out of espionage
than any spy who ever lived. He has written about every
significant spy since the Trojan Horse and lectured on
spying more often than the Security Officer at Cape Ca-
naveral. We are told that, of all his hundreds of spy
stories, "The Lady with the Dolls" is one of his favorites.
We can understand why. After reading it, you will, too.*

ONE MORNING IN 1943, Miss Mary Wallace, in Springfield, Ohio, received a letter from Argentina. An airmail
letter addressed to Señora Inez Lopez de Molinali, in Buenos
Aires. On the back flap appeared Mary Wallace's name and
address.

Across the face of the envelope was a rubber-stamped
message:

"Moved. No forwarding address. Return to sender."

The letter had been mailed from Grand Central Station,
New York, a month earlier. Miss Wallace had never sent
the letter, didn't know anyone in Argentina, and hadn't been
in New York a month earlier.

She opened the envelope and read the letter.

194

Dear friend:

You probably wonder what has become of me as I haven't written to you for so long. We've had a pretty bad month or so. My little nephew the one I adore so has a malignant tumor on the brain and isn't expected to live.

You asked me to tell you about my collection a month ago. I had to give a talk to an Art Club, so I talked about my dolls and figurines. The only new dolls I have are three lovely Irish dolls. One of these three dolls is an old Irish fisherman with a net over his back. Another is an old woman with wood on her back. The third is a little boy.

You wrote me that you sent a letter to Mr. Shaw and he destroyed your letter. You know he has been ill. I saw a few of his family about. They all say Mr. Shaw will be back to work soon.

I do hope my letter is not too sad. There is not much I can write to you these days.

Truly,
Mary Wallace

P.S.: Mother wanted to go to Louville but due to our worry the Louville plan put out of our minds now.

Miss Wallace could make neither head nor tail of the letter. It was true her nephew had a serious brain ailment. It was also true she'd lectured to a club in Springfield about her art collection. But she had no Irish dolls, she hadn't been in New York when this letter was sent, and the letter was typed. She had no typewriter.

She decided somebody was playing a bad joke on her, and teasing her about her hobby of collecting dolls. Piqued, she turned the letter over to postal authorities to find out who the practical joker was.

The Springfield postmaster forwarded the letter to the FBI.

At FBI Headquarters in Washington, the letter was carefully studied. It seemed too strange to be innocent, and too pointless to be a joke. In itself, the letter seemed harmless, but the foreign addressee and the false return name and address made it appear it just might be more than that. Studying it, one Special Agent evolved a theory. It might be all wrong, but it was worth investigating.

His theory—the "new dolls" were code words for warships in the Pacific. "Irish fisherman," he conjectured, meant aircraft carrier, for carriers were draped in safety nets. "The old woman with wood on her back" might stand for a warship with wooden superstructure, and "the little boy doll" might indicate a new destroyer.

The "Mr. Shaw" who had destroyed the letter could be interpreted as the USS *Shaw*, which had almost been destroyed in the Pearl Harbor attack. This destroyer had just been repaired and given a new bow at Honolulu.

The postscript could refer to the USS *Louisville*, a cruiser at sea whose location was a closely guarded secret. The postscript seemed to say that requested information could not be given.

It was a fantastic analysis, if true.

Special Agents called on Mary Wallace. She told them all about her doll collection. She'd recently added to it, buying several dolls at a select shop on Madison Avenue, in New York. The woman who ran the shop seemed a kindred spirit.

"Did you chat with her?" asked one Agent.

"Yes."

"Did you mention family matters?"

"Well . . . I guess I did," recalled Miss Wallace. "Mrs. Dickinson was very nice."

"Did you mention anything about your nephew?"

"I . . . I think so. You see, Mrs. Dickinson spoke with such deep feeling about her husband's last months of life. I guess that made me think of my nephew's condition."

In addition, Miss Wallace cited at least ten others who knew about both her doll collection and her nephew's illness.

Since the Special Agents were in Springfield, they began the investigation there. At the Art Club where Mary Wallace had lectured, and among her friends, no lead of any kind seemed to develop.

In New York, other Agents checked on the Madison Avenue doll shop. It was quite famous among wealthy doll fanciers and antique collectors. Lettering on the window read:

Velvalee Dickinson
Dolls—Antique   Foreign   Regional

Inside, they noted that the stock included no dolls priced under $50. Antiques from the Colonial Period fetched $500. The store resembled a cross between an art museum and a marionette show. There were porcelain beauties dating from the Paris of Victor Hugo. There were exquisite Marie Antoinette figurines. There were stolid dolls from the American frontier, and many others.

Velvalee Dickinson turned out to be a petite, chic, attractive widow with a pert little face, who looked far less than her fifty years.

Posing as browsing customers, the Special Agents made no direct inquiries. As they lingered and looked, they gathered a few general impressions which pointed neither one way nor the other.

Next came a preliminary investigation of Velvalee Dickinson's background. Special Agents in the San Francisco Field Office collected biographical data when it developed that Mrs. Dickinson and her husband had lived there until 1937.

Born in Sacramento, she'd studied at Stanford University. Her maiden name had been Malvena Blucher. She had no criminal record. Her name appeared on the membership list of the American-Japanese Society, and her late husband had his San Francisco office in the same building as the German and Japanese Consulates.

That might or might not have been pure coincidence.

In addition, Special Agents learned, Mrs. Dickinson had worked at one time as a bank clerk, and at another as an employee of the California Fruit Growers Association. When interviewed, both gave Mrs. Dickinson praise-filled reports.

It was also developed that Mr. and Mrs. Dickinson lived for some time in the Imperial Valley, in the heart of the Japanese colony. Having a shrewd business head, Mrs. Dickinson had for several years handled brokerage accounts for Japanese-Americans. Among her customers were Japanese naval officers, but this was before Pearl Harbor, and therefore not necessarily suspicious.

During the last years of her husband's life, Mrs. Dickinson had need of a lot of money, for her husband's heart trouble brought in large doctor and hospital bills. She seemed, though, to have managed very well.

After Mr. Dickinson's death, she'd moved to New York. During the Christmas season of 1937, she took a job in the doll department of Bloomingdale's Department Store. The following year, she opened the Madison Avenue shop. Attracted by Mrs. Dickinson's engaging personality, customers flocked to the store, and Velvalee made a good deal of money.

Sometimes, she'd mention her personal unhappiness.

"Since my husband's death, life means nothing to me," she'd say. It was very touching. She was a frail little woman who seemed to be trying very hard to be gallant. Her clientele thought highly of her integrity. They were positive she'd never try to sell them any forgeries or junk.

In contact with doll collectors in all of the then 48 states of the Union, Velvalee often went on business trips, occasionally to the West Coast to see some of her Hollywood customers.

After a few weeks, the surveillance the FBI was maintaining seemed fruitless. Then suspicions were again aroused. At the FBI's request, the Post Office Department was inspecting Mrs. Dickinson's mail. Tucked into some of the well-packed boxes were little notes buried among the tissue.

The notes referred to dolls. They were worded in a sort of baby language. That might be the parlance of the doll trade, or it might be a code.

One thing was making Velvalee uncomfortable. It was months since she'd heard from Argentina. Had her friends there gotten into trouble? She began to have bad dreams, but by fighting hard, she managed to maintain her poise. She calmed herself by reasoning that if something had gone wrong, she'd have been arrested long ago.

Still, there were those men dropping into her shop. Getting into conversation with them, she realized they couldn't differentiate between a French and German doll.

Who were they?

Again, she rationalized. They must be spies from competing shops. There was a New England dealer from whom she'd taken several very good Hollywood customers. Maybe he was behind it all. He was an unethical person, anyway, she told herself, who'd accused her of forging some of her antique dolls.

Still, she couldn't sleep. One night, long past midnight, she got out of bed and made herself a pot of coffee. As she drank a cup of it, she made her plans.

Her sales assistant, Alma G—, could be left in charge while she went to the West Coast. If anything happened while she was gone, she just wouldn't return. She'd give Alma a false destination. Time was all she needed. Time to see a former Japanese navy officer now hiding in Portland, Oregon. He'd help her. If things went wrong, he'd arrange for a Japanese sub to pick her up in Mexico. But nothing's happened so far, she finally told herself.

Maybe nothing will.

Early the following morning, though, she put her plan into action. She took no luggage—just in case she really was being followed. Alma was at the shop when Velvalee arrived. She sent the girl to the bank to cash a check and gave her enough to run the shop for a few weeks.

Saying good-bye, she left and took a taxi. Glancing through the rear window, she saw a car following. She tried to ignore her fears. There were thousands of cars on Madison Avenue. She couldn't take any chances, though. She told the cab driver to take her to Saks 34th Street. That department store has an overhead bridge from one of its upper floors into an upper floor of Gimbel's, another large store across the street.

In that maze of floors and exits, she was sure no one could follow her.

Losing herself in the crowds, she passed over to Gimbel's, and descended to the basement, which has an exit leading directly into the subway. Through the subway's underground passages, she wended her way to Pennsylvania Station.

She thought she noticed a man who looked suspicious. By now, she comforted herself, all men looked suspicious. Without stopping to buy a ticket, she went through the gates and boarded the next outgoing train.

It was a train for Philadelphia. Paying her fare to the conductor, she decided to continue from that city to Chicago, and then to Portland.

She reached Portland, and went immediately to the restaurant where her contact man worked. Her heart sank. In the window, between two dusty cactus plants, was a sign: CLOSED.

Several weeks later, she was back in New York. There had

been no trouble, Alma reported. No visits from the police. Velvalee felt better.

During her trip, the FBI Special Agents had three more letters to work on. They seemed to be concerned with Colonial and French dolls. None were signed by Mrs. Dickinson or by Mary Wallace. They bore the names and return addresses of three other customers of the shop.

Like the letter signed "Mary Wallace," these were typewritten. Each had been done on a different typewriter. The FBI set out to locate those typewriters. They found them—they were hotel rental typewriters, one in Chicago, one in San Francisco, one in Los Angeles.

All three letters pulsed with nervous desperation. The writer asked for money and answers. Cut off from the rest of the ring, Velvalee was screaming for help.

That first Special Agent's experience with codes had allowed him to make an amazingly quick and accurate deduction. Velvalee Dickinson was one of Nippon's most important spies in the United States.

For a while, the FBI merely waited and maintained its surveillance, hoping Mrs. Dickinson would make contact with any other members of the ring who might appear. Ultimately, Mrs. Dickinson was followed to her safe deposit box in a New York bank. In the box was $18,000 in cash. Velvalee kept that as a getaway fund. After she withdrew the money from the box, Special Agents arrested her.

Before her trial, further funds and valuables were found, amounting to $40,000. The sum was roughly equal to what she owed in unpaid taxes to the U.S. Treasury.

She came up for trial in July, 1944, the first American woman to face a possible death penalty for espionage. Her attorney played for time. Hoping to secure a postponement until the war might be over, he claimed the defendant had fallen ill during detention. Doctors appointed by the court ascertained her physical condition was normal, and that, as a matter of fact, she'd gained a few pounds during her imprisonment.

The United States Attorney revealed how the doll shop had functioned as an espionage front. "The dolls talked," he said at one point, "and the FBI finally learned to understand their language."

She received a ten-year prison sentence.

A Dead Man's Honor

by HERBERT COREY

According to my old friend, actor Jay C. Flippen, the worst two weeks in vaudeville were the week before Easter, and Philadelphia. Jokes have it that Philadelphia is quieter than any other American city. You know this one?

MAN: *A friend of mine died last week in Philadelphia.*
FRIEND: *How did they know?*

No? Well, how about this one, the one about the two pals who meet each other:

PAL ONE: *I spent a year in Philadelphia.*
PAL TWO: *When?*
PAL ONE: *Last Sunday.*

Understandably, residents of the Quaker City always bristle at such overdrawn jibes, which, of course, don't picture Philadelphia truly. The citizens never mind it when you refer to Philadelphia as "The City of Brotherly Love." But that picture isn't an invariably true one, either —as we'll see.

NOT ALL THE DRAMA of FBI operations is punctuated by gunfire. Perhaps the most tragic "quiet" story on record is that of John H. Borden, for forty years an employee of the First National Bank of Philadelphia.

On December 3, 1932, he attended the Army-Navy football game in company with Patrick J. Hurley, then Secretary of War. Suddenly, Borden slumped over in his seat.

"John! John! What's the matter?" asked Hurley.

Borden didn't answer. He was dying.

Two days later, Edward Allen Stoops, head teller of the bank, returned from a hunting trip. Stoops was a genial, active, well-liked man who'd been with the bank 24 years. That afternoon, he came to the cashier.

"Something in Borden's accounts I don't quite understand," he said. "We'd better look it up."

"What's the trouble?"

"It looks," Stoops said reluctantly, "as though John was $70,000 short when he died."

He exhibited a receipt, signed by Borden, on which were two entries. One was for $6,120, representing the usual shipment of cash to the branch bank for the demands of the day. The other entry was for $70,000, in Stoops' handwriting.

"John telephoned me," he explained, "to send him $70,000 in new bills for the branch, for delivery to the Atlantic Refining Company. He said the company would send a check for it, and that in the meantime the amount should be charged against its ledger account, but should not be entered on the statement sent to the company.

"John said that, for a good business reason, Atlantic Refining didn't want the transaction known to its employees for a day or two."

The same thing had happened before, said Stoops, and he had thought nothing of it. This time he had made the entry on the receipt signed by Borden, as directed, sent along the $70,000 in new bills, then left on his hunting trip. He'd probably never have thought about it, he added, if John hadn't died. Vaguely uneasy, though, for no definite reason, he went on, he checked Borden's cage, and then communicated with Atlantic Refining.

The company said it hadn't received the money, and had no knowledge of the transaction. The $70,000 had vanished.

"It's up to the bonding company," bank officials decided.

The bonding company put its experts on the investigation. They found nothing to contradict Stoops' story.

The widow of the dead man said, however:

"I don't believe it. My husband had full right of access to my safe-deposit box. There were cash and securities in there worth much more than $70,000. He could've used them, if he'd wanted to, without asking me, just as he's done before."

She had no proof, though, that the story told by Stoops wasn't true. The bonding company paid the $70,000 to the bank. The incident seemed at an end. Then, one day, a bank examiner mentioned the matter to a friend at the FBI.

"There seems to be something fishy about the case," he said, "but I don't know what it is. The facts have been gone into by the bank officials and the bonding company investigators. They're satisfied. I can't tell you why, but I'm not."

The FBI Special Agents who are accountants are expected to be something more than animated adding and subtracting machines. They must be detectives as well as auditors. In this case, the bank examiner gave the two Special Agents a minor indication of one of the things that troubled him.

"When Borden died," he said, "it was the duty of the bank auditor to check his cage. The auditor would've found his shortage at once."

"Didn't the auditor check Borden's cage?"

"Not immediately. Stoops checked it first."

A year had passed. The trail was as cold as a dead man's hand. No one wanted to be bothered with the case. The Special Agents kept on it, though, working in that peculiarly unaggressive but implacable fashion in which they're trained.

In six days, they had the story.

After more than twenty years of fine service, Stoops had suddenly determined to get rich quick. Someone gave him a tip on a stock. Perhaps the tip was a good one. He got more. Some weren't so good. He began to need money. Like every other gambler in the same pinch, he felt one good play would win enough to recoup everything. He took the money he needed from the bank vault.

This was easy enough, for he was in sole authority over the vault. He could've cleaned it out, and no one would've been the wiser if the counter clerks had enough cash to carry on the day's operations.

The only check he feared was that made at intervals by the national bank examiners. Actually, he didn't even fear that too much, for when the examiners appeared, he merely made a charge against one of the bank's larger customers for the amount of his shortage. When the examiners left, he reversed the charge.

The system seemed unbeatable.

Little traces, however, were noted by the Special Agents as they went over the books. Something else had been going on. One day, they asked Stoops:

"Who are Samuel B. Cross and W.S. Turner?"

"Friends of mine," said Stoops easily. He was a man among men, a good comrade, a likeable, joking, outdoor kind of man. The Agents found him very easy to get along with.

"Have you been handling speculative accounts for them in brokerage offices?" one Agent asked.

Stoops' eyes narrowed. For a moment, he wasn't quite so much the pleasant companion. Then his air of good humor returned.

"Not handling them," he corrected. "I just did the telephoning and bookkeeping. They told me what they wanted to buy and sell."

Oddly enough, Stoops couldn't remember where Cross or Turner lived. His camaraderie began wearing thin. The

Agents continued to press their inquiry. Stoops suddenly lost his temper. He said the fact was that his two friends were bootleggers. It didn't do a bank official any good to be known as the intimate of bootleggers, so he'd kept his friendship with them a secret.

They only communicated with him by telephone, Stoops explained. When their accounts needed fatter margins, they sent him the cash. It was all right, he assured the Agents. His eyes were twinkling again.

"Not precisely conventional," he said, winking, "but quite all right."

The Agents could, he went on, take his word for it. The Agents were inclined to do that, but a rule of the Bureau is that everything must be checked.

"Where are Joe and Harry?" asked one of the Agents, using the first names Stoops had been mentioning.

Stoops didn't know. He didn't even know their real last names, he said. Just that they were bootleggers.

"You know how it is," he said, winking wisely again.

The Agents knew how it was.

They went back through the books once more. They found that coincidental with the visits of the bank examiners, sums had been charged to large customers, and later reversed. The Curtis Publishing Company disclaimed knowledge of an item of $35,000. Other customers were likewise ignorant of charges that had been put on the books, but hadn't ever appeared on their statements.

The Agents re-examined the receipt signed by John H. Borden, and on which "As Borden requested me to do" appeared, along with the figure $70,000, followed by "Atlantic Refining Company."

That entry had been squeezed in between the printed heading of the receipt blank and the notation for $6,120 cash needed for the day's business at the branch bank. It was admittedly in Stoops' handwriting, but it didn't seem to be in the right position. A perfectly innocent notation, the Agents reasoned, would've been entered at the foot of the receipt blank, and initialed by Stoops as having been made at Borden's order.

At first, the bank officials were inclined to doubt there was enough to cast suspicion on Stoops. The more the Agents showed, though, the more they understood.

When Judge Kirkpatrick sentenced Stoops to five years in the Lewisburg Penitentiary, he excoriated the thief who tried to cover his tracks at the expense of a dead friend, and who would've gotten away with it if it hadn't been for the FBI.

There was no gunfire in this case. It is submitted, however, that there may be some who see in it something even more dramatic—the rescue of a dead man's honor.

The Case of the Insurance Conspiracy

by SAM D. COHEN

The clues were all there but they pointed in the wrong direction. What the local law officials soon found out was that one criminal had tricked another. In the end both conspirators paid much more than the price of the insurance premium they had planned on.

T HE ROAD FOREMAN, Esmund Williams, shook his head. The storm the night before had wrought havoc to the highway. The former smooth road was now a mass of ruts and mounds. And as for the road bank . . .

Suddenly Williams was no longer interested in the destruction of the road. He had caught sight of what appeared to be a bundle of clothes lying near the embankment. A few steps, and the road foreman had reached the object. What he saw caused him to scramble to the nearest phone.

It was not a bundle of clothes—it was a man's body!

Sheriff Edgar Fields and Deputy U. S. Marshal Joseph Gailey of Bentonville, Arkansas, soon appeared. The dead man lay as if he had died sitting on the ground. His knees were drawn up under his chin; his arms were folded around his legs. He was a good-looking fellow, well built, and dressed in an expensive dark suit. Near the body was a fine leather bag.

Evidently he had rolled down the road bank. There were three bullet holes just back of his left ear.

According to an identification card found in the man's wallet, he was William Folta, of St. Louis, Missouri. It also said on the card that a Mrs. Mary Folta of Martinsburg, Missouri, should be notified in case of death, accident or serious illness.

The wallet further contained seven dollars in bills.

A letter found in the dead man's pockets was addressed to William Folta, the Muelbach Hotel, Kansas City, and was from a real estate agent named Johnson of Texarkana, Arkansas.

This was all the police had to go by.

Mrs. Folta was notified. She said the dead man could not have been her husband, as he had passed away some time before. Her son, she admitted, had disappeared seventeen years ago and had not been seen since.

The officials then contacted Johnson. The real estate man said he knew Folta and gave a description of him over the phone. There appeared to be no question that Folta and the dead man were the same.

"Why don't you call Dr. Andrew Bass," suggested Johnson. "He's at Columbia, Missouri, and should be more interested than I. Dr. Bass just sold Folta three thousand acres of land there. I put the deal through—a big proposition. If Folta is dead, Dr. Bass would like to know."

A few minutes later Marshal Gailey had Dr. Bass on the wire. The doctor expressed great surprise at the death of the man with whom he had only recently put over a big land deal. He said he would come to the scene immediately.

Bass arrived in Bentonville the next day. He was a tall, strong man. He took one look at Folta:

"That's Folta, all right," he announced. "I wonder who could have done this to him. I had just sold him my farm and land for two hundred fifteen thousand dollars."

His listeners whistled. Several hours later Mrs. Folta arrived. She insisted that by no stretch of the imagination could the dead man be her son.

"There's one way to make sure," she said, "my son was operated on for appendicitis. See if this man has a scar." No scar was found on the man's abdomen.

Dr. Bass had an explanation for this: "Folta and I were talking about science," he said, "and what wonders it can accomplish. Bill told me he had been operated upon. He said it left an ugly scar and when he got into money he had the scar removed by electric needles."

It was a mystifying case. To complicate things further, it developed that Bill Folta had been insured for two hundred thousand dollars, naming his mother as beneficiary. The insurance company assigned investigators who reported that the dead man was unquestionably William Folta.

But, the two hundred thousand dollars she would receive notwithstanding, Mrs. Folta continued to deny that the victim was her son. "He is not my boy," she said, "and I refuse to say he is."

She added that she had ten thousand dollars from an estate—money she had been holding for years for her son.

"Dr. Bass told me I was foolish not to give myself the benefit of the doubt and identify this man as my son and get the property," she continued, "but I don't want anything not rightfully mine, and I told him so."

An idea dawned upon Marshal Gailey. There was something odd about Bass' insistence on getting the body identified as Folta. Furthermore, the sums involved in the insurance and in the property sale—two hundred thousand and two hundred fifteen thousand respectively—were about identical. He sent a wire to the Texarkana police, asking them to check up on the real estate deal. Several hours later he got a wire to the effect that Folta had handed Dr. Bass five thousand dollars in cash, given a demand note for ten thousand dollars, and had given Bass two hundred thousand in life insurance policies as securities for the balance of the land price.

This shed an entirely new light on the deal. Dr. Bass was arrested and locked up in the Benton County jail. He maintained that he was innocent and threatened to sue for false arrest.

Shortly thereafter, police received a phone call from a Miss Pearl Powell. Miss Powell thought the dead man might be someone she'd known.

She appeared the next day. After one look at the body, she identified the slain man as William Pearlman, of Columbia.

"Bill was an automobile mechanic," she said, "but he hasn't worked at that for a long time. As a matter of fact he had been acting strange the last times I saw him. He was out of work, and he suddenly started to wear nicer clothes than he had ever worn. He bought himself a wig, shaved his mustache and was always making trips. Last month he went to Kansas City and sent me a card from the Muelbach Hotel there. He said on the card he was going to Arkansas."

The officers put in a call to Columbia, and the next day four people arrived. They were Mrs. William Pearlman, her son, William Jr., her daughter, and Pearlman's uncle. They were taken inside the morgue, and all stated positively that the dead man was William Pearlman.

Dr. Bass' car was located in Kansas City, Missouri. The officers learned that it had been washed on a farm the physician owned which was situated near the scene of the crime.

It was also learned that Bass had taken a fast train into Columbia from Kansas City.

In the doctor's car were found some .38 shells. There were bloodstains on the front seat.

A service station attendant at Joplin, Missouri, claimed that Dr. Bass had driven into his station and had his gas tank filled on the night preceding the discovery of the body. He said that Bass stood close to him while the tank was being filled and appeared to be very nervous.

Marshal Gailey summoned the doctor. "I'll tell you what happened," he said. "You heard of William Folta, and you looked around for a man of his general appearance—one as crooked as yourself. You found him in William Pearlman, schemed with him, took out a lot of insurance and named Mrs. Folta as beneficiary. That was a smart move, because suspicion would fall on the beneficiary in case of violent death.

"You sent Pearlman about the country, building up his identity as William Folta. You told him that when the time was ripe you and he would find some dupe whom you could murder, and then pass off his body as that of William Folta. But you never intended to do this. You sold Pearlman on the idea, but all the time you intended to double-cross him.

"He was conspiring with you, or thought he was, but he was to be the victim. He *was* the victim! So you came in for the insurance.

"Your farm wasn't worth a nickel because you couldn't sell it. In fact, you were having a hard time keeping up with the taxes. We investigated you, Doctor, and discovered you had to have some money. You couldn't sell any of your property, so you faked this Folta business and traded your largest piece of property for insurance policies, then killed the man you had insured and conspired with."

Dr. Bass went on trial. He caused much astonishment by entering a plea of guilty.

Dallas' Reign of Terror

by KEN JONES

"Dallas' Reign of Terror" is, in our opinion, one of the most dramatic and significant case histories in the book. Extortion is always an ugly crime. In this case, brutality combined with intolerance produced heart-stopping tension throughout an entire city.

IT WAS a bright, soft morning at the end of April 1954. A grim-faced group of Special Agents left the FBI Field Office in Dallas on one of the most unusual missions in the history of the Bureau.

The law enters the scene of most crimes after the offense has happened. Then, it is faced with the exacting, tedious job of reconstructing the crime, developing clues, and attempting to apprehend the transgressors.

This time it was different.

Several of the Special Agents who swarmed out into the sunlit Dallas streets that morning were en route to inform completely unsuspecting citizens that their lives, and the the lives of their loved ones, were in peril. A monstrous $200,000 extortion plot had burgeoned a few hours earlier. When it did, it placed brilliant Jack Mumford, Special Agent-in-Charge of the Dallas Field Office, in one of the most difficult situations of his long career.

214

Julius Schepps, a prominent local businessman, and recent winner of the coveted Linz Award for unselfish civic service to his home city of Dallas, was selected by the imaginative extortionist to play the key role in the fantastic plot. On that April morning, though, when two members of the FBI Squad presented themselves at the handsome Schepps home in Preston Hollow, the senior Schepps was puzzled. A tall, dignified man, with hair graying at the temples, he welcomed the Special Agents warmly. He explained he'd just returned from a fishing trip with friends and members of his family.

"Have you received an unusual communication?" one of the Agents asked.

"Not that I know of," Schepps replied. He added that he hadn't yet looked through the morning mail, but said he'd be more than glad to check.

At this point, Julius Schepps' son, Phillip, entered the study. In his hand, he held an unopened letter. Instinctively, he'd felt this was the reason for the FBI visit. He handed it, still unopened, to the Agents. Reflecting desperate cunning, and dangerous hysteria, it stated:

"You Jews to pay $200,000. How many Jews be dead before you pay. Acid, dynamite, fire, guns will make you pay.

"Law officers can't protect you all the time. One day—one week—one month make no difference. Give lots newspaper story and happen in every city in country.

"Lots people no like Jews. You pay me now and nobody no. Bury husband—bury wife—bury son—bury friends. You pay before you die. Letter go to rich Jews in Dallas.

"Bible says Jews be killed. You put in paper and same thing happen everywhere. You blame. Not me. I tell you pay now and tell nobody.

"You tell Julius Schepps what to do. I wrote him how pay. Children burn, your fault not mine. Somebody get hurt, not me. You. Tell brother, tell sister, tell children, tell friends be ready die. You can not escape. Last letter you get from me. All letters from now to Julius Schepps for you."

Investigation disclosed that the above portion of the extortion letter—copies made with red carbon paper—had gone to the leading Jewish families of Dallas. The remainder of the extortion note was included only in the copy received by Julius Schepps. It read:

"Above letter went to William Susman, Jack Gould, Irvin Weil, Robert Rose, Sherman Kaplan, Albert Susman, Sol Levin, Hymie Schwartz, Harry Shapiro, Milton Weinberger, D.D. Feldman, Louis Tobian, M.A. Rabinowitz, Irvin Jaffe, V.J. Rosenthal, Bernard Gold, Stanley Marcus, and I. Zesmer.

"All the rich Jews in Dallas that do not get on list are just as included anyway. I don't care who I shoot just so he rich Jew.

"Wonder how many Jews I shoot before caught. Lots. I think, as can shoot when and where want to shoot. In no hurry to shoot. Just in hurry to get money.

"Run this ad in personal column in Dallas Morning News, when ready to pay: 'John come home, all is forgiven. Florence.'

"Have $7,500 twenty-dollar bills. Four thousand ten-dollar bills. Two thousand five-dollar bills. Equals $200,000. Do not run ad until you have money, and ready to pay. I smart man like I hear you smart. Not try to doublecross me.

"Want money and going to get money, if have to shoot some of you to get money. Do not mark money in any way as you get in trouble yourself."

FBI interpretation cut cleanly through the gibberish, and isolated the facts. The extortionist's target was juicy, indeed. He was shooting at the whole substantial Jewish community of Dallas. The business and professional connections of men on his list touched all important strata of Dallas life. From the extortionist's point of view, they were very vulnerable targets, for many of them had large families, and, as the extortionist had cleverly indicated, no law enforcement organization, however extensive, could hope to protect all those people indefinitely.

As such things go, it was a well conceived plot. Its successive steps had been meticulously thought out. Julius Schepps was to be the collector—or "bag man"—for the whole Dallas Jewish community, which the extortionist held figuratively at gun point.

After first learning of the plot, via a call from one of the twenty-four families mentioned in the note, SAC Mumford took certain immediate steps. One was to send two Agents to visit Mr. Schepps. Other Agents went to the homes of the remaining families involved. Several first learned of their peril from the Agents.

Next, Mumford conferred with Dallas Chief of Police Carl Hansson, a seasoned law enforcement officer. Chief Hansson immediately offered police protection for all the families concerned.

After that, SAC Mumford, in making his own appreciation of the situation, arrived at two fundamental and inevitable conclusions.

First, the extortionist must be led on adroitly to disclose his identity, and/or place himself in a position in which he might be apprehended.

Second, this must be accomplished without in any way jeopardizing the safety of any of the threatened people.

The first thing to do was to make up a package simulating the cash demanded by the extortionist. Then, run the "John, come home" ad in the newspaper as directed, and follow that by setting up the most flexible plan possible for dealing with the extortionist's next move when that was disclosed.

Meanwhile, however, a subtle terror was working like yeast in the complex of the Jewish community of Dallas. When, they wondered, would the first shot come? The first spray of acid? Who'd be the first victim?

For more than a hundred people, the comforting routines

of daily living fell away to disclose sharp-cold fear. For the Jews of Dallas, a time of terror had begun. As it continued day after day, it was to bring the kindly Julius Schepps close to the edge of nervous prostration.

The "John, come home" ad was inserted in the personal column of the *Dallas Morning News*. Within a few days, a special delivery letter arrived at the Schepps home. It was from the potential killer. Cautious and threatening, it read:

> "You no doublecross. No mark money. No new money. You not be followed when you take money. No tell nobody where you take money. Cops try to get me, your children or grandchildren die.
>
> "ME SAFE, YOU SAFE. NO DOUBLECROSS.
>
> "Think hard about money. If marked you go change. Me give you time to think. Do as told and you safe. Take money home with you Monday, for message. Wrap money in brown store paper. Tie with strong string."

Schepps did as instructed. Then, on Monday night, he waited for the message. At 8:20 PM, his phone rang.

"This is John," said a voice. It spoke in precise, clipped English, totally at variance with the almost pidgin-style language of the notes. "Drive alone to White Rock Lake Park," the voice instructed Schepps. "Drive into the park. Drive approximately eighty yards. You'll see a signpost. At the foot of the post is a brick. Under the brick are further instructions."

A few minutes later, Schepps' car rolled out of the driveway. If the extortionist was watching, he must have been pleased. Schepps' homburg hat was visible. So was the large cigar. Both were almost Schepps personal trademarks. On the seat of the car was the money package, in brown paper and strong string, as directed.

The car, however, was not being driven by Julius Schepps. Nor did the package contain tribute from the threatened

Jews of Dallas. SAC Jack Mumford, dressed to impersonate Schepps, was at the wheel of the car.

Mumford followed instructions, finally leaving the package at the foot of a tree in the park. Then, he returned to the Schepps home. The extortionist did not disclose himself. Instead, at 10:14 that evening, Schepps received another call from John. The extortionist complained that he'd been doublecrossed. He instructed Schepps to return to the park, and retrieve the package.

After that, John went on, Schepps would be given one more chance.

The second FBI attempt to lure the extortionist into the open also failed. However, it added a whole new dimension to the case. Five days after SAC Mumford's first tense ride, Schepps received another phone call.

"This is John," the voice again said. "Do you still have the money?"

"Yes," Schepps answered.

"Take the package to the liquor store at Gaston Avenue and Abrams Road," John ordered. Then, he added: "This time, bring your son with you."

Schepps explained his son was not available. Following FBI instructions, Schepps went on to say he was so nervous he didn't think he could even drive the car. Would it be all right, he asked, if his younger brother, George, kept the appointment instead?

John accepted the substitution.

George Schepps drove to the liquor store. A few minutes later, he received a call there. The call forced Mumford and the squad of Special Agents on the case to a revised evaluation of the desperate problem they were facing.

"This is *not* John," said the caller. The voice and accent were entirely different.

"This is not Julius," replied George Schepps. "This is

George. Julius is very nervous. He's not with me. I have the package. What are my instructions?"

There followed another "treasure hunt" ride—notes left under bricks beside highway markers, notes tacked to fence posts beside railroad tracks, until finally George left the package at the indicated desolate, remote hiding place. Then, he returned to Julius Schepps' home.

At 9:50 the phone rang. A man was calling. He was extremely excited. His speech was so rapid it was garbled at times. Mr. Schepps finally interpreted the essence of the message:

"This is *not* John. What's your brother trying to do? Be a hero? Tell him that's dangerous! He might as well go get the money."

Once more, the package was retrieved. Once more, the Schepps household and the Jewish community of Dallas waited. Waited for what? Originally, there had been just John. Now, at least two men were involved. There might be more.

Would they make another try for the $200,000? Or would they strike with acid, dynamite, fire and guns?

Julius Schepps' position was rapidly becoming intolerable. He feared for the safety of his own family, of course. Because he was a man of charity and compassion, the burden of responsibility to the other families became, if possible, an even heavier burden. Cooperating fully with the FBI, neither Schepps nor any of the other threatened Jewish families revealed the plot in public. Privately, though, and inevitably, the minds of those other families centered on Julius Schepps.

He was the possible key to their continued existence.

The following night, Julius Schepps received another call. It was 8 PM.

"This is John. Have you got the money?"

"Yes," yelled Schepps nervously. "Let me pay. My health, my family's health, can't stand all this."

"It's your family, not mine," John answered. He then gave further instructions. The money was to be taken to another liquor store. This one on Garland Road, leading out of Dallas.

Again Schepps requested that his brother deliver the package. John agreed. He included a warning, though. He wanted George to be alone, and "tell him not to get smart tonight. If he does, he'll never get smart again."

A vicious, stinging rain whirled through the deserted streets of Dallas that night. It beat against the windows of the liquor store as George drove up and parked. He entered the store and browsed. At 8:44 PM the phone rang. The proprietor answered. He called George's name. George hurried to get the call.

"This is John," George heard. "Are you ready?"

"Yes," said George.

"Go back to your car. Drive slowly down Winsted Street. You'll come to a railroad crossing with an overpass. Fifteen yards before you reach the overpass, throw the package out of the left car window. Then drive like hell!"

With that, John hung up.

George returned to his car. As he drove slowly and inconspicuously through the torrential rain, he was the only one visible to other drivers. He was not alone, though—nor had he been on previous trips. Concealed in the car were three Special Agents—Harlan Brown, Joe Hanley, and Dodson Hanes. They were crouched about a walkie-talkie, in constant contact with colleagues circling the perimeter of the area in radio cars—cars closing in with inexorable purpose.

Approximately fifteen yards before the underpass, George Schepps braked his car to a crawl. He peered out through the open front window, as if to make doubly sure he'd reached just the proper spot to throw out the money package. As he did so, the rear right-hand door of the car opened silently. The three Special Agents rolled swiftly into the concealment of high weeds growing beside the roadway. They lay absolutely still in the mud and darkness as George Schepps threw the package from the other side of the car, closed the window, and sped off.

For a moment, there was no sound but the heavy rain.

Then, a gaunt figure raised in silhouette against the sullen sky. He was atop the railroad embankment. He looked around. There was no traffic. No movement of any kind. He jumped down and ran toward the package. He picked it up.

"FBI! Put up your hands! You're under arrest!" yelled Special Agent Harlan Brown. The three Agents closed in on the extortionist. He pulled a .38 and fired. The bullet whistled close to an Agent's head. Before the extortionist could fire again, he was tackled and downed.

He turned out to be James Hollis Jones. Age, forty-nine. Subsequent FBI investigation disclosed he was one of two men involved in the plot. The other was Ralph Franklin Jones, his brother. Both were itinerant workmen, occasionally speculating in oil leases on a shoestring. Lately, their luck had been bad.

So complete was the testimony of the FBI Agents it took the jury but seven minutes to reach a verdict. Both suspects were found guilty. James Hollis Jones was sentenced to serve twenty years in Federal Penitentiary. Ralph Franklin Jones received a sentence of five years.

Guts and Loyalty

by JUDGE HAROLD R. MEDINA

J. Edgar Hoover has too great a knowledge of history, and too ingrained a humility for the unique majesty of American civil liberties—despite the ranting opinions to the contrary of the lunatic fringe on the Right and Left—to want the FBI ever to encroach upon the jurisdiction of local law enforcement agencies. One way he seeks to avoid public and Congressional demands that the FBI assume greater power is to help improve the quality of state, county, and city police. He took a giant step in that direction in 1935 by establishing the FBI National Academy. In twelve-week sessions, the Academy teaches groups of law enforcement officers from every part of the nation the newest and best techniques and skills of modern criminal investigation. A graduation ceremony is held at the end of each semester, to which a prominent public figure is invited to address the graduates as part of the exercises. Judge Harold R. Medina, revered by generations of his students at Columbia University Law School, and by Americans everywhere for his magnificent and successful efforts to insure a fair trial for Communists tried in his court in 1949, addressed the speech that follows to a recent graduating class.

IN A WAY, I am today making a part payment on account of a debt of gratitude which I owe the FBI.

I shall never forget those interminable nine months of the

trial of the Communist leaders in 1949, when FBI men watched over me day and night. The two men assigned to protect me were Charlie Smith and George Sullivan, two of the nicest men I ever met in my life. They kept coming back every once in a while after the trial was over. I never knew why they came, or why they went, but I was grateful. Even last June, when I had a speaking engagement in El Paso, as Mrs. Medina and I got off the plane, there were some FBI men ready to take over.

With these preliminaries, let us get down to business.

Probably the greatest problem which faces the nation on the domestic front today is law enforcement. In my considered judgment, the most significant development in law enforcement in the United States in my lifetime is the Federal Bureau of Investigation.

The FBI has been extraordinarily fortunate in having as its executive head a man with the balance, and the judgment, and the vigor of J. Edgar Hoover.

The reasons why law enforcement officers such as you do their work so well are that you are carefully selected, you are flexible, and you have gone through the necessary discipline and training. The FBI National Academy is today an honored institution in the law enforcement profession of our nation.

Another reason why law enforcement officers do their work so well is that for the first time in the history of our country, so far as I am aware, we have in the FBI National Academy a police training school which is wholly divorced from any sort of political interference, whether the Democrats or Republicans are in power.

The public confidence which the FBI enjoys is in no small measure due to the assurance which everyone feels that no one—and I mean absolutely no one—will interfere with it in the performance of its duties. So far, so good. There is another side of the picture, though, which I hope is equally clear both to you and to the public.

I used to teach at Columbia Law School. My classes always came from nine to ten in the morning. Then, I went downtown to my law practice and my court work. Suddenly, after about twenty-five years, it was discovered that I had some capacity as a jury lawyer. Well, those long, complicated jury trials keep a man on the go practically twenty-four hours a day, so I was obliged to give up my teaching. As I approached my last lecture, after a full twenty-five years at the school, I pondered and pondered as to what I could say, what I could leave with these young men and women as the quintessence of what I had learned as a practicing lawyer.

What I said was something like this:

"Brains are cheap. One can always hire some bright person to do a good technical job. Your position of leadership and influence will depend upon your guts and your loyalty."

There is no point in my talking to you this morning about guts. You men have got the guts. I could probably learn a lot from you on that subject. The subject I really want to talk to you about, though, is loyalty.

Loyalty does not mean marching around waving the American flag, though we all honor and revere that flag. Any person who has goodwill, and justice, and freedom in his heart is bound to be loyal. He will be loyal to his friends, and to his family, and to the institutions of learning he attended, and to his religion, and to his country.

Whether you realize it yet or not, you men will be among those few who will have constant opportunities, even from day to day, to protect our precious freedoms, the rights so plainly written in our Constitution. There will be temptations, almost daily, to do things in your zeal to pursue the violators of our laws which will really undermine these laws.

As you proceed with your work, I would have you always conscious of the fact that your first duty, above all others, is to maintain the integrity of our laws and our freedoms. No convictions based upon some violations of these laws or Constitutional rights can possibly benefit our nation in the long run.

Let me be specific.

The Constitution forbids unreasonable searches and seizures. You know that however guilty a person may be, you have no right to enter premises without a search warrant duly obtained. You know that in the affidavits upon which such search warrants are procured, you must be scrupulously accurate and truthful in your statements. You know that all Constitutional rights are inviolate, including the Fifth Amendment, against which there has been so much irresponsible public clamor. You know that when a suspect is placed under arrest, you are required without undue delay to bring the man before a judicial officer so he may be admitted to bail, and know the charge against him. You know that a man charged with crime is entitled to benefit of counsel.

What I wish to leave with you today is that all these and others are rights of an accused which come to us because men fought and struggled for freedom.

Once lost, these precious freedoms are most difficult to regain. Once whittled away, or disregarded and neglected, they cease to be realities, and vanish.

You men stand at the first line of defense, and I would have you be constantly mindful of your trust.

My first real contact with the FBI was on the occasion during World War II when I was assigned as counsel, without compensation, to defend Anthony Cramer, a German-born American citizen charged with treason for having had some dealings with the saboteurs who landed on Long Island and in Florida from German submarines.

The part played by the FBI in the discovery and apprehension of each and every person implicated in that most serious enterprise, designed to cripple the American war effort, was one of the brightest chapters in its history.

After Cramer's apprehension, a number of FBI Agents interviewed him. He made a series of statements. The contents of his room were taken into custody. A large amount of evidence at the trial derived from the documents and articles found there.

It was, of course, a tremendously important investigation. Yet, Cramer at all times was advised of his rights. The interrogation, while persistent and searching, was conducted in a reasonable and proper manner. There was nothing even remotely approximating any third degree, or any prolonged and unreasonable sessions. The procedure adopted prior to the searching of his room, and taking into possession what was there, was in strict compliance with the law.

Even as defense counsel, I was proud of the way FBI men conducted themselves, and said so to the jury. You men, about to carry these heavy burdens and responsibilities, go forth and do likewise.

And go on your way with my blessings.

Murder in Mid-Air

by DAVID ROWAN

*"Murder in Mid-Air" is included in this book not only
because it is a well-written, well-documented recounting of
one of the most spectacular cases on which the FBI has
ever worked, but also because it is one of the most exciting
stories produced by veteran David Rowan.*

IT WAS JUST ANOTHER DAY for Conrad Hopp, Jr., on his
lonely farm in the lee of the Colorado mountains. November
1, 1955. After a hard morning in the beet fields, he was glad
to get back for his midday meal.

Then something happened to break the routine.

"We had jes' sat down to eat when we heard an explosion
and seen a flash of light in the sky, out through the window.
I run out into the yard, and there was another explosion. It
looked like a haystack on fire in the sky."

From two miles up, the flaming wreckage of a giant airliner plummeted to the ground, scattering fragments of the
fuselage over an eight-square-mile area.

Just another day. The last on earth for the thirty-nine
passengers and five crew members of Flight 629, bound from
Denver across the Rockies to Portland, Oregon. The four-
engined United Airlines DC-6B had taken off only eleven
minutes before.

228

All forty-four on board were killed instantly.

From Denver, nearly forty miles to the south, United Airlines officials and Civil Aeronautics Board investigators raced to the scene. By nightfall, they gathered enough evidence to decide the crash had been caused by an internal explosion.

They called in an explosives expert, notified the FBI, and summoned technicians from Douglas Aircraft, manufacturers of the plane. Forty men were detailed to search for every splinter of wreckage, so the experts might begin the painstaking task of reassembling as much of the plane as possible.

Even as they started, one fact was already evident. This was no ordinary accident.

Working around the clock, they pinpointed the site of the explosion. The rear luggage compartment. The side walls of the compartment were pushed out. Its floor was in pieces. A grayish residue powdered some of the debris. Yet, there were no fuel lines or electric wiring in this part of the plane that might cause an accidental explosion.

Exactly a week later, other findings were announced. The remains of the luggage in the rear compartment had an acrid smell, "like gunpowder, or an exploding firecracker." In addition, whatever had exploded was not a part of the plane, but something "foreign."

In other words, the airliner had been blown up by explosives of some kind contained in the luggage of one of the passengers.

It could still have been accidental. A passenger might have been carrying explosives in a suitcase—illegally, true, but still without the intention of killing himself and his fellow passengers.

The men scouring every foot of the eight square miles of the crash area, however, found two tiny signs to the contrary.

One was a cog from a clock, which might have been used

as a timing device. The other, shreds of yellow wire unlike any of the wiring in the plane. They strengthened the obvious suspicion. This was far from accidental.

This was sabotage.

This was mass murder.

More than two hundred FBI Special Agents went to work on the case. They began with the laborious job of scrutinizing the backgrounds of all victims, their families, and their financial circumstances. The inquiries covered nearly every state. Of the thirty-nine passengers, all but a handful had boarded the plane before it reached Denver. Only one of that handful—a mother en route to visit her married daughter in Alaska—began the trip from Denver, itself. The others were returning home on the second half of round-trip tickets.

Those earlier passengers had started their journeys from places as far apart as Newfoundland, New Mexico, Alabama, St. Louis, New York, Philadelphia, Pittsburgh, and Chicago. In theory, the bomb could have been slipped into the luggage at any one of those places, or at Denver.

Whose luggage exploded? Why? With so many victims, there might be a score of motives. Money? Several of the passengers were wealthy businessmen. A discarded lover? Revenge?

Only the most careful investigation of each victim's private life might reveal the answer. Patiently, the Special Agents sifted hundreds of pasts—not merely those of the passengers and their relatives, but also those of their friends and business associates.

They found that one victim's finances were much less sound than his way of life indicated. They heard a whisper concerning one of the women passengers. Another victim's son turned out to have a police record. Sudden death revealed many secrets which might otherwise have remained hidden.

Of course, none of those circumstances might have any bearing on the crime. Each, though, had to be followed up.

Other Special Agents spread the net still wider—to the victims' destinations, for the vital clue might lie at the end, rather than the beginning of their journey.

Another task force of Special Agents began investigating each passenger's insurance policies—especially the travel insurance bought from slot machines at the various airports. Those policies have a space in which the purchaser writes the name of the beneficiary. The purchaser then gets a copy of his policy, with the machine retaining a carbon duplicate.

Eighteen of Flight 629's passengers had insured themselves in this way, for amounts ranging from $6,250 to $62,-500.

Then, a Special Agent, checking airline records, made an important discovery. Flight 629 had been behind schedule. Why? It had arrived on time from Chicago. One Denver passenger, though, was late. Take-off had to be delayed for twelve minutes.

What made that so important?

The answer was on 629's flight map. If the plane had left on schedule, the explosion would have occurred when it was over the jagged, snow-covered Wyoming Rockies. In that event, the wreckage would have been inaccessible until spring, and detection of sabotage would, of course, have been impossible after all those months.

That made one conclusion seem logical. The bomb had been put aboard at the last possible moment, when such meticulous timing could be planned.

Special Agents promptly centered their investigation on passengers who'd boarded the plane at Denver. They began with the only local resident—Mrs. Daisy King, the 54-year-old mother who'd left to visit her daughter in Alaska.

Things began to drop into place.

It was Mrs. King's son who had the police record. Mrs. King's son was among those who had taken out travel insurance on his mother's life just before the flight. The policies were for medium amounts, but further investigation revealed another important fact. He was in line to get most of his mother's large estate, inherited from her third husband, who'd died the previous year.

The young man's name was John Gilbert Graham. He was twenty-three years old. It turned out that he was Mrs. King's second child, by her second husband, who died when the boy was two years old.

Left penniless, the mother farmed out John and his older half-sister, Helen. The boy went to a Denver orphanage for five years, until his mother married John Earl King, a wealthy Colorado rancher, and regrouped her family.

When young Graham was sixteen, he enlisted in the Coast Guard by lying about his age. After nine months, which included sixty-three days AWOL, he was discharged as a minor. He returned to Denver, and mother. The following year, he got a $50-a-week job as a pay clerk. It was good money at his age, but he had his heart set on a sports car, and disliked the tedious business of saving up for it.

A month later, he stole a batch of company checks, forged the name of an official, and cashed $4,200 worth before vanishing. Eight months later, he was also wanted by police in Texas. They finally arrested him amid a hail of bullets when he tried to ram a police roadblock.

After serving the Texas sentence, he was handed over to Denver police to face the forgery charges. To save him from a heavy sentence, his mother offered $2,500 in partial restitution immediately, and Graham promised he'd work to repay the rest. On those conditions, he was given a five-year suspended sentence.

After the trial, he seemed to settle down. He married, had

two children, and by working hard, managed to make regular payments on the forgery debt. By the week of his mother's death, he had repaid all but about $105.

Nobody had to tell the FBI that Graham's bad record didn't necessarily make him a murderer. They know how surprisingly easy it is for circumstantial evidence to point to perfectly innocent people.

Other evidence, though, also pointing to Graham, began to occupy more and more space in the reports of Special Agents working on every possible angle.

A ticket-counter clerk recalled telling Mrs. King her three pieces of luggage were thirty-seven pounds overweight, which would cost her an additional $27. Turning to her son, she asked:

"You think I'll need all this?"

"Yes, Mother," Graham replied, "I'm sure you will. Christmas in Alaska is cold. You'll be glad you took all those heavy clothes."

Graham's wife was interviewed after Special Agents talked to him. Mrs. Graham upheld his statement that, after kissing his mother good-bye and watching the plane take off, they'd gone to the airport lounge for lunch.

She also revealed other things, however. He'd been queasy all that morning. During the meal, he'd felt sick, and gone to the men's room. As they left the airport, they heard someone say a plane had crashed, but couldn't get any other information. They went home. There, a radio news bulletin confirmed their fears.

"We finally heard his mother's name on the radio," Mrs. Graham said, "and Jack just collapsed completely."

Special Agents dug deeper into Jack Graham's background. A preliminary probation report, made at the time of his trial, commented that "his mother appears to be a type who has overprotected her son."

Agents soon found support for that statement. Although Jack had a good job at a Hertz Drive-Ur-Self agency, Mrs. King paid $35,000 to buy a drive-in restaurant and hamburger stand, The Crown-A, and put him in charge, with the intention of giving it to him later. She'd also made a down payment on a home for the Grahams.

Keeping his Hertz job and running the Crown-A kept Jack busy. So, investigation turned up, did other things. In August, 1955, he'd stalled a truck at a railroad crossing, in the path of an oncoming train. He was fined $50 for careless driving, but the insurance company paid for the wrecked truck. Some time before, a mysterious gas explosion damaged part of the Crown-A. Unable to prove its suspicions, the insurance company reluctantly settled.

One of Graham's neighbors, a Mr. Elvin West, told a Special Agent: "He once said to me, 'I'd do anything for money.'"

Graham's behavior after the crash was also vaguely suspicious. The very next morning, he'd quit the Hertz job, though the company offered three weeks compassionate leave.

Mrs. King's physician, Dr. Earl Miller, said Graham had "some knowledge of dynamite" through working on construction jobs, and that his mechanical ability "bordered on genius."

However damaging to Graham the cumulative effect of all those facts, suspicions, and local gossip, they still amounted to nothing more than circumstantial evidence.

Now, the Special Agents brought Jack Graham into the FBI office in Denver. They questioned him about each item. Six-feet one-inch tall, with stooping shoulders and an almost perpetual pouting expression on his face, he answered mechanically.

He identified some of his mother's belongings without

visible emotion. He showed signs of anger only when it was suggested he'd bought half a dozen insurance policies at the airport. He insisted he'd bought only three, and then only at his mother's request. One for her daughter in Alaska, one for her sister in Missouri, and one for himself.

Then, the Special Agent conducting the interview pointed to the carbon copies of the policies. Despite Graham's protestations to the contrary, the Agent revealed that it was the opinion of FBI handwriting experts that Mrs. King had signed only one of the forms naming him as beneficiary. He could, therefore, never have collected the money, for without her signature, the policy was invalid.

After further questioning, Graham confessed. The hunt was over. It was less than two weeks since the crash. The nation congratulated the FBI on a brilliant job of round-the-clock investigation.

Then Graham's 22-year-old wife, bespectacled, shy Gloria, visited him in prison. During her twenty-minute stay, as she alternately sobbed and puffed nervously on one cigarette after another, a prison guard heard her ask:

"Why, Jack? Why did you sign a confession?"

His reply was inaudible.

It was inaudible, that is, until the following morning, when he repudiated his signed statement. In a tape-recorded interview for a Denver radio station, he said:

"I didn't do it. I have no idea how the explosion occurred."

He signed the confession, he claimed, "because the FBI told me they were going to put my wife in jail, and that I'd better straighten it out myself."

Now the FBI went back to work.

Special Agents located a storekeeper in Kremmling, Colorado, who'd known Graham as a boy. He was "pretty sure" he'd sold Jack twenty sticks of dynamite a few days before the crash. In the pocket of a shirt hanging in a cupboard at Graham's home, they found some wire. Examination at the

FBI Laboratory showed it was identical with the yellow wire found at the scene of the crash.

And it was Mrs. Graham, herself, who unwittingly indicated how the bomb might have gotten into Mrs. King's luggage without arousing suspicion. Jack, she said, was planning a surprise Christmas present for his mother. Mrs. King's favorite hobby was making costume jewelry out of shells, so Jack had bought her a specially designed small drill. He told her, Gloria went on, that he was going to put it into one of his mother's suitcases at the last minute, so she wouldn't find it till she got to Alaska.

When Graham heard about the additional evidence uncovered by the FBI, he again changed his story. Coming to trial on December 9, he still pleaded "Not Guilty"—but this time on grounds of insanity. The court ordered Graham sent to a psychiatric hospital for thirty days' observation.

When that period ended, four psychiatrists testified that, in their opinion, Jack Graham was sane.

One technical legal delay after another delayed the trial until April of 1956. Stubbornly, Graham repeated his claim that he'd signed the confession because the FBI had threatened to prosecute his wife for making a false statement.

Bert Keating, the prosecutor, asked:

You mean you assumed responsibility for forty-four deaths because someone said your wife might go to jail?"

"Yes," Graham shouted.

On May 4, a jury of seven men and five women found Graham guilty of first degree murder, entailing an automatic sentence, under Colorado law, of death in the gas chamber.

Execution was scheduled for the week beginning January 6, 1957. As that date approached, Graham held a press conference. He continued to maintain it wasn't he who'd sabotaged Flight 629. He hinted broadly now that someone else was more to blame than he was. He refused to elaborate or to say another word about his implied accomplice or accomplices.

Speculation as to whether or not the FBI had found the right man continued in the minds of some until the day before the execution. On that day, the Rev. Lloyd Kellams, pastor of the Methodist chapel Graham used to attend, disclosed that the condemned man had twice made a direct confession to him since the trial. They had discussed whether the confessions should be made public, the minister said. Graham had raised no objection.

This time, there was no repudiation.

The Cut-Rate Kidnappers

by LEONARD R. GRIBBLE

Leonard R. Gribble is one of Britain's top-drawer crime reporters. His style of writing conjures the actual rhythm of a working detective's pulse, the pulse that slows as a hot lead peters out to nothing, the pulse that instantly pounds and races as a tiny clue suddenly pumps life into a dying investigation. Naturally enough, Gribble's stories usually follow the activities of Scotland Yard. But the FBI is as widely known, admired, and followed in Great Britain as is the Yard—and Leonard Gribble does as well by the one as by the other. We have a good sampling of his work, here, in "The Cut-Rate Kidnappers."

Ⓘ T WAS DECEMBER, 1937. Outside the apartment in White Plains, New York, a newsboy was shouting: "Extra! Extra!" The big, black headlines were about the latest kidnapping.

Inside the apartment, Mrs. Gertrude Fried, her blonde head sunk over the late edition, read that the secret she shared with the FBI was no longer a secret. Her husband, Arthur, had been kidnapped. The family had received a demand for $200,000. A ludicrous sum. The Frieds were not a rich family.

Only a few minutes before, the voice of the kidnapper had been heard—over the telephone. In a crazy bout of

238

bargaining, tinged with despair, the original fantastic ransom price had come down. Eighteen hundred dollars, not $200,000, was the sale price for the captive.

The tremulous deal was arranged by Hugo, the eldest of the five Fried brothers. He ran a Manhattan garage. He and the kidnapper had agreed on the price and on the time Arthur would be released—ten o'clock that night, after the ransom was paid.

The fear in Gertrude Fried's heart was that the deal would not be carried out. Her son, Arlin, eight years old, played with his toys while waiting for his father to come home. He went to bed disappointed, and fell asleep listening to his mother's choked crying.

Hope for Arthur Fried's return flickered fitfully in the days before and after Christmas. Telephone calls were still coming through to the garage, and Hugo Fried was chasing all over New York. He kept waiting for someone to come up and say "Mr. Roberts?"

That person would tell him where to leave the money, and where to pick up his brother.

No one called him "Mr. Roberts." Soon, the newspapers turned to more topical matters. The brothers met. They decided there was only one thing they could do now for little Arlin and his mother. They offered a reward. By scraping the bottom of the family barrel, they raised $2,500. That was more than the agreed upon ransom.

No one claimed the money.

The FBI, of course, kept working on the case. They had little enough to go on. Hugo Fried's description of the voice that told him to go to cafes and bars, and wait. The fact that the man suggested those places could mean that he was familiar with the pinball machine racket. Possibly, he was interested in the trucking business; the Fried garage serviced heavy commercial vehicles.

Very slender threads to weave into a chain. However, the

inquiries went on. Anything that happened on the night Arthur Fried was kidnapped, and in that general area, was of interest to the FBI. After Fried and his wife had gone to the movies that night—December 5—he'd gone to get their car from a parking lot. He never returned. Worried, Mrs. Fried went home alone. She waited up for him. Just before four in the morning, the phone rang. She heard a hard, metallic voice saying:

"Your husband's in the Bronx, dead drunk. Don't worry."

Then, one of the Special Agents heard a rumor about some high school kids who'd been to a party on the night of the kidnapping. They told a friend that on the way home, they saw a car in front of them cut sharply and force a coupe to the curb. A man with a gun jumped from the swerving car, pulled open the door of the coupe, and climbed in. Then both cars drove off. It was very smooth, and took only a few seconds. The kids were afraid to come to the FBI.

The Special Agent ran down the rumor. It was true. He interviewed the students. They had different notions about the size of the man with the gun, about the actual time, and a few other details. They agreed, though, that it happened near Sound View Avenue, which is where Fried had gone to get his car.

In addition, three of them thought the coupe's license plate began with the letters BM. One said the license plate of the swerving car began with 7N.

That was the last progress made in the Fried case for six months. During that time, however, there were other cases that paralleled the Fried mystery. George Mishkin, who ran the Vijax Coal Company, was held up by a pair of armed men with snapbrim hats pulled down, and coat collars turned up. He was forced into a waiting car, taken to his office, and ordered to open the safe.

The crooks got away with nearly $1,400. Mishkin kept his life. Maybe they thought he was turning into a useful milch-cow. It was the second time they'd tried their tactics on him. By the time he called the police, it was too late.

Max Gross also had a coal company. His was in Wood-haven, Long Island. Thieves answering the same general description took something less than a hundred dollars and a gold watch from him.

"They're running big risks for small returns," the Special Agent noted. "That means they're amateurs. Probably young."

Then, Benjamin Farber was kidnapped. He and his brother, Irving, ran a coal delivery service from the Coney Island district of Brooklyn. Again, the ransom demand was $200,000. Again, the spokesman for the kidnappers agreed to take less than $2,000.

Irving Farber paid. His brother was released. He could tell the Agents nothing. His eyes had been taped, his ears stuffed with cotton. He'd been kept in a hideout he hadn't seen. He had no idea where it was. It was all negative, except for the fact that there were four men in the gang, all young.

Almost four months passed before the same gang's handi-work was apparent in the kidnapping of two young men, Norman Miller and Sidney Lehrer. They'd been to a late movie. Driving home, they stopped for a traffic light. Soon, they were riding in the kidnappers' car.

The car radio was on. Tommy Dorsey's orchestra was play-ing a popular hit of the day, a female vocalist singing, "A tisket, a tasket, I love my yellow basket. . . ."

Suddenly, the radio was switched off. The car pulled to the curb. A door was opened. A gun poked into Lehrer's ribs. He was ordered out after one of the kidnappers had put a dollar into his hand, and said:

"Grab a taxi, and tell Miller we'll get in touch with him."

By the time Lehrer removed the tape from his eyes, the

car was gone. Now, the kidnappers had time to attend to young Miller. They placed another layer of tape across his eyes, filled his ears with cotton, and pushed some spectacles over the top half of his face.

This time, the metallic-voiced spokesman for the kidnappers refused to come down so far. He wouldn't drop lower than $13,000. Charles Miller, Norman's father, followed the rigmarole procedure of the Fried case—going to bars, answering phone calls, being directed to other cafes, and so on.

While he was doing that, Special Agents were interviewing young Lehrer. He told them the time when he and Norman Miller left the movie, how long it took to reach the traffic light, how far they'd gone before the tape was put over their eyes, and where he'd been dropped.

It wasn't very much.

Finally, Charles Miller got explicit instructions. He followed them, paying the ransom as directed. Like Benjamin Farber, Norman Miller was released.

Agents immediately interviewed him. He supplied additional important facts. About twenty minutes passed from the time Lehrer was dropped until Miller arrived at the kidnappers' hideout. The Special Agents got a map of Brooklyn. They drew a circle. The radius was the distance you could reasonably drive in twenty minutes. Approximately on its fringe would be the hideout.

In addition, young Miller estimated that about 25 minutes had elapsed from the time he left the hideout until he was released between 11th and 12th Streets, in Manhattan. They drew another circle. This time, they used the release point as the center. The circles overlapped slightly. Somewhere in that overlapping area, the Agents felt, was the hideout.

Further questioning of young Miller brought more information. While lying blindfolded and tied up, he'd heard a church bell. That would've been for the ten o'clock service, he heard one of the kidnappers say. The others laughed.

He'd also heard sounds of laughter, men moving around, and faint clicking noises.

"What kind of clicking noises?"

"Well . . . like pool balls."

Then, he remembered something else. "When we first got inside, I bumped against a stack of folded chairs. I was taken down some stairs. Afterwards, I heard cars passing. They sounded like they were over my head."

During the following week, Special Agents combed the area between the two circles. They noted churches and assembly halls. It was a large district, and heavily populated. There were many churches, many assembly halls. They had to wait until another Sunday came round before they could check the sound of various church bells with young Miller.

He couldn't identify the sound of any of them.

Scores of poolrooms were visited. One by one, various points in North Brooklyn were eliminated. It was, as it always is, a painfully slow process.

Other Agents meanwhile were tackling another line of inquiry. The attempt, started in January, to check a possible list of cars with a license number beginning 7N for the year 1937 seemed never-ending. They kept at it, of course.

Other Agents worked with young Miller and his friend, Lehrer. Both were interested in cars. Agents took them to a large warehouse. It was filled with all makes of secondhand cars. The boys were blindfolded, put in various models of different kinds of cars, and the motors started up.

It was another slow process of elimination. However, it arrived at a positive point. After days and days, both young Miller and Lehrer agreed on the make and model of car in which they'd been kidnapped. Both said it was a Packard Six club coupe, 1937 model.

That was progress.

Suddenly, more progress was made. Norman Miller remembered something else the metallic-voiced kidnapper said, just after the ransom was paid. As the kidnapper counted the crinkling bills, he commented to young Miller:

"Don't worry. Your old man can afford it. I saw him win a couple big bets at Empire City."

Charles Miller was interviewed. Yes, he frequently went to the track. The Agents checked further. Gross, Mishkin, the Farbers, and the Frieds all went to the races. The Agents discussed this new common denominator. It could be important. The kidnappers now had $13,000 in cash. They liked to go to the track. It was August. August is the month when, as they say on Broadway, Saratoga is in bloom.

A special squad of Agents went to Saratoga. They roamed the streets, looking for a Packard coupe. They found a 1937 model Packard Six club coupe. It carried a current 1938 license plate. Number 6C-6579. The number was checked. The car was owned by Denis Gula. Address: 217 East 6th Street, New York City.

That was an interesting address. It was near the Williamsburg Bridge, and within the overlapping area between the circles on the map.

It turned out to be a place called Ukrainian Hall. That made it even more interesting, because Hugo Fried months before had been told to toss the ransom money for his brother from the fire escape of the building next door. He hadn't done so because the plan had been changed at the last minute.

The Agents now began to investigate Denis Gula. He was of middle age, spoke English with a slurring Slav accent, and made his living by running a combination bar and poolroom in the basement of the hall. He explained that he rarely drove the coupe. Usually his son, Demetrius, did.

The FBI checked the coupe's previous license number.

That number turned out to be 7N-900. 7N? Interesting number and letter.

Other pieces began to fall into place. In the corridor of Ukrainian Hall were stacks of folding chairs. On the next block was a church with a carillon of bells.

Demetrius Gula was put under strict surveillance. He was paying regular visits to a lawyer working to secure the release of one Steve Sacoda, arrested by the police for parole violation. One day, Gula was met outside the lawyer's office by John Virga. They went to Ukrainian Hall to meet another friend. He turned out to be Willy Jacknis.

All had police records. Their photographs were obtained. Each victim identified the entire quartet. The FBI picked up Gula, Virga, and Jacknis. They confessed to the kidnappings and holdups, but accused Sacoda of having decided on his own to kill Arthur Fried.

All were sentenced to death.

Their sentence proved a small consolation to Gertrude Fried as she waited for young Arlin to come home from school.

No Clues

by KARL DETZER

Karl Detzer and your reporter saw some of their World War II service together, fighting Pentagon red tape side-by-side. Karl has been writing top-quality magazine articles almost, it seems, since the invention of movable type. Far from an old man, though, and a newsman to the core, he leaves his Leland, Michigan, home whenever and to wherever his bloodhound-keen sense smells a story in the making. As a writer-reporter, Karl Detzer is, in the language of the trade, a pro—and able to write good copy on anything from murder to problems of economics.

The assignment that produced "No Clues" led him from Kansas to California. Good reporter that he is, he came home, not with bacon, but with the dramatic case history which follows.

SHORTLY BEFORE MIDMORNING the day of the murder—August 4, 1955—thin rain began to fall from a lead-colored sky on Kansas City, Missouri.

In a beauty shop at 6313 Brookside Plaza, Mrs. Wilma Frances Allen, pretty 34-year-old wife of the president of a prosperous automobile agency, was having her hair done. Her mood was gay. She was looking forward to dining out that evening with her husband.

Between 12:25 and 12:30, she left the shop, paused in the door to tie a scarf over her head, and stepped out into the rain. Walking quickly, she hurried toward her convertible in a nearby parking lot.

She was not again seen alive.

At five o'clock, her husband phoned to remind her of their dinner plan. Startled that she hadn't returned home, he spent an hour calling friends, seeking news of her. That evening, he sent out his agency salesmen to hunt for the convertible. They couldn't find it.

Greatly disturbed, Allen notified the police.

It was 2:10 AM when Patrolman Ronald Ehrhardt discovered the car under a dark viaduct near Union Station. The motor was cold, proving the car had been there several hours. Doors and trunk were locked.

Detectives broke in and found bloodstains on the rear floormat and seat cushions. Prying open the trunk, they found most of Mrs. Allen's clothing. It was bloodstained and torn. All jewelry and money, the scarf, and Mrs. Allen's blue handbag were missing.

Experts discovered several latent fingerprints in the car, too blurred to be of value. There were also what appeared to be palm prints, likewise useless because there was no file of palm prints against which to check them.

By dawn, the authorities had dug up only one slim, useful fact. The Allens kept a mileage-gasoline record. That enabled police to estimate the car had traveled some sixty or seventy miles after leaving the beauty shop. They drew a circle on a large map. It covered parts of several counties in two states—Missouri and Kansas. The area included some fifty towns, many suburbs, and some sparsely settled regions.

Somewhere in that circle, police told themselves, somewhere . . .

By eight o'clock that morning, fifty Kansas City detectives were at work on the case. In addition, police and sheriffs in surrounding areas had been alerted. As yet, there was no evidence that any Federal statute had been violated, but Percy Wyly, Agent-in-Charge of the Kansas City FBI Field Office, stopped at Police Headquarters. He offered every cooperation, short of actual investigation. The law rigidly restricts the FBI from participating in local investigations unless a Federal statute has been violated.

Most officers guessed this was the work of what newspapers call a "sex maniac." Before night, a widespread hunt for violent sex deviates was on. All across the continent, unsavory characters were picked up during the next few weeks. All were questioned, then released. During that period, it was estimated that more than six hundred law enforcement officers were devoting full time to the case.

Possible leads poured into Kansas City. All, even the most unbelievable, had to be checked and double-checked.

In Omaha, Nebraska, the Sheriff took into custody a man who'd served a prison sentence for a sex crime, and whose record showed forty-two arrests in the Kansas City area. The man's face was bruised and scratched. He claimed he'd been hurt in a fight in the Kansas City railroad yards.

A bus driver reported that the evening Mrs. Allen disappeared, a man of about forty boarded his bus at Warrenton, Missouri, with his clothes dirty, his lips cut, and his left cheek deeply scratched.

Two teen-age boys the same evening had followed a convertible they were sure was Mrs. Allen's on U.S. Highway 69.

None of those leads proved fruitful.

The first break came Saturday evening, August 6. Late that afternoon, Richard A. Taylor, a Kansas farmer, was driving a tractor on Highway 69 some twenty-five miles south of Kansas City. He saw a blue handbag in a ditch, but didn't stop. Later, on a radio newscast, he heard about Mrs. Allen's missing handbag. He sent his young son back to hunt for it. The boy found the bag, empty. Taylor notified the Sheriff.

The purse was quickly identified as Mrs. Allen's.

The next morning, another farmer, Clifford Erhart, and his son, Milton, were out in their station wagon searching back roads for a strayed cow and calf. On Tibbetts Road, about six-and-a-half miles from the ditch where the handbag was found, they saw a pasture gate standing open, and drove in.

As they bumped across the field, young Milton pointed and cried out, "What's that?"

"It was some distance off," Erhart says, "but I knew right away. We didn't even stop. I just turned and drove fast to the nearest telephone, and called the Sheriff. He came in a hurry."

The body was nude. Mrs. Allen's hands were tied behind her with the striped scarf. She'd been shot twice in the back of the head. Her jewelry, even her wedding band, was missing. Officers immediately roped off the area, but rain had washed away all evidence.

Not a footprint or tire track remained.

Among early arrivals at the pasture was an FBI Special Agent. Now, with proof that the victim had been carried across a state line, the crime became a Federal offense. Special Agents from several Midwest Field Offices converged on Kansas City. Experts were flown in. Files were restudied, in search of some possible stray bit of information that might link this to some other violent crime.

Yet, despite full cooperation among Federal, state, county, and city agencies, the investigating officers couldn't find a single clue.

Medical examination of the body threw doubt on the sex maniac theory. The experts said it was doubtful the victim had been raped. Then how explain the nude body, the ripped and bloody garments in the car trunk? Police asked psychiatrists for aid in forming a picture of the type of criminal involved.

This led nowhere.

As the search dragged on, day after day, night after sleepless night, newspaper headlines shrank to two oft-repeated words: NO CLUES!

Police in most cities always have cooperated with one another. Until recent years, however, this cooperation was hit-and-miss.

Now, though, with the vast network of the FBI covering the entire nation, with a central office in Washington through which pass all reports of serious crimes and wanted criminals, local officers rely more and more on aid from the Bureau.

Even when the FBI can't be called in on a case directly, its records and laboratory stand ready to help all law enforcement agencies. This is frequently a boon to local officers. For example:

Details of Crime A in Seattle and Crime B in Miami arrive in Washington. At first, they seem to have no connection. When Crime C in Chicago is added, though, a pattern may take shape, and the assembled facts may point to a possible solution.

That happened in this Kansas City case.

On August 31, four weeks after the murder, a burglary suspect, believed to be a 30-year-old California parole violator named Arthur Ross Brown, was spotted by a sheriff in Wyoming. As the sheriff was arresting him, Brown shot and critically wounded the officer, and got away.

Brown came from a respected family in San Jose, California. At the age of 14, he'd been charged with forcing a young girl into a car at gunpoint, and driving her into the hills, where she somehow persuaded him to return her to her home.

There were other arrests on his record: another abduction

—with a gun—of a woman, and twice he'd been apprehended while stealing lingerie from women's bedrooms.

However, nothing in his record showed he'd ever been in or near Kansas City. He was married, but his wife's whereabouts were unknown.

Shortly after shooting the sheriff, Brown stole a car in Sheridan, Wyoming. He drove to Rapid City, South Dakota. There, he robbed a liquor store. He was later identified from photographs.

He then stole a series of cars, in several states. One was recovered in Omaha, Nebraska, with his fingerprints—but no palm print—on it.

Next, a man answering Brown's description held up liquor stores in Pensacola, Florida; El Paso, Texas; and Evansville, Indiana. In each case, a woman clerk, alone in the store, was the victim.

During that period, the FBI and California police kept close watch on the homes of Brown's relatives and friends. They still didn't connect him with the Allen case, though.

Then, on November 9, a frightened householder called the Kansas City police, and also the local FBI Field Office. The caller reported that a neighboring woman had been visited by her estranged husband, and forced to accompany him in his car.

Her name? Mrs. Arthur Ross Brown.

A search was launched immediately—without result. Four hours later, Mrs. Brown returned home, so unnerved she was incoherent. Brown himself had escaped again. This time he fled to California, the move the FBI had been anticipating.

Local officers and FBI Special Agents interviewed all members of Brown's family, wherever they lived. They also talked to all persons with whom he was known to have had previous contact. His mother, in San Jose, was convinced her son was mad. She begged officers to apprehend him before he could do more harm. She also promised to notify the authorities if she heard from him.

She did, on November 13.

That evening, she thought she saw a prowler outside. A little later, her son telephoned. He'd tried to see her, he said, but had fled, fearing a trap. Now, he told her, he'd kill himself. Then he hung up. The frantic mother called the FBI. Special Agents went into quick action.

Several of them rushed to keep close watch on the mother's house. Others went to an uncle's home, in Oakland. Still others to an aunt in San Francisco.

A car parked on a dark street near the aunt's house quickly drew their attention. One of the Special Agents approached it silently. He saw a man, his face hidden by a blanket, apparently asleep on the front seat. Car windows were closed, and the doors locked. The Agent backed away. This might be Brown. It might also be somebody sleeping off a drunk.

Just then, a San Francisco Police cruiser rolled past, turned its spotlight on the house occupied by Brown's aunt, and went on. The Special Agents drove after the cruiser, and overtook it. The police told them the aunt had reported a prowler a little earlier. They'd responded, and found nothing. Now, they were making sure he hadn't returned.

A few minutes later, eight officers—half San Francisco Police, the others FBI Special Agents—quietly surrounded the car. They turned three spotlights and half a dozen flashlights on it, and ordered the occupant into the street. He obeyed. They studied his sullen face.

The hunt for Brown was over.

The Special Agents sped him to the San Francisco FBI Field Office. They quickly made prints of his palms. Then they questioned him. He admitted some robberies, denied others, contradicted himself. He confessed his mania for handling women's undergarments.

The Agents continued to probe. They mentioned the

Wyoming sheriff. The Mrs. Allen case. At first, Brown denied his guilt. Finally, he told the whole horrible story.

He'd never seen Mrs. Allen until she walked out of the beauty shop. "I was looking for someone to rob," he explained. "She looked wealthy."

As she got into her car in the parking lot, he climbed in beside her—gun in hand. He directed her on the long drive. She pleaded with him, talking about her children. He "just was lucky" in finding the open gate to the pasture.

Thus ended a classic case of cooperation among Federal, state, county and city law enforcement agencies. Working together, with the FBI coordinating their far-flung efforts, they solved a mystery without clues in 101 days, and brought to justice a ruthless killer.

Homemade Money

by HARRY EDWARD NEAL

*A Secret Service Agent who works under cover may be
flirting with death. If his masquerade is discovered, his
fate will depend upon his own resourcefulness and quick
thinking. If he is dealing with killers, he may expect to be
killed or wounded.*

SECRET SERVICE AGENT GABRIEL DAMONE had succeeded in
winning the confidence of a gang of Italian counterfeiters
near Scranton, Pennsylvania. In the Scranton case he was
able to arrange to buy fifty thousand dollars in counterfeit
ten-dollar bills from Tony Scalzi, a hoodlum long suspected
of masterminding various holdups, burglaries and knifings
in and around Scranton.

On the night before the counterfeit money was to be delivered, Scalzi met Damone in a small restaurant which they
had used several times as a rendezvous. Not far away, other
Secret Service men took up inconspicuous posts where they
could observe the restaurant, but they did not go in for fear
they would make Scalzi suspicious.

Scalzi was very cordial. "I got a surprise for you, Joe."
(Joe was the name Damone had assumed for his undercover role.)

"Yeh? A surprise, huh? A good surprise?"

Scalzi laughed. "Very good. You and me—we're going to celebrate."

"That's fine," Damone said, smiling. "What are we celebrating?"

Scalzi registered surprise and held out both hands, palms up. "Our deal! What do you think?"

"Oh, our deal. Okay. That's good, all right. What are we going to do?"

Scalzi stood up. "Come on, I take you for a ride. You'll find out."

They entered Scalzi's automobile and drove toward the outskirts of the city. Soon the city lights were behind them and they were in open country. In a few minutes Scalzi slowed down and turned left onto a narrow dirt road flanked by open fields. Instantly Damone realized it would be impossible for the other Agents to follow without being discovered, and he knew that they would at least wait until Scalzi's car was out of sight before they attempted to travel in the same lonely area.

Scalzi drove along the dark, rutty road for perhaps two miles before they came to their destination, a farmhouse. Lights glowed from most of its windows, and as they approached the front porch, Damone could hear music and the sound of voices from within.

Damone tried to make a quick survey of his surroundings, but the darkness was complete. He could not see the lights of another house anywhere, and there were no woods nearby in which his fellow officers might take cover. He knew now that he was strictly alone and on his own.

In the farmhouse Scalzi and Damone were greeted with cheers and laughter by three men and four women. Two of the men were Rocco and Vincenzo, whom Damone had met previously with Scalzi. The other, Ugo, was Scalzi's brother-in-law. He brought Damone a water glass filled with red wine, and held a half-filled one himself. Damone was introduced to the women, none of whom he had seen before.

In the dining room a large table was set. Scalzi had a glass of wine which he clinked against Damone's. "To our big deal, Joe!" he said, and they drank. Then Scalzi pointed to the table. "You see?" he said. "I told you it was a good surprise! We got real good food, none of that restaurant stuff. We got antipasto, minestrone—ah, such minestrone!—spedini, lasagna, spaghetti—everything! The works! All for you, my friend."

Feeling considerably relieved, Damone joked and talked with his hosts. Before the dinner was served, he saw one of the women whisper something to Scalzi, who went with her into the kitchen. A few minutes later Scalzi emerged and went directly to Damone. Scalzi's eyes were cold and angry. In a low voice he said, "Joe, I want to talk to you. Private." His strong fingers grabbed Damone's arm and guided him into the kitchen. There Damone saw the woman who had whispered to Scalzi.

Scalzi let go of the Agent's arm. "Go ahead," he said to the woman. "Tell him what you just told me."

She stepped nearer and faced Damone, a sneer on her lips. "Your name ain't Joe," she said. "You're Gabriel Damone. You're a cop. I seen you in court once."

A hundred thoughts bubbled through Damone's mind and burst. There was no time to think, for if he groped for a defense, he would surely betray himself.

Calmly he stared at the woman and at Scalzi, and a grin grew into a chuckle as he began to stroke his black mustache with one finger, first on one side, then on the other.

"I knew I should have shaved off this mustache," he said. "This is the third time I've been mistaken for that cop. I guess I must look something like him, all right, but it's the mustache that does it. He's got a mustache like mine, hasn't he?"

The woman nodded.

"You say you ain't Damone, huh?" Scalzi demanded.

"Tony," the Agent said with a tone of disgust, "you ought to know better. I've never even seen the guy. Besides, if I was a cop, would I have come out to this place with you—alone? You know about my connections in New York—and here, look at my stuff." He pulled out his wallet and began laying cards on the table, a driver's license, membership cards, a Social Security card—all in his assumed name. He glanced at the woman. "I don't blame her, though. I told you I've been taken for this cop before. Look," he added, hiding his mustache with one finger, "now do I look like him?"

The woman took two or three steps to the right, then to the left, her eyes intent upon the Agent's face and figure. Finally she looked at Scalzi, shrugged and made a face as though to say, "Maybe I was wrong."

"Is it him or not?" Scalzi asked.

The woman picked up some of the identification cards and examined them closely. "I could have sworn it was him. But it was seven years ago I seen him."

"Yes or no?" Scalzi growled. "This is important, Maria!"

After another glance at the smiling—and anxious—Damone she said, "No. I guess I didn't remember so well. I'm sorry, Joe."

So the dinner went off as planned, and the next afternoon Scalzi delivered the fifty thousand dollars in counterfeit bills to Damone. The instant the package changed hands Damone placed Scalzi under arrest and signaled other Agents, who came to his aid.

An angry Scalzi spat at Damone. "I should have listened to Maria last night," he said. "If I had believed her, you would be where you belong—buried in the pigpen on the farm."

Scalzi and his accomplices went to prison for several years, causing a lot of passers of counterfeit money to lose a good source of supply.

Alias Me

by PHILIP WYLIE

Noted author Philip Wylie tells what it was like to be impersonated by someone who used his name not only in conversation but also on checks which bounced from coast to coast. The imposter, a charming old scoundrel named Frederick Emerson Peters, supplied proof of the old adage that crime doesn't pay when he died in New Haven, Connecticut, at the age of seventy-four, almost penniless.

AMONG LIFE's most peculiar experiences is the discovery that somebody else, somewhere else, is publicly impersonating you. I know.

Some years ago, in a national magazine, a man confessed that "purely for fun, and to while away long train rides," he often introduced himself as somebody else—somebody with a modest national reputation, and hence a touch of glamor. Such deceit he held to be harmless. It brightened up the trip for his dupes, and in no way damaged either them or the good name of whoever he pretended to be.

That innocent impersonator, however, almost certainly gave less innocent ideas to other travelers. His confession had not long been in print when I received a letter that read about like this:

258

"Dear, dear Philip:

"How wonderful it was to get to know you so well on that lovely, unforgettable trip from the West Coast!

"I never realized that an ordinary parlor-car could be the bower of romance! But I am growing terribly worried about your failure to keep your date with me here in Amberville. You promised to come out to New Jersey last weekend!

"Of course, I realize you are dreadfully in demand, and you said you had a great many conferences scheduled with editors and publishers. But I'm sure you'll soon find an opportunity to renew the wonderful relationship with

"Your very loving Ellen."

Enclosed in that missive were two snapshots of the lady. She was a most attractive young woman. One of the photographs was signed "Your me, with love." The other stated, in a neat, feminine hand "Me—two years ago—just after my divorce." The notepaper on which she'd written was expensive and tasteful.

Her letter was forwarded to me in Southern Florida, where'd I'd been continuously for many months with my wife and daughter.

I set myself to the painful task of letting Ellen down as easily as I could by writing to her. After gently informing her that she'd been deceived, and cautioning her about such deceivers, I added firm proof that the "I" writing this letter was the actual Philip Wylie. That was necessary, for the dupes of imposters are often very hard to undeceive.

I told Ellen that by telephoning my literary representative or my lawyer in New York City, she would find that I hadn't traveled to or from the West Coast for several years. Then, to try to make my letter a shade less distressing, I wrote that she was far from being the only person who'd been similarly deceived.

Even so, I mailed my letter to Ellen unhappily. I was not

in the least surprised when she didn't trouble herself to thank me for putting her straight.

Another imposter, a professional, gave me a decade of intermittent dilemma—as well as one moment, at least, of welcome revenge. That gentleman, all those ten years and more, was trailed by the FBI, for I was only one of several semirenowned Americans whom he impersonated.

His existence became known to me when my literary representative in New York wrote to me in Florida that a large carton of books—purchased in Cincinnati—had been sent to me in care of a national magazine, and forwarded by the magazine to him. He had paid the express charges. I wrote back that of course I hadn't ordered those books, and, as he suspected, an imposter must be at work.

The books kept coming—cartons of them—from all over the United States. Harold Ober, my literary agent, kept sending them back, express collect, not to the magazines, but to the bookstores that had shipped them. Soon, he learned my imposter's operating method from the aggrieved and swindled stores.

The man would saunter into a bookshop. He would browse. Eventually, he'd engage a clerk in literary chitchat. As they talked, he'd begin to select numerous books for purchase. The clerk's interest would rise, and finally, the man would introduce himself—as Philip Wylie. There would follow a great deal of talk about his writing, his life, and his habits. The impersonator—whose real name finally proved to be Peters—had gone to great pains to learn about me.

Once he'd established his "identity," and been introduced to other clerks and the store manager, he'd really pitch in and buy books. Old and rare editions, as well as dozens of the newest novels and leading works of nonfiction. He'd then say he was on a leisurely trip to Hollywood to write for one of the motion picture companies—something I often did at that time, though never in a leisurely way—and he'd explain that since he was moving to a new home in Florida, he'd like the books sent to such-and-such a magazine.

By then, he was in solid with the store and its management—and ready for his final gimmick. To pay for the books, he'd offer a check on the Estate of Edna Edwards Wylie. That was the name of my mother, who died when I was five —and left no estate.

The printed check and my mother's printed name looked very convincing, though. I've seen some of those checks. They were made out on a check-writing machine for an amount which the swindler said was a "quarterly payment from the estate." That amount was always for about $200 more than the value of the ordered books.

Mr. Peters—alias me—would ask for the change in cash, and get it.

Then he'd walk out—not even quickly.

When I first heard of his con game, it seemed to me that whoever was impersonating me went to a lot of trouble for a rather small return. Eventually, though, I was to learn that Mr. Peters, during his years of wide and rapid travel, impersonated not only me but about a dozen other men of modest prominence, and various occupations. For all of them, he had printed checks, and about all of them he had considerable knowledge. So I came to realize that, even though he passed only ten or twelve such checks a week— paying hotel bills with them, buying merchandise other than books—he was probably netting $1,000 a week!

During Mr. Peters' active years, he gave me that opportunity for a riposte mentioned earlier. At Metro-Goldwyn-Mayer Studios, where I was working one winter, the writers' building became so crowded that several of us were assigned offices off the Culver City lot, in hastily purchased bungalows. Across the street from them, a huge steel-frame building was under construction. The clangor, not surprisingly, disturbed our efforts to compose screen plays. We complained to the studio manager. His futile reaction was to erect an enormous billboard beside our quarters. It said:

QUIET. AUTHORS AT WORK.

The sign did nothing to tranquilize the construction workers, but it did a great deal to amuse our fellow movie workers. We demanded that the sign come down. No use. We requested to be moved to quieter surroundings. In vain. The studio manager did not care much for writers. I, especially, protested so vehemently that he came to loathe me.

Late one afternoon, he phoned me at my apartment. With the greatest glee and unction, he commanded:

"Come to my office at once!"

Since it was past working time, and Culver City was miles away, I said:

"Sorry. Tomorrow."

He screamed back gloatingly, "Come now! Fast! The FBI is waiting for you in my office!"

I thought over my imperfect past. I hadn't kidnapped anybody, joined gangsters, or cheated on my taxes. I was jarred, but not panicked. "If the FBI wants to see me," I answered, "tell 'em to come here, to my place."

"It's the FBI!" he thundered. "You come to them, not—" There was a pause. Then his voice came again, chastened. "The FBI man says he'll come to your place."

What the gentleman from the FBI wanted of me was this. He had several hundred photographs of men who might be that impersonator of me. I was asked to look slowly through the collection on the chance that I might recognize one of the faces. I didn't—but the best part of that session came the next day.

Oozing unction, trying to hide his burning curiosity, the studio manager called at my sonorous bungalow office to try to find out what the FBI had wanted that made its representative come willingly to me, not vice versa. All he got from me was this:

"Just asked me to give them a little help. Confidential matter."

The writer-hating manager was awed. And I soon had a quiet office.

Mr. Peters was finally trapped, mainly by Stanley Rinehart, my publisher. Hearing me complain one day of the crates and cartons of books that kept coming, Stan had an idea. He took advertising space in *Publishers Weekly,* a trade journal that reaches every bookstore. There, he printed a warning about my imposter. It suggested that any bookstore where I was not personally known should call him by phone, collect, if anybody claiming to be Philip Wylie bought books and offered a check in payment.

The busy Mr. Peters didn't read trade magazines. Some while after the warning appeared, a bookstore in San Francisco called Stan Rinehart in New York. "A man who says he's Philip Wylie is in our store right now, picking out a large selection of expensive books."

Stan knew I was in Miami, but he asked: "What does the guy look like?"

"Light hair, blue eyes, about five-seven . . ."

"Call the FBI!" Stan interrupted.

Thus was Peters apprehended.

Toward the climax of those uncomfortable years in which I constantly wondered what my unknown imposter would do next in my name, I had one very startling experience. My wife, Ricky, and I went from Miami to Baltimore for a stay of some months. After we'd settled in an apartment, Ricky went out one day to establish relations with the department stores, and I walked to a nearby bookstore to buy some books. I picked out more than I wanted to carry, so I asked one of the clerks to deliver my order—giving my name and starting to give my address.

Suddenly, the man's face paled. "Just a minute," he said. "Pardon me."

He hurried to the rear of the store. For a moment, I was puzzled. Then I remembered Stan Rinehart's ad. In alarm I rushed after the salesman, and found him whispering feverishly to a colleague.

"Look," I said nervously. "I *am* Philip Wylie. I'm going to pay for these books in cash." I whipped out my billclip. "Furthermore . . ."

Beating my way back to the contemporary novels section, I hunted for one of my books on the back jacket of which was a large and recent photograph of me. Luckily, that novel was in stock. I held up the book so they could compare. It was the proffered cash, though, rather than the photograph, which convinced them.

"We were just going to call the FBI," the clerk said, wiping his sweat-beaded forehead.

I nodded—and mopped my own.

I disagree with the man who confessed that he often impersonated others as an innocent, time-passing game. He misrepresents the people impersonated, and his sport can lead to a circumstance I've encountered myself—in which somebody just introduced to me announced:

"Why, I know Philip Wylie well. This is somebody else!"

Well, can you always prove offhand and beyond doubt that you are you? Nobody can. Hence, if you've had an imposter, you may wind up, any day, highly embarrassed and innocent—but in the clink!

Lady in Love

by RONALD SETH

*What moves a person to spy against his or her native land?
There are, perhaps, as many reasons—some romantic, the
rest mundane—as there are spies. Ronald Seth, another of
our British contributors, and an internationally famous
expert on espionage, suggests the possible reason behind
an American front-page spy case which began in New
York's Museum of Modern Art, and ended in—but, this is
Mr. Seth's story.*

THIS IS THE STORY of Judith Coplon.

In December, 1949, it came to the knowledge of the FBI,
through a thoroughly reliable source, that the Soviet Embassy in Washington had come into possession of a number
of top-secret documents.

Some of those documents emanated from the FBI, itself.
Others, from elsewhere in the U.S. Department of Justice.

The information was incomplete. The only idea that could
be given of the nature of the documents was that they contained particulars of certain known foreign agents, diplo-
mats, and American Communists.

The information also gave an indication that the supplier
of the documents might be a woman, that possibly she was

employed in the Foreign Registration Office of the Department of Justice, and that she may at one time have worked in the New York office of the same department.

Only one woman in the Foreign Registration Office in Washington fit this description. Her name: Judith Coplon. The FBI began an investigation.

Judith Coplon, a college graduate, was twenty-seven, attractive, and so efficient at her job dealing with matters of external and internal security that she was marked for promotion shortly after her transfer to Washington. That promotion came in May, 1948, after she received the commendation of Attorney General Tom Clark for a piece of brilliant political analysis.

She came of good family. Her father was a well-to-do manufacturer, and something of a philanthropist. Mrs. Coplon was quiet and retiring.

When Judith Coplon first came to Washington, she lived in an apartment at 2634 Tunlaw Road. Her landlord and neighbors later described her to FBI Special Agents as a quiet, intellectual type who never brought men home. Later, to be nearer her work, she moved to a one-room apartment in Jefferson Hall, McLean Gardens.

After a month of probing and surveillance, about all the FBI discovered was that Judith was socially active. She enjoyed more than the usual quota of dates with many men.

The following week, however, she asked her Section Chief, William Foley, to let her see the Most Secret report on Russian agents in America. She said she needed it in her work. Foley knew she was under surveillance by the FBI. He stalled, and telephoned the Bureau.

FBI Director J. Edgar Hoover, himself, came to see Foley. He brought a faked letter marked Most Secret. It stated that three Soviet agents working in the Amtorg Trade Division were really undercover FBI Special Agents, who were shortly to be submitted to a loyalty test.

Hoover asked Foley to give this letter to Miss Coplon, and ask her to work on the case. He pointed out the obvious strategy—if Judith Coplon really were in league with the Communists, she'd warn her friends.

This was done.

On Friday, June 14, 1949, Judith requested of Chief Foley that she be allowed to leave at the end of the morning, so she might have a long weekend. Foley granted her request.

When she took the one o'clock train to New York, she was unconsciously accompanied by four FBI Special Agents.

When they arrived at New York's Pennsylvania Station, Judith went to the terminal's ladies' room. She stayed there approximately forty-five minutes. When she left, she deposited her suitcase in a cloakroom, visited a bookstore, then went to a drugstore where she ate a sandwich at a counter. After that, she took the subway to 191st Street.

It was dark when she arrived there, and the street lamps were already lit. She walked aimlessly down the street for about ten minutes. Then, she stopped and looked in the window of a jewelry store. She remained there, continuing to look in the window, for about seven minutes. This, of course, is an old, well-worn espionage trick—watching the street via reflections in the glass.

Presently, a well-dressed, dark, husky but short man appeared. He did not speak to her. When he walked away, however, she followed him. They went into a restaurant. Once inside, they occupied the same booth.

To keep anyone from overhearing their conversation, they continuously fed coins into the jukebox. They remained in the restaurant for about an hour. For most of that time, Judith spoke with apparent animation. She was still in an excited mood when they left and took the subway downtown together.

As the train was about to pull out of the 125th Street station, the man suddenly jumped to his feet, squeezed

through the closing doors, and was away. Despite his unexpected moves, and speed, one of the Special Agents got
off with him.

The man's sense of security was good. He didn't know he
was being followed, but he was leaving nothing to chance.
By taking a series of taxis, buses, and trolleys, he succeeded
in shaking off the Special Agent following him.

From his appearance, the FBI men guessed "the man" was
a Slav. Probably a Russian. If so, possibly a member of the
staff of the Soviet Consul-General in New York.

Working on this assumption, Special Agents maintained
a surveillance outside the Russian offices. At ten o'clock that
evening, they saw their man entering the building. He remained inside for an hour. When he came out, he took the
subway to his apartment at 64 West 108th Street.

The janitor there identified him for the FBI. He was a
Russian engineer. His name was Valentine A. Gubichev.

By this time, of course, Miss Coplon was denied access to
Most Secret documents, at least until the investigation was
concluded. Now, to make certain she didn't accidentally get
to see any, she was transferred to another office.

She demanded a reason for her transfer. Foley told her
that her new job had to be done, and that she was the one
best equipped to do it.

She accepted the inevitable. Every day, though, she
visited her old office. She explained her visits by helping the
girl who'd succeeded her. In that way, she still had access
to certain files.

On February 18, she made another move. She requested
another long weekend from Chief Foley. Again, the request
was granted.

This time, she took the two o'clock train to New York.
And this time, the Special Agents "accompanying" her took
along a female secretary from the Washington FBI Field
Office.

In turn, they kept Miss Coplon under continuous surveillance. Once more, she went to the ladies' room at Penn Station, where she made a phone call. Then, she went to the subway.

Ultimately, she again repaired to a side street off Broadway. Again, she met the man the FBI now knew was Gubichev. They were together only a very few minutes. Though it was too dark to be certain, the Special Agents were almost sure she handed him an envelope.

Once more Gubichev embarrassed the Special Agent following him by shaking him loose in a crowd of commuters.

On March 3, Judith again asked for the extra half-day off. Again, Chief Foley granted the request. This time, she spent the weekend with her parents.

During the following week, though, she asked Foley if she could see some of the Most Secret files. Foley nodded, and wondered if she recalled the three Amtorg men who were FBI Special Agents acting as Soviet agents. She did. Foley said he now had more information on that case.

He handed her a file.

Among its papers was a "copy" of a letter from J. Edgar Hoover to the Assistant to the Attorney General. It purported to set out that Amtorg had recently been making inquiries about some instruments called geophones, which measure blast pressures. These geophones had first been manufactured in connection with the original atomic bomb tests. Mr. Hoover, according to the letter, was asking the Attorney General's advice as to what would constitute a violation of the law on the part of Amtorg.

The letter was devised to settle once and for all whether Judith Coplon was passing information to Soviet agents.

Shortly after that interview with Foley, she again went to New York. Once more, there was a repetition of all that had happened on previous occasions, with only a few variations. One of the variations was rather important.

This time, the FBI made its move.

Both Miss Coplon and Gubichev tried to escape arrest. They almost succeeded in escaping by car. At 16th Street and Third Avenue, though, Special Agents in pursuit forced Gubichev's car to the curb. Both Miss Coplon and the Russian were arrested.

They were taken to FBI headquarters in Manhattan. There, they were searched. Gubichev had on him $125 in cash, but no incriminating documents. Judith's handbag contained a sealed advertising circular extolling a particular brand of nylons. The matron supervising the search brought the circular to the Special Agents.

They opened it. Inside, they discovered copies or résumés of thirty-four Most Secret documents, including Hoover's "letter" to the Attorney General about Amtorg, and a covering note explaining she'd been unable to get a copy or even more than a quick glance at the FBI's Most Secret report on Soviet and Communist Intelligence activities in the United States.

Despite those thirty-four papers, Judith denied everything.

The evidence against her, though, was too strong. At her trial, she was found guilty under the Treason Act of stealing Government documents, and of conspiracy against the United States. She was sentenced to a term in prison.

Why was there ever a "Judith Coplon case"? Maybe for an old, old reason. She said she was in love with Gubichev; that they'd met by chance in New York's Museum of Art; that he told her he was married, but she hoped to become his wife "as soon as he got his divorce."

The United States Government didn't wait to find out if romance would triumph. It declared Gubichev *persona non grata,* and deported him.

The Unhidden Persuaders

by VANCE PACKARD

You know Vance Packard as the author of books in which he dissects American life with the fervor of a sociological Mayo brother. In the story that follows he is in especially good form. He brings tough facts to face. His conclusions are just as tough.

EVERY SIX MINUTES, someone is being assaulted, raped, or slain.

Every two minutes, someone's car is being stolen.

And every single minute tonight, burglars will be entering someone's home or place of business.

These startling statements are based on reports of the Federal Bureau of Investigation. They show we are now nurturing the biggest flock of thieves, robbers, and murderers on record—and their number is still growing. Last year, there were about 175,000 more major crimes committed in the United States than the year before.

Our criminals cost each voter in the country an average of about $320 a year—vastly more than we pay for education. The price will continue going up, for the criminal's "take" is increasing to match the rising cost of living. The average loot of robbers, for example, rose last year from $113 to $146.

271

Altogether, our bustling criminals perpetrated well over a million and a half known major crimes, or about one for every ninety people in the nation. That means that, on an average, criminals reached into every block of every city and hamlet in America.

The FBI figures show that some areas in our land breed many more criminals than others.

Some of the old gangster-hunting grounds are now among our quietest, most law-abiding areas, and Vermont has not shown a murder in the FBI's "Uniform Crime Report" for two years. New Hampshire, next door, is the nation's most all-around law-abiding state. It has the fewest robberies, the fewest burglaries, and the fewest auto thefts per 1,000 population of any state.

In contrast, the West today is really wild. Thieves roving our Western states are causing more nervousness than the two-gun badmen of the old Wild West.

Nevada burglars pulled six times as many second-story jobs per 1,000 population last year as burglars in New Hampshire. Arizona thieves committed seven times as many larcenies as thieves in Pennsylvania. California robbers were guilty of fifty times as many stick-ups as robbers in New Hampshire. Last year, your car was six times as safe in New England as on the West Coast.

Why the great upsurge in crime in the Far West?

There undoubtedly are many reasons. One of the main ones given by FBI officials and other authorities is that the Western states have swelled so tremendously in population within the past thirty years. Thus, a feeling of restless turmoil has pervaded many of those Far Western cities.

When America is considered sectionally, our least crime-ridden areas are all east of the Rockies, and north of the Mason-Dixon line. The Northeastern section of our country has the least crime per 1,000 inhabitants. The Midwest comes next. It's notable, however, that within the Midwest itself, the states in the Plains west of the Mississippi scored consistently lower on all types of crime than the states east of the river—Illinois, Indiana, Michigan, Ohio, and Wisconsin.

While criminals in the Far West accounted for more major crimes proportionately than those in any other region last year, their offenses were primarily "against property"— that is, burglary, theft, robbery.

When it comes to crimes of violence "against the person"— murder and aggravated assault—the South is way out ahead. There were, for example, twelve times as many murders per 1,000 people in the South last year as in New England.

Georgia had more than fifty times as many murders as New Hampshire.

Southern Negroes certainly accounted for their share of the murders, but the Negro does not seem to be the main explanation for the high proportion of murders in the South. Dr. Ellsworth Huntington, Yale's demographer, has found that if you consider only white populations, the ten worst states for homicide are still all in the South.

The white residents of Kentucky, for instance, kill one another ten times as often as the white residents of Vermont.

Not only are most of our murder-ridden states in the warmest part of our country, but the twelve least murder-ridden are in the coldest part of the continental United States, in the fringe near the Canadian border. In fact, as you go down the Atlantic Coast from New England to Florida, the murder rate rises so uniformly it's startling.

The same thing happens when you go south from Idaho to Arizona.

If you need more evidence that hot weather seems to encourage violence—as most criminologists believe—consider a study made by O.E. Dexter of some forty thousand New York City arrests for assault and battery. He found that brawls follow a beautiful seasonal curve, increasing gradually from January to July, then subsiding gradually until December. He concludes:

"Temperature, more than any other condition, affects emotional stages which are conducive to fighting."

FBI officials showed me charts portraying the seasonal curves of various crimes. While robberies and burglaries rise sharply in the fall, when days get shorter and nights longer, the violent crimes of murder, rape, and assault reach a decided peak during the hot-weather months.

It seems to be a fact that our citizens with weak wills and constitutions most often go berserk, commit suicide, start riots, or kill somebody during the summer months.

If stealing is involved, the chances are the culprit is just a kid. Half of our major crimes last year were committed by young toughs under twenty-five, the greatest number of them only seventeen. The teen-agers are interested primarily in robbery, burglary, and car theft. Older men, on the other hand, starred in homicide, assault, arson, rape—the emotional crimes.

How can we cope with our rising tide of crime?

Basically, we cannot abolish crime until we stop producing incompetent misfits. Most criminologists believe we can bring crime under control faster—and end our disgraceful and costly crime waves—if we, as Americans, take a coldly hard-boiled attitude toward our criminals.

Virtually all of them mentioned to me that we should stop coddling our prisoners with an oversentimentalized parole and pardon system, and stop trying to reform those who are unreformable.

J. Edgar Hoover probably voiced the lament of all law enforcement agents when he said:

"We grow tired of risking our lives time after time apprehending dangerous men who are allowed new opportunities to prey upon society. I know of nothing which would help choke off the growing crime wave more effectively than a general tightening of our attitude toward the criminal who has established the fact that he is completely untrustworthy."

A Baby Is Missing

by ALISTAIR COOKE

In the eyes of many literate Americans, Alistair Cooke is Britain's greatest gift to this nation since Yorkshire Pudding. Because of his appearances on "Omnibus" and other programs, Cooke's face and voice are familiar to those whose TV tastes demand something intellectually stimulating. Alistair Cooke, however, is not primarily a TV performer, but a reporter viewing the American scene for his British newspaper readers. It is a traditional conceit among literary snobs that newspapermen can't write very well. Read, then, "A Baby Is Missing," and decide for yourself. We think you'll join us in regarding that particular snobism as being as outmoded as cash payment of restaurant checks.

I SUPPOSE EVERYBODY who ever stops at a newsstand has at the back of his mind a very simple distinction between a good newspaper and a bad one—or better, between a "heavy" newspaper and a "light" one.

It's a curious thing that the heavy newspapers in most countries tend to steer clear of the great human interest stories in the news, while the light newspapers eat them up. Surely it's odd that light newspapers should be the ones to take an instinctive interest in such profound things as murder, kidnapping, rape, and infidelity, for surely the deepest human feelings are involved in such goings-on.

Another curiosity is this: people who write for heavy newspapers are just the people who, on their own confession, pretend to a superior taste in literature. They will brood long and talk strenuously over a murderer in Dostoevsky, a pickpocket in Dickens, a spy in Conrad.

Lift the murderer or pickpocket out of literature, though, and they assume no journalist worth the name would give his talent to such squalid stuff. The result is, it seems to me, that the best stories get badly written up, while the dull abstractions that are the same in all countries and all generations—politics, economics—are treated with solemn care.

Luckily, the United States is not yet blasé enough to keep up this artificial distinction between life and literature. The result is that the most serious newspapers in the country—and there are no better newspapers anywhere than the best three or four American dailies—always have in their active employ a small stable of feature writers who are very much aware of the teeming life that is going on all around them.

In the spring of 1950, a story broke in New York which swept Germany, Congress, and the risk of war right off the front pages of *all* the light and heavy newspapers. It seems to me to have been one of the most poignant news stories of the century, and I think it's worth telling over to anyone who has ever felt a pang for somebody else's disappointed hopes.

It's a story about a Negro girl, eighteen years of age, and a Negro baby, ten days old.

The first day of spring that year came into New York with a spatter of snowflakes. The night of the 21st of March was no time to be out. It was raw and misty, and even the midnight movies on Broadway were doing poor business.

That night, a young Negro woman, a Mrs. Holden, was taken uptown by her anxious husband to Lincoln Hospital, and delivered of a premature baby. It was put in an incubator right away. It weighed two pounds and a few ounces at birth. The doctors told the trembling couple they could do no more than their best. Nine nights later, the 30th of March, was a wheezing, freezing night. The night nurse of the incubator ward came in to see how the premature babies were doing. She peeked at the thermostat, looked around and into the Holden incubator and—the Holden baby was gone.

She brought an orderly and a doctor running. Sure enough, the baby had vanished. When the parents arrived, they were almost crazed. The doctor had to tell them the pitiful truth. The baby then weighed two pounds, eleven ounces. Taken outside on such a night, it might live for an hour, two hours at most.

The parents shuffled off home. The doctor put a tentative stroke across the baby's progress chart. A police siren whined outside, and the next morning's tabloids reported a routine kidnapping. The FBI was called in, and that was apparently the end of the story.

Three weeks later, a pleasant housewife who lived uptown was doing her housework one morning and listening to the radio. Up came that tune again, a pleasant jingle going the rounds of the dancehalls and the disc jockeys—a song called "Don't Call Me a Nosey Man."

This woman couldn't get the thing out of her head. She decided she'd clean up a bit, then go out and buy a record of it. She went to a little store on 125th Street, in the heart of Harlem, and asked the clerk to play it first. While it was jingling away, a chunky, strutting Negro girl in her teens strolled up and said, "Oh, I *like* that record."

The housewife turned to look at her, and suddenly she knew the face. She'd seen it once before, weeks ago. She looked again, and knew it was the face of a girl holding a baby on a very cold night. The housewife was sure it was the same girl. Where three weeks ago the girl had been a forlorn, ignorant mother, she was now in the housewife's eyes "a person wanted."

The housewife, too, read the papers. Before the girl could say another sentence, the woman dashed from the store. She grabbed the nearest cop. He was an old-timer. He'd seen hysterical women before.

"Take it easy, lady," he said. "Now, what's all this about a blanket?"

By the time he was up and on the job, the teen-aged girl was gone.

Then, a week after that, by a mad coincidence, a little strutting, chunky Negro girl went into a bus depot on 42nd Street. Of all things, she went up to a cop. She wasn't too consecutive in her story. It seemed she'd had some trouble lately in a store in Harlem. The cop motioned to another cop, who came up and said: "I know that girl. She lives in my hotel."

So she did. It was a seedy little place over on the West Side. Well, the cops phoned the station house, and the FBI connected in no time, and the word went out over the police-car radios that a young colored woman "wanted" had hopped a bus on 42nd Street, the terminal for buses that serve the South. In fact, though, the girl had not taken a bus. She'd wandered out of the terminal and gone across the street to her hotel.

Next day, the FBI found her in her tiny hotel bedroom. She was married to a porter in the hotel. She wept out her story. She'd done nothing wrong. She was unhappy because only lately she'd given birth to stillborn twins. Please, would they get out and leave her alone.

At last, she broke down and said it. She'd kidnapped the baby. The Special Agents knew as well as she did that the baby was dead. They'd already cast a roving eye around everything, tapped the tattered wallpaper for hidden panels, and looked under this and that.

All right, then. Sorry, ma'am. They'd have to book her. Too bad about the baby.

They were at her door, and on the way out, when one of them held up his index finger. From across the hall came a thin, broken wail, like the complaint of a powerful kitten. Jumping across the hall, they broke the lock on a small door, and pulled it open. The heat from inside came at them like a ten-pound roast. It was a room no bigger than a linen closet.

And there was the baby.

Now, we can go back to the nipping, frosty night of the 30th of March, and straighten everything out. The girl, eighteen years old, had, as she said, just had stillborn twins. She was fairly frantic for a baby. In the active memory of her loss, she decided "straightforwardly" to go get one.

On the afternoon of the 30th of March, she somehow got into Lincoln Hospital. I said, I think, she had a plump, confident strut. Well, the nurses and doctors probably thought that she was a charwoman, or kitchen worker, or something.

She marched around the corridors, took elevators up and down, sallied into this room, this lab, that dispensary, and kept her eyes open. By nightfall, she had the premature-baby section very well located. She went there, walked straight in, unhooked a door, lifted the top of the first incubator she saw, and took the baby out—two pounds and eleven ounces. She put it under her coat, took an elevator down, and walked out to the street.

This is where the good Lord and neighborly sense did more to help her than the split-second timing of a bank robbery.

She walked three blocks to the subway station, went into a rest room, took off her bright red skirt, and wrapped it around the baby. The train came in. The conductor said: "Lady, that's no way to warm a baby on a night like this. You better go and get a blanket some place."

She went upstairs to the street and walked straight into a

nearby apartment. In no time, she was back with another woman, holding a blanket. She thanked the woman, hailed a cab, put the squawling baby on the seat, and started to put on her red skirt.

The driver was mildly outraged. "I'm sorry, miss," he said. "You can't dress in my cab." They tossed it back and forth a while, and the cabbie said: "Just can't *do* it, ma'am."

He knew a nice lady who'd let her dress at her place, though. So he drove her to the home of a friend—the house-wife we met with the tune on her mind. There the girl dressed, thanked the housewife, and the taxi driver drove her downtown to a bus terminal.

Somebody who worked around there remembered this bulging sight when, three weeks later, FBI Agents started asking questions in the same terminal.

None of this answers the aching question: "How did she possibly keep the baby alive?"

When at last it was returned to the hospital, it weighed three pounds, one ounce—a gain of six ounces—and was squealing a little more lustily. The doctors said—"a miracle." "An act of God," said others.

Well, we all know that God helps them that help them-selves. And what had this forlorn, half-crazed, illiterate Ne-gro girl done to nurture this miracle?

She'd bought a twenty-five cent book, a reprint about baby care, at a drugstore. She'd nosed around a clinic and talked with nurses. And when the FBI Agents broke into the little room, they found some paperback books: *The American Woman's Cook Book*, a Bible, *The New Modern Home Physi-cian*, and two pulp magazines.

They also found a folding carriage lined with an electric blanket. There was an electric grill. By its side, a row of baby formulas and twelve bottles with those sterilized nipples that pop up without touching. A pan of water and sterilizing tweezers, the proper vitamin extracts, baby powder, absorbent cotton, baby oil.

And the essential feeding instrument for a child that size—an eye-dropper.

At the hospital later, an obstetrician, still full of doubt, said: "But there were two things she *couldn't* know: the atmosphere around a premature that size has to be humid, and the temperature must be maintained strictly at ninety-six degrees."

"Well," said an Agent who was on the expedition to get her, "she had a pan of boiling water on the electric grill, steaming the place up like mad. And, oh yes—up against the inside lintel of the door was a thermometer."

He remembered he'd seen it and noted the temperature. He opened his pad and turned the pages. It was right there. The thermometer had read precisely ninety-six degrees.

They brought the girl into court about a month or so later. Very reliable psychiatrists had looked her over, and simply testified the truth: she was quite mad, a psychotic.

And, since psychotics are beyond the intelligent handling of life, not to say a threat to you and me, they put her away.

A Liberal Looks at the FBI

by MORRIS L. ERNST

On the next few pages, Morris L. Ernst examines a problem which, next to world peace, is probably the subject most vital to every American—civil liberties. As a counselor for the American Civil Liberties Union, he has a distinguished record as a defender of the inherent right of every citizen of the United States to enjoy the freedom to dissent—including those with whose opinions he violently disagrees. Mr. Ernst is Jewish. Yet, shortly before World War II, he diligently defended without fee a number of German-Americans openly sympathetic to Adolf Hitler. A liberal in the noblest sense of the term, he understands only too well that unprotested abridgement of the civil liberties of our ideological enemies is an invitation to abridgement of our own.

At seventy, Mr. Ernst is not only a very active partner in the New York law firm of Greenbaum, Wolff & Ernst, but also finds the time and energy to write books. The most recent—his fifteenth—is Touch Wood, *the fascinating diary of an exciting year of his life.*

AN OFFICIAL who has acutely affected our way of life, through generations of kids who have grown up since he became a front-page figure, is J. Edgar Hoover. I've known him for a good many years, and have had an increasing admiration for him and his staff of Special Agents.

I began with suspicions.

I listened to the blank, indiscriminate attacks on him by my Civil Liberties friends. It was fitting that my friends should be on guard against anyone in Mr. Hoover's position. A national police force carries implicit dangers within itself.

After listening at meetings of liberals to repeated assaults on Hoover and the FBI, I took the time to look into the facts. Since J. Edgar Hoover assumed command of the Federal Bureau of Investigation, the FBI has uncovered facts which allowed prosecutors to secure convictions in over 95 per cent of the cases brought to trial.

> [When challenged that such figures are "justice by box-score," and indicate that prosecutors are more anxious to secure convictions than justice, Mr. Ernst gave this reply:
>
> "As one with a long record as a liberal, I'm always inclined to view such a record with a wary eye. You find yourself wondering how those convictions were obtained.
>
> "The Nazis and the Communists have taught us that a plea of 'guilty' may prove nothing more than that a human being's power to resist mental or physical torture is not unlimited. In this country, fortunately, we have Courts of Appeal, where defendants may protest unfair treatment, or violations of Constitutional rights.
>
> "Do what I did. Check the record of those Courts. You'll find not only that the charge is almost never raised against the FBI. You'll also discover that the FBI has a magnificent record of respect for individual freedom."]

At a time when there was agitation for permitting wire-tapping, despite the Holmes-Brandeis opinions in the Supreme Court, Hoover suggested to the Attorney General that Judge Ferdinand Pecora or I should make an investigation, and report. It should be made clear that J. Edgar Hoover was then, and has remained, opposed to any free use of wire-tapping. He believed that, given the power of indiscriminate wire-tapping, investigators would ultimately stoop to the level of the criminals, themselves.

If Thomas E. Dewey had only learned that much when he was New York's District Attorney, the City would have been spared some of its subsequent unhappy history of the use of information procured over tapped wires.

Some twenty years ago, a great liberal who died unde-feated as a champion of individual liberties, gave the follow-ing opinion of wire-tapping:

> "I do not believe wire-tapping should be used to prevent domestic crimes, with the possible exceptions of kidnapping and extortion. There is, however, one other field in which, given the conditions in the world today, wire-tapping is very much in the public interest.
>
> "It is the duty of our nation to take every step to protect our people. I have no compunction in saying that wire-tapping should be used against those persons not citizens of the United States—and those few citizens who are traitors —engaged in espionage or sabotage against this country."

That opinion was important not only because the man who said it was a true liberal but also because he happened at the time to be President of the United States. His name was Franklin D. Roosevelt.

That established the limits of FBI wire-tapping to this day. FBI Special Agents may not—and, more important, do not—decide on their own judgment or authority to tap a wire. Not even J. Edgar Hoover has (or wants) the power to grant such permission. That must come in writing from the office of the United States Attorney General.

It has been Hoover's job to be concerned about American Communists and Fascists, and he has stood silent while some reporters, disregarding the facts, continue to spread less than the truth about him and the FBI.

Almost invariably, such critics turn out to have confused the FBI with some other Government agency. Stupid questions about whether or not one reads *The Nation,* belongs to the American Civil Liberties Union, and the like, have been asked by investigators questioning a suspect's loyalty.

I have yet to see documented and proved a single case, though, where such nonsense was asked by any FBI Special Agent. I have tried to find such proof. So has J. Edgar Hoover. It always turns out the accuser "remembers hearing it from *somebody.*" Somehow, even critics with otherwise superlative memories never can recall exactly who that "someone" was.

The assaults on Hoover and his men simply do not stand up in the eyes of anyone desirous of looking at the complete, unbiased, documented record.

In all the kidnapping cases in which the FBI has been involved, for example, only one charge of violation of Constitutional rights has been made. That lone accusation was completely disproved by recordings the Special Agents had made of their interviews with the suspect. In only two or three cases on which the FBI worked in cooperation with a local law enforcement agency have similar charges even been voiced, let alone proven.

That's a great record for any police, especially in a land this vast, with a buccaneer people.

J. Edgar Hoover is a great constable. He knew Justices Holmes and Brandeis, and their philosophic interpretations of the value of our Bill of Rights. He understands that this nation was founded on a tremendous gamble—on the theory, for which men died, that if all opposing viewpoints were allowed to be expressed freely, truth and justice would triumph over falsehood and evil.

He supplements that philosophy in the daily administration of his job as director of thousands of employees, intelligently chosen without discrimination as to race, creed, or color, and superlatively trained.

Perhaps his greatest accomplishment was his Bureau's unbelievable control over and limitation of sabotage before and during World War II. Few people know that FBI investigations resulted in over one thousand convictions for technical sabotage; or that, immediately following Pearl Harbor, FBI Special Agents arrested thousands upon thousands of suspicious enemy aliens without the use of duress, without holding any incommunicado, without ever employing anything that could possibly be construed as "third degree."

I know. I defended some of those people, and was able to free a few of them. Without any question, though, the FBI had been justified in every case in picking up and questioning my clients.

These words will not, and should not, prevent future criticism of either J. Edgar Hoover, or the FBI. I hope, though, they inspire any such prospective future critics to do what the FBI does so superbly: get the facts.

One-Man Narcotics Squad

by ANDREW TULLY

*Dope peddling is one of the most international of all crimes.
The major producing areas for dope are in the Middle East;
the major distribution lines are through Italy; the major
market is the United States. Recognizing that the best
method of combating this menace would be to cut the
lines of distribution, Federal Narcotics Commissioner
Harry Jacob Anslinger, in 1951, appointed one of his best
agents, Charles Siragusa, to a permanent post in Rome.
"One-Man Narcotics Squad" is a vivid presentation of
Siragusa's activities. Though the war against dope peddling is never-ending, Siragusa has achieved—almost sin-
gle-handedly—some notable victories.*

DURING CHRISTMAS WEEK, 1957, Charles (Lucky) Luciano
showed up at a respectable Christmas party at a Naples
orphanage and was seen in deep conversation with an Amer-
ican-type Santa Claus provided by a Yankee expatriate to
give the shindig a home-town touch.

"Take a look at Lucky over there," an American correspondent told his companion. "He's asking for Charlie Siragusa in a block of concrete."

Possibly they were libeling Mr. Luciano, who often affects
a charitable outlook, even toward cops. But there's no doubt

he would reward handsomely any Santa Claus who could deliver Charles Siragusa in such a package. For Siragusa is kind of a one-man Federal Narcotics Bureau in Europe, and he has been a pain in the neck to Lucky Luciano's dope syndicate.

Operating out of a wing in the United States Embassy in Rome, Siragusa's little police force of himself and two assistants since 1951 has cut the dope traffic from Europe to the United States by forty per cent. During that time, he has staged more than one hundred raids from Rome to Beirut, Lebanon, has arranged the arrest of nearly two hundred narcotics racketeers, and has seized forty-four hundred pounds of opium, heroin, hashish and cocaine ticketed for the United States. At the retail level, the value of the stuff seized runs into millions of dollars.

Siragusa roams about Europe and the Middle East, spreading his reign of terror in the underworld, because his boss, Federal Narcotics Commissioner Harry Jacob Anslinger, believes in the approach direct. Shortly after the end of World War II, Anslinger was troubled by the increase of heroin addiction in the United States and by evidence that the illicit drug was pouring into the nation's East Coast cities from Europe, notably Italy. It seemed like more than a coincidence that the Justice Department had recently deported a passel of Italian-born American hoodlums—mugs who had a fat hand in the dope traffic here. By arrangement with the Italian government, Anslinger sent a couple of his agents to Italy for a look-see in 1948 and 1949. In 1950 he sent Siragusa on a similar errand, and then the next year he assigned Siragusa to a permanent post in Rome, with orders to go anywhere in Europe and the Middle East where he thought he could do some good.

Siragusa had both the background and the personality for the assignment. A brash, glib-talking, second-generation American whose parents emigrated from Sicily, he had grown up in New York's Bronx, where he spent a typical rough-and-ready childhood on the fringes of the teen-age Sicilian gangs which roamed his neighborhood. New York University was his education background; he had gone on to a stint with the Immigration Service and a wartime interlude with the intrigue-laden Office of Strategic Services (OSS) before joining up with Anslinger's outfit. By 1951 he was sporting black horn-rimmed glasses, a thin mustache and an insatiable curiosity.

During his 1950 tour, Siragusa had picked up enough information to give him a start. In Greece, Turkey, Syria and Lebanon he had seen the flourishing acres of marijuana and he had peeked into huts stacked with bags of opium. Police officials and underworld informants had showed him evidence indicating that the raw opium from Turkey and Iran was smuggled into Syria and Lebanon, then into Italy for processing into heroin, and finally shipped to the United States. Everywhere he went, he saw the fine hand of those expatriates from Uncle Sam's paternalism—Frank (Three Finger) Coppola, Little Joe Peachy and Nick Gentile.

Siragusa also was properly impressed with the fact that Italy at that time imported twice as much raw opium as it needed, and produced four to six times the heroin required for legitimate medicinal demands. So one of his first moves was a quiet investigation of the five legal heroin plants near Milan. Working with Italian police, he seized twenty-two pounds of bootleg cocaine and evidence that the owner of one of these plants was diverting heroin to his good friend Lucky Luciano. A few months later he joined Italian police in a raid on a little Sicilian village, where they came up with a green trunk filled with heroin and some interesting papers that implicated fourteen well-known recent deportees from the United States. Siragusa was convinced that American mobsters had muscled in on the racket, and that Lucky Luciano was the chairman of the board of this new organization. It was, in fact, the old Mafia with some new bosses.

One of the first tasks was to convince the Italian government that steps should be taken to curb this illicit traffic. So Siragusa, and our then Ambassador Clare Boothe Luce, started a campaign to get Italy to ban the legal production of heroin. They were helped by the scandalous Schiaparelli Affair, in which a top official of a heroin plant admitted he had diverted eight hundred thousand dollars' worth of heroin to hoods known as close associates of Luciano. But it wasn't until March, 1956 that Italy finally banned heroin production.

It wasn't enough to crack down on the distributors in Italy; in order to curb the traffic, something had to be done about the source of supply, which meant the Middle East. American Agents have no police powers abroad; they must depend on the cooperation of police officials of friendly countries, and to get that cooperation they need the combined talents of a Machiavelli, a Winston Churchill and a Madison Avenue account executive.

Siragusa showed he had these talents, in spades. Prowling about the Middle East, choking over a popskull called raki, he impressed the cops in countries like Syria, Turkey, Lebanon and Greece with his sincerity. He accepted their confidences about political throat-cutting and never tattled. He lent a hand in solving an occasional local crime. He convinced them that he was a friend they could trust. A Greek police chief named Gerasimos Liaromatis—who is "Gerry" to Siragusa—says, "Charlie is the only honest man I ever met."

Thus, when Siragusa was ready to launch his drive in the Middle East in the fall of 1954, he had a lot of tough and efficient cops all over the area going for him. The operation took five months of planning and was climaxed by nearly simultaneous raids in three countries—Turkey, Lebanon and Syria. Siragusa's right-hand man in the operation was his old pal, the Greek police chief, Liaromatis. Siragusa, a man with a flair, calls it "Operation Old Goat."

In mid-November, 1954, Siragusa was tipped by an informant in Greece that circumstances were favorable for rounding up the gang they were after, a gang whose exports had an estimated retail value in the United States of more than a million dollars a year. Siragusa picked up Gerry, and the two set off for the Turkish town of Adana, an ancient cotton center where Uncle Sam had set up an Air Force base.

The man they wanted was an opium supplier named Ahmet Ozsayar, but in order to get him to do business with them, they had to have a convincing story. Siragusa solved that problem. He drove out to the Air Force base and had a chat with one of the two Air Force officers stationed there. An hour later he drove off in an Air Force jeep, wearing one of the officer's spare uniforms.

"You're a big Greek gangster," Siragusa told Gerry. "You want to buy opium. I'm a corrupt Air Force pilot who's willing to smuggle it out."

Confronted with this tale, Ahmet was charmed. He would be glad to sell them five hundred and fifty pounds of opium. It was agreed the stuff would be delivered the next morning, and the trio then hied themselves to the nearest night club, where Ahmet belted himself stiff with raki and insisted on covering Siragusa's cheeks with kisses. That's when Siragusa started calling him the "Old Goat."

Siragusa chose well the rendezvous for the next morning. It was at a lonely road intersection near Adana's airport, and there was a railway shack nearby in which were hidden a platoon of Turkish police. Ahmet showed up promptly at five o'clock with a British truck loaded with opium, and after submitting to a moist buss on his cheek, Siragusa started helping Ahmet and his two assistants unload the truck. Suddenly, the Turkish police burst from the shack with what sounded like Indian war whoops and tethered Ahmet and two helpers together with a chain.

At police headquarters, the Old Goat was persuaded to mention the name of his supplier. A few minutes later, Siragusa and Gerry, supported by a half-dozen Turkish policemen, took off for a mountain village in Anatolia. It was a three hundred mile drive through wild brush and desert prowled by hundreds of wolves, and when they reached the village, they were nearly mobbed by a knot of some twenty peasants. But they grabbed their man and an accomplice with four and four-tenths pounds of opium.

Things were happening in Beirut by that time. One of Siragusa's Rome assistants had donned the uniform of a Pan American World Airways pilot and was making a deal with another member of the gang to buy eighty-eight pounds of opium. This gangster's name was Abou Sayia. He was an irritable little Lebanese who was the Old Goat's branch manager in Lebanon.

Abou refused to make the delivery anywhere but in his apartment, so at the agreed-on time the Agent showed up and flashed his roll—a few hundred-dollar bills wrapped around a wad of paper. This was the signal for the Lebanese police to break into the place. As they did, one of Abou's teen-age sons staged a one-man battle with the cops, which gave his mother time to flush a quantity of the dope down the toilet. Still, the cops seized eighty-eight pounds of opium, nine of hashish and an ounce of morphine, and made five arrests.

The final raid was set for the next day in Aleppo, the famous walled city of Syria. The quarry was known as a dangerous man, a huge Syrian-type gangster named Tifankji, who had a potbelly and a face slashed with scars. Two weeks before, according to one Undercover Agent, Tifankji had tackled three rivals in a raki joint and had departed, leaving one of them with a broken neck and the other two with fractured skulls. As one Agent put it, "Maybe we should raid that guy with a tank."

No tanks were pressed into service, but the enforcement clan gathered for this one. On hand were Siragusa, Chief Gerry, the original Greek informant, a Turkish police chief, the Agent who had nabbed Abou Sayia in Beirut, and two other Agents.

They separated into two groups and started dickering with Tifankji in an assortment of coffeehouses. To give it an old-school authenticity, the two groups represented themselves as competitors, and Tifankji had the time of his life setting one group against the other, while the bid price soared. During one stage of the negotiations, he also demonstrated his strength by punching a hole through the coffeehouse wall. The wall was three-inch-thick mortar.

Finally Tifankji had had enough fun, and he closed a deal with Agent X for one hundred and fourteen pounds of opium. That night Agent X drove to Tifankji's home, a fourth-floor apartment in a respectable section of the town. In the street below were Siragusa, his policeman friends, and six Syrian cops dressed in civilian clothes.

Tifankji emerged a half hour later, after telling Agent X he had to go to get the opium. He boarded a streetcar, with Siragusa behind him; the police followed in a truck. Tifankji got off at the end of the line and made his way to a collection of unlighted huts; his pursuers spread out behind him. When he entered one of the huts, Siragusa and his cohorts burst in at his heels, and Tifankji was nabbed without a struggle. Also arrested were two accomplices; the one hundred and fourteen pounds of opium were seized.

The two-day raid had netted thirteen dope peddlers and seven hundred sixty-five pounds of drugs, which if successfully smuggled into the United States, would have sold at retail for upward to a half-million dollars. In one month's time, Siragusa's combined operations in cooperation with officials of Turkey, Syria, Lebanon and Greece knocked off thirty-four drug traffickers, one thousand and thirty-eight pounds of opium, forty-six pounds of morphine base, fifty-three pounds of heroin, nine pounds of hashish, and a laboratory for the conversion of opium into heroin.

That Middle East campaign was a classic in international cooperation, and Narcotics Bureau men like to savor it, because there are times when things can go wrong. Often, countries just don't have the diplomatic channels necessary to work together, as shown by an incident in April, 1955.

Siragusa had tipped off the Lebanese and Egyptian police to a hashish shipment scheduled to be smuggled from Lebanon into Egypt, aboard a Lebanese vessel. During the voyage, the vessel encountered a terrific storm and had to make for Israeli waters. Israeli Customs Agents boarded the vessel and arrested the captain when they discovered eight hundred and twenty-five pounds of hashish aboard. Obviously, it was now Lebanon's move—an investigation of the charter of the ship was indicated. But since the Lebanese were not on speaking terms with the Israelis, nothing was done about it, and the ship was freed to resume its illicit trade.

The snafus, though, are becoming more and more infrequent. International cooperation, fostered by Siragusa's personable persistence and Commissioner Anslinger's devotion to daily negotiations with officials abroad, is making life miserable for traffickers whether they do business in Aleppo or Albany. And the key is the free and mutually trustful exchange of information.

Thus there came a day in January, 1955 when Narcotics Bureau Agents in Detroit learned that one Hussein Hider was getting regular shipments of heroin from Beirut. Authorities in Beirut were advised, and meanwhile an Agent went undercover and struck up an acquaintance with Hider, by posing as a dope pusher. Hider was willing to sell, but he had a better plan. He suggested that the Agent go into partnership with him. Hider said he was dissatisfied with the man who was bringing in the dope from Lebanon, and he hired the Agent as his courier.

Beirut is a long way from Detroit, but any trip is worth while when the result can be the cutting off of a source of supply. So the Agent flew to Beirut and, after the usual negotiations through contacts, got himself an introduction to Hider's supplier, one Mounib Goureyeb. After buying a kilogram of morphine base, the Agent tipped the Lebanese police, and they seized Goureyeb's secret processing laboratory and put the pinch on Goureyeb. The same day, Hider was arrested in Detroit.

A tip from Lebanese police to Narcotics Bureau headquarters in Washington in January, 1957 had even wider ramifications. Beirut authorities had seized a cache of heroin and had persuaded somebody to talk. The information they received led Narcotics Agents to Detroit, where they hauled in Fauzi El Masri, a courier for the Beirut ring. Two days later, on the same information, French police grabbed another member of the ring in Marseille. He turned out to be Ibrahim Mabrouk Khalil, a resident of Brooklyn, New York. Agents found a supply of hashish in Khalil's apartment.

Much of the credit for these cracks in the wall of secrecy built up by the syndicates of international dope gangsters belongs to Charles Siragusa. On a monthly budget of only four thousand dollars, he has set up a vast network of informants from Hamburg to Rome to Naples to the little villages in the Middle East. The information he receives from these Undercover Agents is checked and then filed and crossfiled in an imposing array of filing cabinets in his Rome office. United States and European intelligence agencies feed him vital tidbits; so do members of Uncle Sam's armed forces scattered over the continent. As he puts it, "Everybody helps; I'm just the guy who sorts out the stuff."

This is partially true, of course. But both the Treasury Department and the Italian government regard Charles Siragusa's contributions with considerably more esteem. He has been awarded Treasury's highest award, the Exceptional Civilian Service Medal, "for outstanding courage in the face of danger while performing assigned duties." And in 1956 he was made a knight of the Ordine al Merito, which is the Italian equivalent of the French Legion of Honor.

Charles Siragusa, son of Sicilian immigrants, occasionally must savor a kind of poetic justice in those awards. "My uncle would get a kick out of it," he says. That, of course, would be the uncle who was murdered by Mafia mobsters on New York's Lower East Side forty years ago for refusing to kick back part of his pay envelope.

Dead or Alive

by FREDERICK AYER, JR.

Frederick Ayer, Jr., is one of several contributors to this book who have been, or presently are, members of the Federal Bureau of Investigation. This is his report of a manhunt in which he was one of the hunters, hunting for a dangerous killer, a "mad dog" killer, who was wanted as much alive as he could be taken.

KARL STRAKA, of Steubenville, Ohio, was a machinist by training, a criminal by persuasion, and a multiple killer by intent. He had the instincts of a hunted fox, and was, by necessity, an uncannily accurate observer.

He was courageous, brilliant—and damned.

Straka was wanted by the police in at least three states, and by the FBI. He was wanted for robbery, theft of government property, flight across a state line to avoid prosecution, and a dozen other offenses. First and foremost, he was hunted as a safecracker and killer. He'd often stolen nitroglycerin from the torpedo plant at Wheeling for use in his safe burglaries.

In addition, he'd shot and killed four policemen.

For these killings, he would be hunted to the death as long as a policeman anywhere remained alive. There were a great many policemen in West Virginia, Kentucky, and Ohio. Plus that, the Bureau had been on the case for almost two years.

Nevertheless, Karl Straka remained at liberty.

In this chase, the FBI was represented almost permanently by Jack Delaney, a 230-pound, ex-star tackle from Holy Cross. For nearly two years, he did little else, night and day, but run down leads on Karl's whereabouts, and attempt to lay successful traps for the fugitive.

This was no easy task. The Steubenville area was a difficult hunting ground for a Special Agent. Here, to be wanted by the police was sometimes to be among friends. Straka had dozens of relatives in the area. A few were on the police force.

Straka enjoyed another advantage. People were more afraid of him than of the law. It was said he traveled armed with a submachine gun. He was known to have killed. He'd been widely quoted as saying that at all times he carried on his person a half-pint bottle of nitroglycerin. It was his promise that he'd take with him in a deadly blast anyone— G-Man or private citizen—who had him cornered.

Little by little, the scales began to balance as Delaney and all of us working with him continued our dogged pursuit. With increasing frequency, we raided places from which Karl had fled only minutes earlier. Time after time, he narrowly escaped roadblocks. I participated in several raids. Two came just before the drama's closing scene.

At about 2 AM on the morning of February 6, 1943, Agent-in-Charge Al Belmont, of the Cincinnati Field Office, to which I was then assigned, called me from Steubenville, 289 miles away.

"Jack has a very hot lead on Straka. This might be it. Get five other men. Bring two cars. Load up with searchlights, loudspeaker, tear gas guns, and anything else you think you'll need. And be here in time for breakfast."

I did as directed, and assembled five other Special Agents.

We set out for Steubenville in a lot of rain and a little sleet. When we finally got there, Belmont greeted us with:

"Lie down for an hour, and sleep if you can. Then come back to my room."

When we got together an hour later, Belmont briefed us. One of Delaney's contacts had told him about a hunting cabin where Straka had holed up several weeks before. Karl had told this man that "later today, after it gets dark, I am coming back to pick up a packet of money and a machine gun stashed under the floor boards of the cabin."

We were quietly to move four Agents into the shack around nightfall, and station four men in two cars well off the road to the hideout—in case Straka didn't come on foot.

Shortly after dark, with the added cover of heavy clouds, we moved into position. We quickly found that every time one of us took a step, or shifted his weight, one of the boards in the floor of the old building would creak. It was bitter cold to remain motionless; yet, during the two hours of a light snowfall that followed, I think it's fair to say none of us consciously moved a muscle.

Then the snow clouds blew away, and a bright moon appeared. Thus, all approaches to the cabin were brightly illuminated.

About an hour after moonrise, Delaney grabbed my forearm. He pointed through the open door. About 200 yards away, I finally spotted a figure. He was approaching warily. He'd advance a few feet, halt, turn his head from side to side, and resume his progress. After a minute or so, he began to circle first for twenty or thirty yards to the right, then back and to the left. Finally, he came so close he couldn't have been more than seventy yards away.

Then, suddenly, he threw up his head like a startled animal, and remained, it seemed, frozen for seconds, before turning and sprinting into a clump of trees. I thought Jack Delaney would burst into tears.

By the light of morning, we examined the ground for a great distance around the cabin. We found Karl's footprints circling it twice at a distance of nearly an eighth of a mile. We were unable to follow the tracks he left when running away.

I still don't know what thing he noticed that night as being out of place—or what instinct warned him that all was not well. I do know we found a packet containing over $500 in bills, as well as a Navy-issue Thompson submachine gun under the cabin's floor boards.

Later that morning, we picked up another important piece of news. On the previous day, Straka, or a man closely matching his description, had been surprised by a store owner while attempting to blow the latter's safe. He shot the store-owner, who was now hospitalized and on the danger list.

Washington then placed Straka in the "mad dog" category.

A flat-out manhunt began. Four Agents hunted while four rested. That was the theory. In truth, for three days none of us really slept. The tension was far too great.

We carried out an almost frenzied series of raids, interrogations, and searches. Some of us even scoured a couple of abandoned mine shafts and a few caves. Not a trace was found. Then, one of the men Delaney had already questioned came to the hotel. He wanted to see Jack again.

"Mr. Delaney," he said, "I just thought of something I forgot. Straka, he's hiding up with Jan Karolik's family. On Plum Lane they have a house."

"I know Karolik," Delaney said.

We acquired map plans of the neighborhood. Our informant sketched out the location of the Karolik house and indicated its surroundings. It stood on a dirt road in a nearly deserted tract. It was bordered on one side by the railroad, by vacant lots on two other sides.

This, therefore, would be a raid with three cars converging on the dwelling. Two men would patrol the tracks. Searchlights would be used to illuminate the area. And, if needed, tear gas shells would be fired into the house.

In practice as well as theory, it was a textbook operation. About 9:15 that night, I drove Al Belmont to within about three hundred yards of the house. Then we coasted the rest of the way, with the headlights off. The other cars also arrived quietly. They took their allotted positions. Suddenly, on signal, the searchlights blazed on. Al bellowed at the top of his voice:

"OK, Straka! We're Federal officers! You're completely surrounded! Come out with your hands up!"

Almost at once a door opened, and a man ran out into the circle of light. He was dressed in what appeared to be pajama pants and a lumberman's jacket. For a moment, he stood as if undecided and bewildered. Then, he plunged a hand toward his jacket pocket. He would then have been a dead man, save that at the very same split second Delaney yelled:

"Don't shoot, for God's sake! It's Karolik!"

As he yelled, he leaped forward, and brought the man to the ground with a diving tackle.

We all rushed up. Delaney, sitting on the recumbent figure, announced, "I was right. This is Karolik, OK, not Straka, and he's not armed." Then, turning, he went on, "For God's sake, Jan, why did you reach for your pocket? We damned near shot you full of holes."

A quavering voice answered, "I am having coffee. Then comes yelling and screaming. Lights in my face. Guns all over. I am a nervous man. I sweat. I need a handkerchief, and you jump on me. What is it I do?"

After we searched every inch of the house, we were able to show Jan what he'd done. With him lived his wife and three small children. The guest he'd sheltered for the past 48 hours had left, under his cot, a submachine gun and a 50-round drum of .45 caliber ammunition. Not only that, but in a kitchen closet, not five feet from the baby's crib, I found a glass bottle.

It was filled with a viscous, burnt-orange liquid. It was giving off acrid and visible fumes. This is the appearance of nitroglycerin when it's begun to decompose. In this state, it's even more unstable than fulminate of mercury. A very slight jar will cause it to detonate.

After we had ordered the family out of the house, I found a packing case. I stuffed it with old socks and such, then very tenderly laid the bottle on this padding. Then, walking as if on eggs, I carried it out of the house. One of the other Agents took a photo at this juncture, which is probably a classic study of a terrified young man.

Gingerly I poured the liquid onto a pile of chips and sawdust we had gathered from the woodpile. I then touched a match to it. It burned very rapidly, with an angry, hissing, yellow flame, exactly as described in the Bureau instruction manual.

Straka, of course, was nowhere in sight. We learned from Karolik that he'd gone out to steal a car, feeling, for some reason, that Karolik's house was no longer a safe refuge.

The manhunt resumed. Apparently, Karl had taken entirely to the woods and to abandoned shacks. No one reported seeing him for the next three weeks.

Then there appeared a very slender clue. A nine-year-old boy had been on an errand for his mother to an out-of-the-way grocery store. There he'd seen a heavily bearded man purchase half a dozen quarts of milk and a couple paper bags of sandwiches. For some reason, the boy mentioned what he'd seen to his teacher. The teacher repeated it to the principal, observing casually that you didn't see many men wearing beards any more. The principal had heard about the manhunt. He told the village constable. The constable got hold of Jack Delaney.

Jack, together with Jeff Baker, of the Wheeling Field

Office, put a stake-out on the store. The whole thing seemed a very tenuous lead, but by then Delaney was ready to try anything. They chose a place of concealment across the road, and maintained an all-day watch on the off-chance that Straka would be careless enough to return to the same place for supplies.

For four days, nothing happened.

On the fifth morning, a bearded figure appeared in the roadway. He carefully surveyed the surrounding territory. Then he approached the store.

Delaney yelled, "Straka! Hands up, and down on your knees!"

Instead of obeying, Karl whirled and swept his hand to his belt. He was felled immediately by a blast of buckshot. In the belt and pockets of his blood-soaked clothing, the Agents found a .45 caliber automatic, a .38 caliber revolver, and a glass vial of nitroglycerin. This, miraculously, had failed to explode.

Sometimes our concepts of justice are hard to explain. Straka did not die at once, so he was taken to a hospital and given massive transfusions of whole blood in order that he might live long enough to stand trial.

He didn't.

The FBI Goes Hunting

by CARL B. WALL

There are some who feel that the case recounted here may well be the FBI's most brilliant spy investigation. As Carl B. Wall points out, in support of that view, all the Special Agents really had to work with was the fact that there was a spy. It was suspected that he lived in the vicinity of New York City. Within the Metropolitan Area, some ten million people live, work and play. Which one of them is the spy?

THIS IS A SPY STORY minus false whiskers, cloak and dagger, and the like. There is no beautiful Mata Hari. No desperate cliff-edge struggle. Not a shot is fired. Yet this case is one of the most intriguing in the annals of the Federal Bureau of Investigation.

It is the story of the hunt for an unknown man lost in the swirling tides of New York City's millions of people.

It begins on the night of February 20, 1942. An alert postal censor, scanning mail destined for Portugal, plucked a typewritten sheet from an airmail envelope. It was apparently harmless. The sort of letter one old friend writes another. The address, though, was one of those listed by counter-espionage agents abroad as a "mail-drop" for German agents.

Within hours, it was at the FBI Laboratory in Washington.

305

An expert in secret inks stroked the blank side of the paper with a chemically saturated sponge. From the empty whiteness, secret writing slowly appeared. It twisted in the curious hieroglyphics of German hand-printing.

The message conveyed information on troopships and freighters making up for convoy in the Port of New York. In the hands of Nazi U-boat commanders, it would be a deadly threat to the lives of soldiers and seamen, and to the tons of arms and equipment produced in this arsenal of democracy.

Obviously, the letter came from a Nazi spy in New York. The FBI's job was equally obvious. Capture that spy. The lab, though, could furnish only one thin clue. The letter had been typed on an Underwood 3-bank portable. Special Agents began to check sales and rentals of that type of machine in the New York area.

Within the next ten days, there was a second letter. Then, a third. All were mailed from New York post offices. Did that mean the spy lived in New York? Maybe yes. Maybe no. And what did he look like? Usually, when the FBI is hunting for a criminal, they have some description to go by.

Here, the Special Agents began with nothing.

One night, one of the Agents was mulling over photostatic copies of the letters. Suddenly, a theory occurred to him. It might be brilliant. It might be worthless.

The theory hinged on the fact that certain passages of the typed sections of the letters had a curious aura of truth. Most of them, he guessed, were probably sheer invention. However, the spy might be telling the truth about the inconsequential trivia of his everyday life.

The Special Agent jotted down these things, which seemed to him to be true:

X is married. He owns his own home. He has a dog. The dog has been ill with distemper. X has a regular job. He leaves his home between seven and eight every weekday morning. He recently had his eyeglasses changed. He is an air-raid warden.

There were at the time 98,338 air-raid wardens in Greater New York.

When the SAC—the Special Agent-in-Charge—at the New York Field Office heard about the idea, he grinned. "That's a lot of air-raid wardens," he said, "but it's better than eight million John Does. At least it gives us a toenail hold."

So the handful of Special Agents began the task of checking almost a hundred thousand wardens. How many are married? How many own homes? How many own dogs? Which wear spectacles?

While they investigated those angles, more letters were intercepted. From them, a further image of X began to take shape. These items were added to the list:

He has a "Victory Garden."

His home is threatened by mortgage foreclosure.

He'd like to own a chicken farm.

The shadow of the invisible spy was still indefinite, but it could no longer be cast by millions. Day by day, night by night, the hard-working Agents cut the figure. 98,000 . . . 88,-000 . . . 81,000. Progress, but even 81,000 is a lot of possible suspects.

On the night of April 14, letter number 12 was intercepted. From it the Agents plucked this apparently innocent, nostalgic passage:

"It is very warm here, and the trees are beginning to bud. The Spring always reminds me of that wonderful week we spent on the beach at Estoril. . . ."

Estoril! The FBI knew Estoril. A resort a few miles outside of Lisbon. They also knew it was a clearinghouse for Nazi espionage agents.

Immediately, a hurried conference was called. What was the best way to check every citizen and alien entering the

United States from Lisbon since the Spring of 1941? There was no photograph to compare with passport photos. No fingerprints. No name. Then, one of the Agents said:

"We've got a fairly good specimen of his handwriting—the "Fred Lewis" signature on the letters. The name is undoubtedly phony, but the handwriting isn't."

"Go on," said the SAC.

"Everybody entering the country," the Agent continued, "must fill out a baggage declaration for Customs. Why couldn't we go through the files at the Customs House, and compare the handwriting on the declarations with that signature?"

Early the next morning, FBI handwriting experts, armed with photographic copies of the spy's signature, went to work on the mountain of Customs declarations. There were, of course, thousands and thousands of them, for the spring of 1941 had been high tide in the flood of refugees pouring out of Lisbon.

The work of the handwriting expert is an exact science. Clues hang on the slightest twist of an e, or the looping of an l. Spotting a similarity so slight meant examining each declaration with meticulous care. For days, they burrowed their way through stack after stack.

And this was only one phase of the great manhunt, now in full swing. Every scrap of information that had been sweated from those 12 letters was being checked, and double-checked. Of the original 98,338 air-raid wardens, nearly 60,000 had by now been eliminated. They had been eliminated by Special Agents who got their answers by asking questions, waiting, humoring silent folks, and enduring the talkative ear-benders. That all consumed precious time. Time for the spy to be doing more damage.

At 9 o'clock on the night of June 9, 1943, a Special Agent wearily picked up one more form from the stacks at the Customs office. The 4,881st.

Suddenly, as his eyes focused on the signature, his weariness vanished. He reached for his magnifying glass. Yes. He was sure. There was the same looping e. The same slanting f. The identical sloping s.

The Agent startled his colleagues with a bellow.

Later that night, at the FBI lab in Washington, enlarged photographs were made of the signature. Then, they were compared with the spy letters. Now, the experts were sure. At 1:45 AM Washington called the New York Field Office. "Check the name Ernest F. Lehmitz."

The list of air-raid wardens was consulted. On it was a man named Lehmitz. He lived at 123 Oxford Place, Tompkinsville, Staten Island, New York.

Less than an hour later, Special Agents strode down the gangplank of the ferry from Manhattan to Staten Island. A blustering show of automatics? A duel in the dawn? Nothing quite so simple. There are other questions to be answered. Are there accomplices? Where and how is the spy getting his information? Is this man really a spy? In this country, even spies get a fair trial, and legitimate evidence must be legally obtained to convince the jury.

The Special Agents set up a surveillance on the house in Oxford Place. At 7:15, a tall, spare man walked out of the door, and hurried along the street.

He wore *spectacles*.

Casually, one of the Agents followed him. Not far from the house, the man turned and went into a restaurant. Despite the early morning hour, the place was filled with waterfront workers, soldiers, sailors. The Agent went in. He ordered coffee. And he watched. His "man" donned a soiled apron, and started mopping the floor. He seemed to be about fifty-five, with mild blue eyes, and wispy brown hair. The kind of a man you wouldn't look at twice.

The other customers were talking. Like most people, they

were talking business. Cargos. Ships movements. Sailing dates. The Agent finished his coffee and left.

The man was shadowed for the next sixteen days and nights. Other Special Agents, posing as salemen and talkative barflies, unearthed additional facts about Lehmitz.

"Ernie? Sure, I know Ernie. He's *air-raid warden* for this block. Brother, you should've heard how he bawled people out for not dimming their lights. Ernie takes the war real serious."

"Ernie? A kind-hearted guy. Last summer, you'd've thought he lost his best friend when *his dog died of distemper.*"

"Ernie Lehmitz? He had one of the best *Victory Gardens* on the Island. Too bad the bank *foreclosed on that mortgage.*"

"Sure I know him. He usually stops in here for a glass of beer on his way home. He's a quiet kind of guy. Usually talks about the *chicken farm* he's gonna buy one of these days."

One by one, the pieces fell into place, jibing perfectly with the chit-chat of the spy letters. At eight o'clock on the morning of June 27, 1943, Lehmitz was brought to the New York FBI Field Office. It was one year, four months, and seven days after the first letter was intercepted.

He was shown the letters. He was shown the great mass of evidence so painstakingly accumulated. The avalanche of facts was too much. He signed a complete confession. He'd first arrived in the United States in 1908, as a clerk at the German Consulate in New York. There were several trips to Germany. During the last one, in 1938, he was recruited by the German espionage network, and trained in the use of secret inks.

In the spring of 1941, the Nazis ordered him to return to the United States, find steady employment on the waterfront, pose as a good U.S. citizen, and lose himself among the millions of other loyal Americans.

How well Lehmitz played his role was indicated by the stream of Staten Island neighbors who offered their sympathy. "It can't be anything bad," they said, before the charges were made public. "Why, Ernie wouldn't hurt a flea."

The FBI disagreed. So did the judge and jury in Federal Court, which sentenced Lehmitz to thirty years' imprisonment. And so ended the manhunt. To the FBI, it was one of the most tedious jobs of World War II.

To the American people, it is still one of the most brilliant.

The Scales of Injustice

by ASA S. HERZOG
and A. J. EZICKSON

Like several other contributors, Asa S. Herzog is a New York attorney. In "The Scales of Injustice," he collaborates with New York Times-Wide World photographer A.J. Ezickson. Together, this Gotham double-play combination digs into one of the most important and fascinating aspects of criminal investigation—criminal identification. It's an unspoken axiom among many law enforcement officers that eyewitness identifications are always wrong. That, of course, is not invariably true, as we shall see.

IN ONE CASE, witnesses to a holdup identify a photo in the "Rogues' Gallery." In another, a small-town sheriff recognizes the picture of a "wanted" forger as "that friendly newcomer who's already cashed some checks." In a third case, a man arrested in Philadelphia for a petty crime is found to be "wanted" in Nevada for homicide.

Has the right man been identified in each case?

Over the centuries, criminal identification progressed at a maddeningly slow rate until the advent of the camera. Beginning, however, with the first photographic method, Daguerre's wet plates, accurate identification was off to its first real start. With the advent of dry-plate photography, it was definitely on its way.

Photography alone, of course, could not solve the problem. How could a particular criminal's photograph be extracted from a collection of hundreds of thousands? Filed by names, the collection is rendered almost valueless by the criminal's use of aliases.

And so we come to the magic name of Alphonse Bertillion.

In 1881, the French Parliament was discussing a burning political question—the deportation of habitual criminals. How, members asked, could it definitely be established that a felon was a habitual criminal unless he could be positively identified, and his criminal record produced?

Bertillion presented a system a thousandfold superior to any known before—the first really scientific method of criminal identification.

Formerly, photographs had been taken full-face. This method gave no clear picture of the nose and ear, the two most important features in distinguishing between persons.

Bertillion "mugged" his criminals by taking both full-face and profile views, the method still universally used today. He employed standardized camera equipment, and fixed a scale so bodily measurements could be calculated from the pictures.

This idea was based upon the scientifically proven fact that the bony structure of an adult remains constant.

It seemed foolproof.

Then, in 1903, one Will West was committed to the Federal Penitentiary at Leavenworth, Kansas. Questioned as to whether he had ever previously been in the penitentiary, he made firm denials. The clerk, however, had his doubts. He took West's Bertillion measurements. Then, searching his files, he found a card.

On it was the name William West.

Will West insisted the card wasn't his, despite the almost exactly similar appearance and measurements.

Turning the card, the clerk was shocked. William West was already an inmate, serving a life sentence for murder!

That brought about the adoption of the fingerprint system. Is fingerprint identification really infallible?

No!

There is a possibility of duplication. It is one chance in a novemdecillion. For those who like to be precise, that exact statistic is one chance in 1,606,937,974,174,171,729,761,809,-705,564,167,968,221,676,069,604,401,795,301,376.

An additional, vitally important fact is that fingerprints cannot be altered. That's been tried, notably by John Dillinger.

On March 3, 1934, Dillinger, being held on a charge of murder, escaped from the Lake County jail in Crown Point, Indiana. Later, it was found he'd resorted to plastic surgery to conceal his identity. Not only had his face been remolded, but an attempt had been made to mutilate and change the markings on his fingertips.

The attempt was a failure.

FBI fingerprint experts detected more than 300 points of similarity in prints taken before and after the operation. Twelve are sufficient to establish positive identification.

Photography is vital to the system. When police take a criminal's fingerprints, photographic copies are made and distributed to all law enforcement officials. Obviously, those prints can be decisive in establishing a criminal's guilt.

Even more imporant, they can help the FBI prove that J. Edgar Hoover and his men are more interested in justice than in convictions.

May 28, 1938, for example, was a black-letter day for the citizens of Lamar, Colorado. Four particularly ruthless bandits held up the First National Bank of Lamar, killed the president and the cashier, stole more than $200,000, and kidnapped two employees, one of whom was later found murdered.

The bandits fled from Colorado into Kansas, breaking through a police roadblock en route. At Dighton, Kansas, they spotted the shingle outside the home and office of a Dr. Weininger. One of the bandits, shot during the roadblock breakthrough, needed a doctor badly. They stopped the car on the outskirts of town, and hid it among some trees.

Through a ruse, Dr. Weininger was persuaded over the phone to drive into the country to meet them.

Arriving, he attended the wounded bandit. Then, to prevent him from ever identifying the four men, they murdered the doctor, and threw his body into a canyon. His car was pushed over after him.

Days later, Dr. Weininger's body and car were found by the police. There were no clues—none, that is, except a single, blurred, rather indistinct latent fingerprint impression, found on a window of the car.

That single print was developed, photographed, and circulated throughout the country. FBI fingerprint technicians were requested in a memo from J. Edgar Hoover to impress the print carefully upon their minds.

Months went by.

In Lamar, public indignation was mounting. People demanded action from the authorities. They wanted arrests, not excuses. A new wave of "Wanted!" notices went out. They repeated descriptions of the four bandits by the few surviving eye-witnesses.

This time, the notices produced results.

William Jennings Bryan (alias "Whitey" Walker), Charles G. Clinton, Floyd Jarrett, and Al Oliver—all with long criminal records—were apprehended in various parts of the country.

Returned to Lamar, they were promptly identified as the bandits and held for trial.

It was a quick trial. All were found guilty and sentenced to death. They appealed the verdict.

More than a year later, an FBI clerk, engaged in routine filing of newly arrived prints, suddenly came upon a set that nagged him. They belonged to one William Harrison Holden, alias Joseph Reed, according to the card from the Sheriff's office at Stockton, California.

Searching the files produced no previous record for Holden or Reed. The clerk shrugged. Maybe he was wrong. Maybe he'd never seen that print before.

Then he remembered.

Comparison showed one of Holden's prints was identical with the print on Dr. Weininger's car. In addition, a more complete search of the files showed that the prints of the man in California belonged not to a William Harrison Holden but to a notorious criminal and known killer named Jake Fleagle.

"Detain Prisoner Holden," the FBI wired the Stockton Sheriff.

Unfortunately, Jake Fleagle was no longer in custody. At the Fleagle home in Colorado, the FBI questioned Jake's father and others. Information led to the apprehension of Ralph Fleagle, Jake's brother, in his Kankakee, Illinois, hideout.

Brought back to Lamar, he confessed, and named as his accomplices Jake, Howard L. Royston, and George Abshier. Royston and Abshier were soon located. Not Jake Fleagle, though. The FBI launched one of the first of its soon to be internationally famous manhunts.

On October 14, 1930, Jake Fleagle was found at Branson, Missouri. He tried to shoot his way out. The following day, he died from his wounds.

Ralph Fleagle, Royston and Abshier were tried, convicted, and executed more conventionally. The charges against the four men originally arrested were, of course, dropped.

The Frugal Forger

by CHARLES DENTON

Charles Denton—currently TV Editor of the Los Angeles
Examiner—*is one of the crop of good, young writers whose
exciting reportage is bringing the American public back
to the habit of reading newspapers. In this contribution,
Denton illustrates one of the most important reasons for
the FBI's spectacular record of achievement—to J. Edgar
Hoover and his Agents, no crime is unimportant, and no
criminal is pursued with anything less than maximum
effort.*

*As many lawbreakers can testify, this attitude leads to
constant interruptions in their careers, and makes it difficult to plan for the future.*

THE COST of bringing a criminal to justice often outweighs
the purely financial significance of his crimes—though seldom
as heavily as in the case of Homer James Adkins.

The principal misdeed for which the FBI spent a solid
year running him to earth netted Adkins only $5—and the
money itself was of no interest to the elite defendants of
Uncle Sam's law.

Homer James Adkins was a tall, spare, nondescript man
who'd compiled an impressive record of burglary, larceny,
mail fraud, bad checks, impersonation, and confidence games

in the full vigor of his youth. Like other men, though, Homer felt his energies fading as his sixties overtook him. His incentive for crime seemed to be going dull. He yearned for a quieter, less pretentious life. His needs were few. He wanted only to enjoy himself in his declining years, to take things easy—without, of course, descending to the level of honest employment.

So, being a man who believed he was one of the two sharpies born each minute to fleece the sucker entering the world at the same time, Homer hit on a scheme which might easily have provided for him through the sunset of his life— if only his sense of geography and Federal law hadn't failed him.

On April 14, 1956, he dropped in at a real estate office in Gresham, Oregon. He introduced himself as Clyde C. Owens, a frugal farmer who for years had saved his money to buy a place of his own.

Homer was ideally suited to the role. He exuded an earthy sincerity, seasoned with just the right amounts of shrewdness and naivete. The real estate agent was properly helpful.

Homer consulted the agent's list of offerings, and decided he wanted to see a small farm about eight miles out of town. The agent cheerfully drove him there. Together, they surveyed the land and house. Homer's performance did him credit. He tested the soil in his hands, talked knowingly of crops and planting, and generally appraised the farm with the perception of a veteran agriculturist. Then he and the agent returned to Gresham. At the real estate office, Homer wrote out a check for $1,000 drawn on a Chico, California, bank as earnest money to bind the deal.

Later the same afternoon, Homer returned to the farm for more discussion of weather, plowing, and the like with the outgoing owner. When Adkins was ready to leave, the owner agreed to drive him back to Gresham. On the way, they talked more of farming. They became close enough friends that when Homer remarked casually that he was a bit short on pocket money, his new friend gladly advanced him $5.

That was the last anyone in Gresham ever saw of Homer Adkins.

In due time, the $1,000 check bounced back from Chico marked "Unable to Locate Account." Homer's choice of banks was decidedly injudicious. Had he written the check on an Oregon bank, the case would've remained in local jurisdiction. And, since the actual cash loss involved was only $5, probably no one would've wasted much time looking for him.

Forging a check on an out-of-state bank, though, is a Federal offense, regardless of whether or not the forger realizes any profit on the crime. The FBI takes no account of the extent of lawbreaking. Just to crack a Federal statute is enough to send it into action.

Special Agents in Oregon promptly identified "Clyde Owens" as Homer James Adkins, in whom they had still another interest. Homer had been sentenced to Federal prison in 1947 for mail fraud. Paroled in 1951, he'd been returned two years later for violating that parole. In 1954, he was again given his conditional freedom, but failed to report even once to his parole officer.

The FBI scarcely had time to enter Homer's latest mischief in his record before it became painfully apparent that it was no isolated caprice. Two months later Homer called on a Seattle realtor. This time he gave his name as Charles W. Thompson, and negotiated to buy a local grocery store. Now, though, he was more careful about where he did his illegal banking. He wrote a down payment check for $5,000 on a bank in the state of Washington.

This bank, however, wasn't there at all.

While the negotiations were in progress, Homer contacted the happy owner, turned on his grass roots charm, and borrowed $30. Then he left for California before the down payment bounced higher than the victim's temper.

He repeated the scheme again in the latter part of August. This time, it was an Ontario, California, chicken ranch which had caught his fancy. Laboriously, he wrote out a $500 down payment check with the proper agony of a thrifty man parting with hard-earned cash.

The real estate broker got the touch in that one—$15.

Another chicken ranch deal in San Dimas, California, reportedly provided Homer with an even better score less than a month later. Besides tapping the ranch owner for $6, he persuaded the real estate agent to help him cash a $30 check worth just as much as his down payment—nothing.

Homer wearied of picayune deals in December, however, and switched his pose to that of a well-heeled businessman looking for a good thing. He wasn't up to the part. He agreed to purchase a $30,000 grocery store in Pomona, California, and allegedly handed the owner a rubberized $2,000 check on a Lodi, California, bank. Somehow, though, Homer's approach failed to reach the owner as effectively as it had the others. He turned down Homer's request for a $40 loan, and advanced him only $5.

As the months went by, the pattern was repeated all over Southern California with a frequency that drove FBI Agents to distraction. What bothered them most was Homer's motive. Why, they asked themselves repeatedly, would anyone go to so much trouble for so little reward? Not that it mattered in the long run. The investigation went forward as efficiently as if Homer were reaping fortunes from his victims.

Homer had too much underworld know-how, though, to be taken easily. He ambled aimlessly around Southern California, soaking up the climate, enjoying himself—and playing his pixieish game just often enough to keep a few dollars in his pockets.

His trail wound from Santa Barbara to Riverside, through Long Beach, on to Anaheim and Hemet, and back again. How many of his scores escaped official notice because they were too minor to bother reporting, no one knows.

His bad checks assertedly ran as high as $5,000, and his personal profits as low as $2 per deal. That didn't bother Homer. It was playing the game that counted, not the score. As one chagrined victim after another identified Homer as the culprit, the FBI's dossier on his activities swelled to the proportions of a tome.

In Riverside, he reportedly issued a $2,400 check as down payment on a $30,000 rest home, borrowed $10 from the owner, and moved on to Los Angeles, where he tapped the manager of a downtown hotel for $5 while arranging to purchase the place.

And so it went.

Finally, in February, Homer acquired a new, and, as it turned out, fateful interest. He discovered an exhilaration in riding ambulances. This new phase of his remarkable career became evident when he allegedly turned up at a rest home in Bakersfield one afternoon, and explained solicitously to the operator that he wished to have an invalid sister moved there from another rest home in Los Angeles.

The operator arranged to have an ambulance go to Los Angeles to pick her up. At the last minute, Homer announced that he wanted to go along for the ride. He left the ambulance at 8th and Hope Streets after giving the driver detailed instructions on how to find the rest home. The driver found it, all right—but no invalid sister.

No one knew it at the time, of course, but this proved to be the break in the case that Agents had been hoping for. Since Homer's customary prey were realtors, information on his operations had been circulated in the trade. The circulation list now expanded to include ambulance services, rest homes, and others Homer might approach to satisfy his new-found appetite for ambulance riding.

He called at a Glendora sanitarium on April 13, gave his name as C.C. Thornton, and discussed plans for transferring his invalid mother to the home. In the course of the discussion, he managed to borrow $10 from the owner.

The scheme was still working.

It seemed to retain its customary smoothness until a Covina ambulance service was called to transport the alleged mother. A secretary thought the whole story had a suspiciously familiar flavor. Then, she recalled reading about Homer in a trade magazine. She checked back, and sure enough, Homer and the prospective customer told strikingly similar stories.

An ambulance was sent to the rest home to bring Homer back to the service's office to complete the deal. Instead of supplying a free ride to wherever the mother was supposed to be, though, the operators put him on the griddle with detailed questioning.

Homer squirmed nervously. Then he became righteously indignant, and informed his inquisitors that if they didn't want his business, he'd make arrangements elsewhere. He stamped out in high dudgeon—but he didn't get very far.

Before FBI Agents took him away, however, the sanitarium operator inquired about the fate of his 10-spot. Homer steadfastly denied having borrowed it. Agents and Covina police went over him like vacuum cleaners. He was as barren of $10 bills as a Skid Row drifter. Finally, one of the Agents discovered his ingenious hiding place. Homer had rolled the bill tightly and stuffed it into the stem of his pipe—hoping, no doubt, to cling to it as a scrap of memorabilia.

Adkins proved to be much less loquacious with the FBI than he had been with his victims. He confessed to the

Gresham caper, but insisted he had only a "dim memory" of his other dealings.

"It's a good racket if you work it right," was his only grudging explanation.

The Federal District Court in Portland, Oregon, agreed. It ordered Homer removed from circulation for four-and-a-half years.

Is John Jones a Communist?

by LEO ROSTEN

Loyalty oaths and loyalty investigations have been the subjects of a rip-roaring controversy for several years. They are, however, a fact of life. The important question, therefore, is "Are such investigations conducted fairly?" Leo Rosten, famous for his humorous writings, was deadly serious when he examined this problem.

O N THE MORNING of April 29, 1950, an anonymous letter arrived at FBI Headquarters in Washington.

Postmarked Philadelphia, it bore no sender's name, no return address. The letter was poorly typed. Only the signature—"Friend"—was handwritten.

"Just heard a guy in Pittsburgh, name John Jones—we call him Ted—is up for a govt. job. He is no good. I saw him go in C.P. headquarters Pittsburgh many times—1940, '41, '42. Find out if he got a Party card. I bet he had one— '41 or '42? He was a lousy Commie spy in the O.C.W. Union and sold out.

'Friend.' "

The letter was routed to the office of Allen Rowan on the fourth floor of the Department of Justice Building. Rowan is Chief of the FBI unit which investigates employees of the Federal Government under the loyalty program.

A week earlier, the FBI had received a batch of routine "loyalty forms" from the Civil Service Commission. The form filled out by John Theodore Jones, an employee in the Pittsburgh office of Department X, was among them.

> [*Everyone who works for the Federal Government must be* cleared. It is not the FBI, however, that gives or withholds clearance. *The FBI only investigates. It is strictly a fact-finding agency. It reports the facts it uncovers. The Loyalty Board in each Government agency decides whether an individual shall enter into, or continue in, the Government service.*]

While Allen Rowan read the anonymous letter, Special Agent Robert Nesbitt on the floor below was about to stamp Jones' form:

"No disloyal data, April 29, 1950."

Nesbitt had read the report on John Jones from the FBI's Identification Division, which checks fingerprints and criminal records; and from the Records Section, where every scrap of information collected by the FBI is analyzed, filed, and cross-referenced. In none of the FBI's voluminous files was there any derogatory information on John Jones.

The case was about to be closed.

Then Special Agent Nesbitt's phone rang. It was Allen Rowan. "Come up, please. Bring all the material on John Theodore Jones."

In Rowan's office, Nesbitt read the anonymous letter. "That's odd," he frowned. "There's nothing in Jones' file to support this."

"How did we happen to have a file on him at all?" asked Rowan.

"The War Department asked us to check him in 1939. He was up for a job with a Pittsburgh concern which involved restricted information. His record was clean as a whistle."

Nesbitt handed FBI File No. 62-490215 to Rowan. John "Ted" Jones, forty-two years old. Born and raised in Gary, Indiana. Moved to Chicago, 1935. Married Lois Tannen. Went to Pittsburgh, 1938. Worked for the Rossmore Corp.

Rowan turned to the loyalty form which Jones had filled out. In 1940, Jones took a job with a union called the Organized Clerical Workers. In 1942, he enlisted in the Army. Overseas service. Wounded. Honorably discharged, 1945. Took a Civil Service examination. Temporary appointment in Department X. Assigned to Atlanta, Georgia. Transferred back to Pittsburgh in 1950.

Rowan put the documents down. "If Jones ever figured in Communist activities, or if his name ever appeared in our files on the Party—"

"The Records Section would certainly have picked up some reference," Nesbitt interjected, tapping the anonymous letter.

> [*Everything which comes to the FBI is filed. To give any investigating agency the power to "screen" material, to remove material unfavorable to a person, also means to open the gates for the removal of favorable material—for reasons of personal malice, political advantage, or bureaucratic strife.*]

Rowan called the Washington Field Office of the FBI. "Check the Civil Service files on John Theodore Jones." Then he called the FBI Liaison Agent at the Pentagon. "Jones was in the Army. Check Military Intelligence." Then Rowan dictated a letter to the Special Agent-in-Charge of the FBI's Pittsburgh Field Office:

"Re: John Theodore Jones a/k/a Ted Jones, Department X, Pittsburgh, Pa.

"Subject: Loyalty of Government Employees

"You are instructed to conduct a full field investigation

concerning the captioned individual. The Bureau's files contain the following unverified information:

"An anonymous communication alleges that during 1940, 1941, 1942 Jones entered Communist Party Hq. in Pittsburgh many times, that Jones may have held a CP membership card in 1941 or 1942, and that when employed by Pittsburgh Chapter, Organized Clerical Workers Union, he knowingly followed either the orders or the line of the CP.

"For your assistance, there are enclosed copies of the following documents: loyalty form and application from Federal Employment.

"You are requested to submit your report by May 29, 1950."

Rowan sent copies of this letter to the FBI Field Offices in the areas where Jones had previously lived or worked: Indianapolis, Chicago, Atlanta.

Jones' loyalty form was returned to the Civil Service Commission bearing the following stamp:

"Files of this Bureau reveal unverified information concerning this employee, bringing the employee within the purview of Executive Order No. 9835. Investigation being conducted. If this employee is assigned to a sensitive position, a résumé of present information in the files of the FBI will be furnished on request."

The Commission would put Department X on notice that the FBI had launched a "full field investigation" of John Theodore Jones.

On May 1, Special Agent Harold Newman, of the FBI's Pittsburgh Field Office called on Mr. Merle Wollans, at his office in Department X.

After presenting his credentials, Newman said: "Like some information on one of your employees. John Jones."

Wollans looked surprised. "He in trouble?"

"No. It's a routine investigation. Loyalty program."

"Jones is a good man," Wollans said. "I'd recommend him without hesitation."

"You know of any activities that might reflect on his loyalty?" Newman asked.

Wollans shook his head. "None. Talk to Vern Foster, though. He and Jones are good friends."

Newman did. "Ted?" Foster exclaimed. What're you checking on him for?"

"He's a Government employee," Newman answered.

"And he's okay," Foster said emphatically. "Some people don't like him cause he's not a back-slapper. So what? My wife and me know Ted and Lois pretty well. He's strong for labor and civil liberties. But he's no Fascist or Commie, if that's what you want to know."

"On what do you base that opinion?" Newman asked.

"That's not an opinion. That's facts. Ted was against the Nazi Bund, and he's against the Communists. He says the Commies aren't just another party, but a Fifth Column. He says a lot of guys who mean right get sucked in by the Commie slogans.

"Ted got pretty worked up when those Ku Kluxers down South beat up a couple of Commie organizers. He said he was against Commies, but he didn't like the idea of a mob beating anybody up."

In the next few days, Newman interviewed two of Jones' neighbors, a man with whom Jones had once worked, the minister of the church Jones' wife attended, and three members of Jones' veterans organization.

Some obviously liked Jones. Some didn't. None offered any facts which might link Jones with Communist activities.

On May 6, Newman went to the headquarters of the Organized Clerical Workers Union. Barney H_____, President of the Union, was a big, barrel-chested man with a rough-and-tumble manner, and a very quick temper.

When Newman presented his credentials, Barney said: "Who are you guys snooping on today?"

Newman made a wry face. "John Jones."

"You're nuts," Barney roared. "Ted went on a couple of picket lines. So he's no scab. So he's against Franco. So he doesn't like the way hit-and-run congressmen smear a man's reputation. That's no reason for messing around in people's private affairs—like a Gestapo."

"The Bureau isn't a Gestapo," said Newman. "We haven't that kind of power, and Mr. Hoover doesn't want that kind of power. Congress wanted to allow the Bureau to clear people under the National Science Foundation Bill. Mr. Hoover took such a strong stand against it that the Senate killed the idea. Our job is to investigate."

"By listening to every Tom, Dick, and Harry who has a grudge against a man?" asked Barney. "You've probably tapped Ted's wire, and—"

"No, we—" Ted tried to interrupt.

Barney made a sound signifying extreme distaste. "I suppose now you'll tell me the FBI doesn't ever tap a wire."

"We do," said Newman, "when we're authorized to in writing by the Attorney General. And that's only in cases involving internal security—espionage, sabotage—or where human lives are in danger, like kidnapping or extortion."

"You're breaking my heart," Barney answered. "I'd be more impressed if you guys knew the difference between a liberal and a Communist."

"We think we do," said Newman. "You can help us by cooperating."

"Okay. I'll cooperate. Just serve me with a subpoena. Do all this in a court of law—the way it ought to be done."

"There's nothing to go into court about," Newman countered. "Jones hasn't committed any crime. Even if he were a Communist—"

"He isn't," Barney snapped. "He's as good an American as

you or me. Now, you'll have to excuse me. I've got a conference."

On May 8, Special Agent Newman met a man called "Whitey." "Whitey" was known to the FBI as Pitt-649 (Confidential Informant No. 649, Pittsburgh Field Office, FBI). His real name was locked in the Confidential Informant file. Pitt-649 had been a Communist for 18 years—until the Russians took over Czechoslovakia. Then, embittered and disillusioned, he'd gone to the FBI. He offered to stay in the Party and give information to the Government. He'd been doing that for the past year.

Whitey studied a picture of John Jones.

"No. He wasn't tied in with the Party any place I operated. Of course, I wasn't in Pittsburgh from 1940 to '44. Let me ask around."

Meanwhile, in Gary, Chicago, and Atlanta, FBI Agents were conducting interviews—with John Jones' high school principal, his oldest friend, his ex-landlord, people he'd given as character references, and some people he hadn't mentioned.

May 10, 9:45 AM. A call came into the Pittsburgh Field Office for Special Agent Harold Newman. It was Pitt-649.

"About that fellow Jones. I think I've turned up something. Call BArkley 7-0336. Ask for Joel. He's jittery, and scared of your outfit, but he wants to talk. If he does, he'll level with you."

Newman called the number. It was a furniture store. He asked for Joel. After a minute, a man's voice answered. Joel sounded scared. He wouldn't come to the FBI office. He suggested Newman register at the ____ Hotel that night, adding, "I'll try to make it. I won't promise. Don't use your name."

"I'll register as Frank O. Martin, from Toledo," Newman said.

It was almost 10:30 before Joel showed up at Newman's hotel room. He was a young man, in his early thirties. "It mustn't ever get out I talked to you," he said quickly. He moved a chair so his back was to the window. "You'll have to promise my name'll never figure in this."

Newman nodded. "If those are your conditions, the Bureau won't reveal its source."

"I want to break with the Party," Joel said tensely. "That's why I'm here. To prove it." He studied his palm for a minute. "My full name is Joel H____."

Newman pulled a photo from his briefcase. He handed it to Joel. "That's Ted Jones," Joel said. "He was a Party member."

"How do you know?"

"He was in my cell. Back in '41."

"Where?"

"Right here. I ought to tell you. I hate Jones' guts, and he never liked me. We always tangled on Party tactics. But he accepted Party discipline. I'll say that for him. He was getting instructions from the Party all the time he was working for the OCW."

"Would you be willing to put all this into a signed statement?" Newman asked. "The Bureau prefers—"

"I won't sign anything!" Joel yelled. He took a handkerchief from his pocket. "My God, if it ever got out that I even talked to the FBI—"

"Would you be willing to testify orally, before a Loyalty Board?"

"Why should I appear before any Board? Why should I stick my neck out?"

Newman hesitated. "You've given no proof, except your word. There's no evidence—"

"Evidence! You can get the evidence. But not under Jones' name. His Party name was Theodore Jonathan."

Newman wrote the name. "Can you prove that?"

Joel stood up. "I don't know. Maybe I can. Maybe I can't." He walked out hurriedly.

The next morning, Newman dictated a teletype to Washington for Agent-in-Charge Dorne's signature:

"FBI Pittsburgh 5-11-50 10:18 AM
"Director   Urgent
"John Jones aka *["also known as"]* Ted Jones, LGE *["Loyalty Government Employee"]*. Informant claims to be in position to have secured fact that Jones member CP 1941 under name Theodore Jonathan. Check and sutel *["submit teletype* immediately"]. Dorne."

The next day, Washington answered:

"John Jones aka Ted Jones, LGE. Reurtel *["Re your telegram"]* May eleven, fifty. Records reflect one Theodore Jonathan member CP forty to forty-two. No proof Jonathan and Jones identical. Secure verification. Hoover."

Newman phoned Pitt-649. "Your friend made a pretty strong allegation about Jones, but we need more than his word."

"I'll try to talk to him," Whitey promised.

May 13. Joel H—— telephoned Agent Newman from a public pay-station. He sounded uneasy. He suggested Newman sit in the last row of the reading room at the Public Library at 3:15.

At 3:25, Joel came in. He sat down next to Newman. He put an envelope on the table, thumbed through a magazine, and left, leaving the envelope. Inside was a photostatic copy of an application for membership in the Communist Party.

It was signed "T. Jonathan."

Newman sent it to Washington. Agent Robert Nesbitt took it to the Documents Section of the FBI Laboratory.

Technicians analyzed the handwriting of "T. Jonathan," then compared it with the signature of John Jones' fingerprint card.

Both were written by the same person.

An hour later, Agent Newman returned to Barney H____'s office. "We're double-checking something," he explained. "We want to be absolutely sure."

Barney stood up. He walked to the window. After a long, thoughtful silence, he turned to Newman. "Okay. I'll give you the dope. Ted Jones joined the Communist Party in 1940, but he was never a Communist. He joined on orders."

"Orders? Whose?"

"Mine. In 1940, the Commies were trying to take over this union. They worked in the dark. They always caught us by surprise. The only way to lick 'em was to plant somebody in with 'em. It was a lousy assignment. Ted turned me down two weeks running. Finally, he agreed. For two years, he tipped us on what they were up to. And for two years, he kept working to convince them to move slow. It worked—both ways."

"Will you put all that into a statement, and sign it?" Newman asked.

"Sure."

"Could anybody . . ." Newman hesitated. "Could anybody else confirm your—"

"My word's not enough, huh? Okay. Talk to Abel White. He was our treasurer in those days. He's out on the West Coast. I'll get you his address."

That night a teletype went out to the FBI Field Office in Los Angeles.

The next day, Special Agent Arthur Riggs interviewed Abel White. White confirmed Barney's story detail by detail, and signed a statement.

On June 16, on the basis of information in the FBI reports,

John Jones was "cleared" by the Loyalty Board of Department X.

Only one question remained unsolved. Who sent the FBI that anonymous letter? Joel H——? The Bureau had a file on him. His handwriting didn't match the person's who signed the word "Friend" on the note. The FBI may never know who wrote that letter. It may have been sent by someone who scarcely knew Jones, but was alarmed by newspaper accounts of Communist activities. On the other hand, it may have been sent by an enemy of Jones.

Whichever is true, one thing is certain. The writer helped the man he tried to destroy, thanks to the FBI.

In Defense of Wiretapping

by DOROTHY THOMPSON

The late Dorothy Thompson was a gifted writer and a sound thinker. In the essay which follows, she takes a position on the question of wiretapping with which we find it difficult to agree. J. Edgar Hoover often has voiced his dim view of wiretapping, and for some years forbade his Special Agents to employ the technique. A Presidential Directive issued by Franklin Roosevelt authorized limited use of wire taps, but the FBI rarely seeks authorization to tap a wire. Despite the stepped-up espionage and counterespionage activities engendered by the cold war, the FBI stated officially to a Congressional committee that it had only ninety-five taps in the entire country. But let us hear Miss Thompson.

As a result of recent hearings, Congress has been asked to consider new laws to facilitate investigations of espionage and subversion.

One would permit the Federal Government to use in Federal courts evidence obtained by tapping telephone wires.

Whether or not Congress passes such legislation, there will be vigorous and continued discussion of the subject, with opposition by no means animated by sympathy for suspected spies, traitors, or other criminals.

I doubt whether many Americans are familiar with law and practice as they govern the tapping of telephone wires. If a public debate is to generate light, rather than heat, the facts should be known.

No law forbids the tapping of telephone wires by authorized investigators as a means of obtaining evidence of suspected criminal activities. The criminal investigation bureaus of all states do it, and so, legally, does the FBI.

The policy of the FBI on wiretapping was set by the late President Roosevelt on May 21, 1940. Whenever a tap is under consideration, the Attorney General must authorize it. It has, under successive Attorneys General since then, been authorized only in tracing espionage, sabotage, and kidnapping.

It may surprise our citizens to know, in view of hysterical charges against the FBI, that the FBI uses this means of tracing criminal activities *far more sparingly* than do the states.

Although the FBI is charged to protect the security of the whole country, there are fewer than two hundred telephone taps in existence at this time. In contrast, the number of wire taps made in New York County alone equals, if not greatly exceeds, that of the FBI. The FBI taps wires only in the course of investigating the very serious cases I have listed.

The states use wiretapping to get evidence in any and all sorts of cases, from petty racketeering onward.

Information thus obtained can be introduced as evidence by the prosecuting attorneys in state courts. Under existing Federal law, however, Federal prosecutors may not produce in court evidence obtained by wiretapping.

Nevertheless, wiretapping is one means by which the FBI may eventually obtain evidence leading to an indictment. By recording telephone conversations, the investigator learns appointments made by suspects; finds, if they exist, odd and continuous associations; gets clues of meeting places, and hints of dubious activities; traces, in espionage cases, links to foreign embassies, and so on.

It has been claimed in some cases that the mere record of such telephone conversations would be sufficient to secure an indictment. This I think dubious, since the criminally active are likely to be more circumspect. It is more reasonably claimed that the records of such conversations would, in some cases, have clinched the Government case in trials which have left the public only partly convinced that justice has been done.

American feeling reacts strongly against invasions of privacy.

Criminal investigation, however, must obviously invade privacy. The criminal wants to keep his goings and comings as secret and private as possible. It is an invasion of privacy for a detective to seat himself at a tavern table near a suspect to overhear a conversation, and perhaps record it; or rent a house or apartment opposite the suspect's living quarters to watch his movements; or plant a stenographer in his office, or an Agent as a member in good standing within a conspiratorial organization.

Government detectives are "snoopers" for the law, against lawbreakers, as they are a shield of the innocent.

To bar the records of wire taps as evidence in Federal courts, when they are admissible in state courts, and when they are legally used by the FBI as aids to gathering further admissible evidence, seems to me illogical.

I would not, though, like to see a Federal law like that of the State of New York, which is almost totally unrestricted.

Such indiscriminate practice opens opportunities for blackmail over matters having nothing to do with law enforcement. Many people have things in their lives that are not illegal, but which could cause them pain and suffering if they were known, publicly or to intimates. That is the opportunity for the blackmailer.

If Congress is to revise the Federal law to make evidence obtained by wiretapping admissible in Federal Courts, it should, I think, take up the basic question of when, by whom, and in what circumstances wires may be tapped.

It should continue to limit wiretapping by Federal authorities to cases involving national security and kidnapping. The number of such wire taps should be reported. Permission to tap any wire should continue to require the written approval of the Attorney General, and be confined exclusively to his office and to the FBI.

The possibility of Military Intelligence, the Counter Intelligence Agency, and even Congressional committees using this device should be quashed.

Clues in Wood

by HENRY MORTON ROBINSON

Arthur Koehler, as introduced by Henry Morton Robinson, is one of a great number of people who could not properly be called "law enforcement officials" but whose specialized knowledge is invaluable in the tracking and prosecution of criminals. These individuals work so far from the frontiers of crime-busting, in fact, that their existence often provokes cries of outrage when they are called in to present testimony.

Wood expert? There is no such animal as a wood expert," cried Attorney Pope, defense counsel for Bruno Hauptmann, as the State of New Jersey announced its intention of qualifying bald, keen-faced Arthur Koehler, Government authority on wood, as an expert witness at the Lindbergh trial. "There may be men who know about the bark on trees and all that Boy Scout business," continued Pope, "but we maintain that the identification of wood and objects made of wood is not yet a science like ballistics or dactylography."

Pope's contemptuous dismissal of wood experts as non-existent animals merely indicates that he, along with some hundred and twenty million other Americans, has not kept

pace with the amazing strides made by investigative crimi-
nology in the analysis and interpretation of "wooden clues."
But the testimony of Arthur Koehler instructed him fully
and focused the attention of the nation on a type of scientific sleuthing that has been developing for the past ten
years: the tracing of wood instead of men.

Arthur Koehler, who more than anyone else "wrapped
the kidnap ladder around Hauptmann's neck," is a carpenter
and the son of a carpenter; literally there has never been a
time in his life when the tang and touch of wood, or the
glisten of tools used in fashioning it, have been far from
his daily experience. But he is more than a carpenter; he is,
one might almost say, a biologist and anatomist of wood. He
studied forestry at the University of Michigan, took his
Bachelor's degree in that subject in 1911, and returned to
the University of Wisconsin in 1928 for a Master's degree in
the same field. He became the Government's expert on wood
identification, stationed at the United States Forest Products
Laboratory at Madison, Wisconsin. He is the author of a
book entitled *The Uses and Properties of Wood,* and has written no less than fifty-two Government bulletins on his special
subject. Briefly, he is a combination of scholar, scientist and
practical woodsman—and a living refutation of the charge
that a wood expert is nothing more than a glorified boy scout.

"But what on earth," you ask, "are the daily duties of a
wood expert?" Well, a tennis racquet manufacturer may
accidentally come across a piece of wood that is particularly
suited to his purpose. He wants more wood of this type, but
before he can place an order for it he must find out exactly
what kind of wood it is, where it can be purchased most
economically, and how it should be treated to obtain the
best results. He sends a sample to the United States Forests
Products Laboratory at Madison, Wisconsin, where Koehler
examines it with his batteries of scientific apparatus, adds
his own practical wisdom to these findings, and writes the

manufacturer the full story on this particular piece of wood. Or perhaps a dock pile goes wrong in service—crumbles, splits, or decomposes prematurely. Again Koehler studies the sample presented to him and analyzes the trouble. In "survey cases" he frequently receives a fragment of stump or buried root, and is asked to say what type of tree it came from. The tree in question may have originally been a boundary mark; now it has decayed or been destroyed, and only the root remains. Is it the veritable larch, oak or chestnut mentioned in the old "rod and link" survey? Koehler's opinion, based on the evidence laid before him, must decide this question and thus determine the true boundary line.

Koehler's entrance into the Lindbergh case in May, 1932, was accompanied by no fanfare of trumpets; at that time he was a very humble private in the army of investigators assigned to that crime. Bruno Richard Hauptmann was still at large, and his name was utterly unknown to Koehler or anyone else when the Government expert started tracing the materials used in making the kidnap ladder. Other scientists had viewed this wooden exhibit and had pored over it for indications of its maker's identity; they had daubed it with silver nitrate in an attempt to find fingerprints; they wrapped it in blankets and shipped it all over the countryside to more or less informed "experts," who, after scrutinizing it blankly, had shipped it back in its woolly blankets, as mute and as impenetrable as ever.

A more provoking clue could scarcely be imagined. Here was a crude but not inexpertly constructed engine of crime; it had borne its maker's weight while he climbed to the Lindbergh nursery, but had treacherously failed him as he descended with the added burden of a stolen baby in his arms. A cleat had broken; Lindbergh himself had heard the crash —"a sound like a falling crate"—which had so alarmed the kidnaper that he hastily abandoned the ladder, and thus permitted it to become, under Koehler's probing, the most eloquent of witnesses against him.

Koehler's preliminary observations were those of a practical carpenter and woodsman: he noted that the ladder was made in three sections and contained four kinds of wood. All the lumber was ordinary run-of-the-mill stock; to the layman's eye there was nothing distinctive about it, nothing that could possibly reveal its origin or the identity of its maker. The uprights or rails were of North Carolina pine; the pins or dowels that held the sections together were made of birch, and the crosspieces, or cleats, were fashioned of Ponderosa pine. The man who had built the ladder had evidently run out of material, for the upper left section (afterward known as Rail 16) had been pieced out with an odd board, probably a strip of fir flooring. There were four nail holes in this fir board; the nail holes showed no sign of rust, and Koehler therefore concluded that it had previously done duty in some protected interior. One of his first thoughts on seeing those nail holes was, "If I ever run across four similar nail holes in another piece of lumber, I shall be fairly near the end of my search for the man who made this ladder."

Koehler now entered the second phase of his scrutiny. He knew from experience and from thousands of laboratory tests that no two instruments or tools, no two chisels, knives, saws or planes, ever make identical marks on a piece of wood. He hoped, therefore, that some distinctive tool-markings on the ladder, acquired during the planing, sawing and fitting of its timber, would give him a clue—however fragile —that would orient him properly in this needle-in-the-haystack search for the author of the ladder.

Aided by his microscope and a special kind of oblique light, Koehler soon found the first of the marks he was looking for—the planer-marks of the machine that had dressed the side rails. To understand exactly what these marks were, and why they gave Koehler's heart a little bobble of joy, requires a brief explanation of planing machines and their peculiar habits. When lumber is machine-dressed at a mill, it is fed through a planing machine that simultaneously smooths all four surfaces by means of revolving knives. These knives are set in circular "cutter heads," which whir around like the edges of a lawn mower. Each revolving knife-edge makes a cut at the board as it is pushed through the machine; these cuts are so small that we ordinarily fail to notice them, yet if we inspect a piece of planed stock quite carefully, we observe that it has a wavy appearance as the result of these flying, circular knives. Furthermore, if all the knives are in good condition, and functioning properly, all the waves will be of the same size and spaced at equal intervals.

Suppose now that one of the knives has a nick in it. Every time this knife comes around to the board, its nicked edge makes a tiny mark. The other knives make no such nicks; therefore, if we can count how often the nicked edge comes around, we know how many cutting blades the planer has. Koehler determined that most of the ladder rails were dressed with an eight-knived plane, because every eighth wave showed a tiny nick, spaced regularly at intervals of ninety-three hundredths of an inch—the distance that the board traveled during a complete revolution of the cutter-head. He also discovered that knife Number 5 was not aligned properly with the other knives and consequently made shallower cuts at the board. And because there were seven comparatively deep waves between every shallow one, Koehler was certain now that the planer he sought had eight knives on its top cutting-head.

Examining the edges of the board, Koehler ascertained that the waves here were spaced in a series eighty-six hundredths of an inch apart, and that one wave in every six showed a characteristic defect in the knife blade that made it. He concluded, therefore, that he was looking for a planing machine with eight knives in its top and bottom cutting-heads, and six knives in the cutting-heads that dressed the edges.

Here was a clue that would serve admirably to start him on his hunt for the mill that originally planed the rails in the kidnap ladder. Koehler's next step was to visit the two planer manufacturers who made machinery for finishing lumber of this type; from these manufacturers he got a list of the mills throughout the country that had installed their planing machines. There were one thousand five hundred and ninety-five such mills spread over an area extending from New York to Alabama; in one of these mills was the plane that had dressed the wood in the ladder. But which mill? It would have been physically impossible to visit every mill personally, so Koehler did the next best thing: he asked these mills to send him samples of work done on 1 x 4 pine stock.

Among the samples sent to him, he found one bearing the same highly individualized plane marks as the lumber in the ladder rails

This sample was from the mill of M. G. and J. J. Dorn Company of McCormick, South Carolina. Off to South Carolina flew Mr. Koehler to take a look at the planer in the Dorn mill. He discovered that it fitted his specifications precisely, and that when a certain type of feed pulley was used on this machine, it made revolution marks exactly like those on the ladder rail.

Fact Number One was now established: the lumber in the kidnap ladder had been planed in the Dorn mill. But where had it gone from there? Fortunately for Koehler, a limiting time-element entered the search at this point: the particular feed pulley on the planer had been purchased in September, 1929; therefore, the stock in the two ladder rails must have been dressed between that date and the time of the kidnaping. With the "theater of time" thus narrowed down to approximately thirty months, Koehler consulted the shop records of the Dorn mill and discovered that it had shipped, during this interval, forty-five carloads of 1 x 4 pine stock to twenty-five different firms in various parts of the country.

Deep-lying question Number Two, "What lumber company purchased the wood that went into the kidnap ladder?" still had to be answered.

Koehler, far from discouraged, began visiting the twenty-five lumber companies that had purchased North Carolina pine from the Dorn mill between 1929 and 1932. He examined thousands of boards in a score of states, always looking for a piece of wood bearing the characteristic marks that were now seared in his memory. For eighteen months he searched, and then in November, 1933, long after everyone else had become skeptical of his methods, he discovered the board he was looking for! It was part of a bin in the National Lumber and Mill Work Company of the Bronx, New York City. The remainder of the shipment had been sold long before, and only the luckiest of contingencies had led the foreman of that lumberyard to make a small bin out of this predestined wood.

If the fate that hovers over scientific investigation had inserted one more link here, Hauptmann would have been captured a year sooner than he was. That link—the one that Koehler now eagerly reached for—was a record of the names of all persons who had bought 1 x 4 pine stock from the National Mill Work Company. He asked for these names, but there just weren't any. The owner of the yard informed him that the company sold only for cash and that no itemized sales records were kept.

There can be no doubt that if Koehler had secured the list of persons who had bought pine from the Bronx lumber company, he would have snared Hauptmann single-handed and thus achieved the widest renown ever won by a scientific detector of crime. But Koehler was denied this distinction. He had gone as far as he could go, so without a murmur of complaint he went back to his Madison laboratory and held himself in readiness as a corroborative witness, a secondary role to be sure, but one that would claim a large part of the spotlight when the big break came and the abductor of Lindbergh's baby was finally captured.

The big break occurred when Bruno Richard Hauptmann was picked up for passing a five-dollar bill of the ransom money. One of the first things that Hauptmann admitted was the fact that he was a former employee of the National Mill Work Company. A search of the cash sales slips showed that he had purchased ten dollars' worth of unitemized lumber there in December, 1931. The shipment from the Dorn mill had been made the first part of the same month, which just about supplied the missing link in the long chain of evidence that Koehler had so patiently built up.

But there was another kind of evidence to be examined now, and Koehler sprang to the task with damning ingenuity. Time and again he had told the police, "If you ever seize a suspect, let me examine his premises for a board containing four nail holes." The opportunity had now arrived. Koehler entered Hauptmann's home and a half an hour later found exactly what he had been looking for. In Hauptmann's attic he found four nail holes in a floor joist, corresponding precisely to the four holes in Rail 16 of the kidnap ladder. Now there are probably in this world many millions of boards with four nail holes in them, but according to the laws of probability there could never be two boards with nail holes corresponding so identically as these did. When I say *never*, I actually mean 1 in 10,000,000,000,000,000 times—which are the chances as calculated by mathematicians. The holes in the two pieces of wood were made by nails of the same type and size: when Koehler laid Rail 16 over the attic floor joist, he could push nails into the four holes with the merest finger pressure. Furthermore, there was some sawdust directly under the place where Rail 16 had been sawed off the attic floor. Was it not as clear as a fish in a milk bottle that Hauptmann had run out of material for his homemade ladder and had used a board from his own attic floor to piece it out? It seemed so to Koehler, and he managed to convey his belief with dramatic force and clarity to the Hauptmann jury.

But Koehler went even further; he proceeded to "match up" the grain, pitch streaks and annual rings in the two pieces of wood, i.e., the attic floor board and Rail 16. By counting the annual rings he found that they were identical in number, shape and location. True the graining of the floor board did not exactly coincide with the graining of the ladder-rail, because Hauptmann had sawed off an inch or two of the latter to make it suit his purpose. But the similarity was strong enough to be conclusive, especially when Koehler showed that the presence of a knot in the sawed end of the ladder-rail had distorted the graining adjacent to it in the floor board.

The final straw in the weight of evidence was the testimony of Hauptmann's own plane. With this tool the kidnaper had smoothed down the material in the ladder, and in so doing had left unmistakable marks of the plane's identity on every cleat and rail. When Koehler laid hands on Hauptmann's plane, which he found on a dusty shelf in the garage, the wood expert trembled with the fierce delight that comes to a man when he is on the verge of solving a difficult problem. He could scarcely wait to shove its dull edge—unsharpened and neglected ever since Hauptmann had secured the big ransom payment—across a piece of lumber. Koehler knew exactly the marks that he wanted the plane to make; he had examined those marks on the kidnap ladder a thousand times, always noting the scuffed ridges left by the abused tool. To make these distinctive markings visible to others he resorted to a trick well-known to every school child. Fixing a sheet of paper over the plane marks on the ladder-rail, he rubbed a lead pencil back and forth across the surface of the paper until a black and white diagram of the plane's imperfections was transferred to the white sheet. Then, taking a fresh piece of lumber, he pushed Hauptmann's plane across its surface. Now for a second time he got out a sheet of paper, placed it over the newly planed board and rubbed it as before with his lead pencil. Comparing the two pieces of paper he could easily demonstrate that they contained the same markings, the same ridges and longitudinal striations! This he demonstrated to the Flemington jury, and the case against the ladder-maker was complete. The ragged track of that dull-edged plane probably did more to convict Hauptmann than all the rest of the evidence combined.

Robbery in the Cathedral

by FRANCIS X. BUSCH

The FBI sometimes has no other way to get solid evidence on a gang of criminals than to plant an Agent in the gang so he can help them do whatever it is they're doing. For the Agent, it is play-acting all the way. The gang are his stage partners in playing out a crime. But—they are his audience, too. For them, he must say his lines perfectly and turn in a great performance. He's got to kill them in the aisles—or else . . . In "Robbery in the Cathedral," Francis X. Busch gives us the true story of an actor-Agent who got rave reviews for his performance—a character as colorful as his name, Jean Pierre Lafitte.

THE QUIET LITTLE TOWN of Bardstown, Kentucky, is the second oldest permanent settlement in the state. It was founded by pioneer Roman Catholics in 1808, when they established the first bishopric or diocese west of the Alleghenies. In 1819, they built and dedicated St. Joseph's Cathedral.

The Cathedral, built of native limestone, bricks molded by hand from native clay, and giant poplars from the surrounding forests, still stands today.

Bardstown is at the center of a circle that encompasses some of America's most noted shrines. It is thirty miles from

Hodgenville, birthplace of Abraham Lincoln, sixty miles from Frankfort, where Daniel Boone lies buried, and within a dozen miles of John Rowan's manor house, "Federal Hill," where Stephen Foster wrote "My Old Kentucky Home."

Our story concerns St. Joseph's Proto-Cathedral. The first bishop of St. Joseph's was a priest named Benedict Joseph Flaget, a man of much executive ability as well as great piety. His fame spread far beyond the limits of his western bishopric. St. Joseph's became a landmark in the pilgrimages of the faithful. Bishop Flaget's jurisdiction was broad, and the churches in his diocese widely scattered, so he took numerous journeys.

He had also traveled widely before coming to Bardstown, and on one of those earlier journeys, in 1788, he met and gave spiritual consolation to Louis Philippe, Duke of Orleans, then in exile in Cuba. Legend has it that Bishop Flaget not only gave Louis Philippe and his brothers spiritual comfort but presented them with a handsome purse made up by the Catholic inhabitants of Havana, who sympathized with the exiles.

When Bishop Flaget came to Bardstown, early in the nineteenth century, paintings of religious subjects were common in the churches and galleries of Europe. They were, however, practically nonexistent in America. There were some in the Catholic churches in Maryland and Delaware. There were few, if any, in all the Protestant churches. There were none in any of the widely scattered churches in the far western diocese of Kentucky.

In 1826, Bishop Flaget determined to send some of his trusted associates to Europe to beg and, within his limited means, to buy religious paintings for distribution among the churches of his diocese. He chose four priests—Fathers Nerinks, Chabat, Badin, and Martial.

Father Martial was the one assigned to produce some particularly fine paintings for St. Joseph's Cathedral. When he left, Bishop Flaget gave him a letter addressed to Louis Philippe, who by now had not only returned to France but was the richest man in the nation.

The Duke of Orleans gave Father Martial a number of religious paintings. The bishop's other deputies also fared well in that undertaking, securing in all more than one hundred and fifty paintings. Some of them, along with other gifts of Louis Philippe, found their way to the little cathedral in the backwoods of Kentucky.

The bishop took a justifiable pride in having them suitably mounted and framed. They were then assembled, primarily on the basis of matching sizes, and hung. A number of the larger ones, measuring five by seven feet, were mounted to a common line on the west wall, about fifteen feet above the floor.

Three of those, the choicest of the collection, are involved in our story.

One, bearing the title "The Descent of the Holy Ghost," depicts a dove hovering over Christ's disciples. Another, called "The Crowning of the Blessed Virgin," shows Mary surrounded by cherubs. She holds the infant Jesus, who is placing a star-pointed crown upon her head. The third, "The Flaying of St. Bartholomew," shows the naked saint, suspended by ropes, and an unbeliever with a small knife in hand, in the act of stripping the flesh from the victim's arms. The last two had inscribed on their frames "From the Gift of Francis the First, King of the Two Sicilies."

The fame of the pictures spread. Thousands of persons from beyond the boundaries of the parish journeyed to Bardstown to see them. Among the thousands were students and connoisseurs of art, who naturally speculated as to the identity of the artists of the unsigned paintings.

By the early part of the twentieth century, visitors to the cathedral gallery were hearing some details from the priests who acted as guides. Also, they could buy pamphlets giving a romantic history of the pictures.

One of the younger visitors to the cathedral gallery in the later 1920's and early 1930's was Kenneth D. Donohue. A native of Kentucky, he was a devout Catholic, and had gone with his father to Bardstown on numerous occasions to view the paintings. He entered the University of Louisville as a candidate for the Bachelor of Arts degree. As a result of either the impression made on him by the cathedral pictures or a course on art by the celebrated Dr. Richard Krautheimer, Donohue decided to major in Renaissance art.

In 1947, he left the United States to continue his art studies in Italy. His interest became centered in establishing the identity of the painter of "The Flaying of St. Bartholomew." Painstaking research "made the conclusion inevitable," to use his own language, that the picture had been painted by Mattia Preti, a celebrated Neapolitan artist.

A number of the leading Italian authorities on seventeenth century art unanimously agreed the cathedral painting was an authentic Preti. By 1952, these facts were common knowledge in the upper and under worlds of art.

November 13, 1952, started out much as any other day in the life of Monsignor Willett, pastor of St. Joseph's Cathedral. Following his usual custom, he entered the rear door of the church just after daybreak. The sight which met his eyes was far different from the usual orderly and fixed arrangement.

Nine of the large canvases, including "The Flaying of St. Bartholomew," had been cut from their frames.

One of the empty frames had fallen off the wall to the floor. Two carpenter's ladders, taken from the parish school building, stood propped against the walls.

Monsignor Willett hurried to the front of the church. The

open front door's lock had been forced by a burglar's jimmy.

The robbery of St. Joseph's Cathedral captured headlines from coast to coast. Local and state police examined the vacant frames, the ladders and the broken door for fingerprints. There were none. They made a broad search of the countryside. They found no trace of the thieves or the paintings.

It was logical to assume the thieves wouldn't try to hide the paintings in Kentucky. Until they could be smuggled to Europe, they'd probably be cached with someone in New York or Chicago, or some other large city.

The FBI has jurisdiction over the law which makes it a Federal crime to receive, conceal or possess merchandise valued at more than $5,000 which is known to have been stolen and transported across state lines. Special Agents began an investigation of the theft. Five months went by. The newspapers carried follow-up stories about the paintings and the theft, but there was not a hint as to what authorities were doing to recover them or to apprehend the thieves.

The long silence was broken on April 3, 1953.

In Chicago, at about 5 PM that day, a large blue Cadillac sedan turned right from Michigan Avenue into a parking lot just across the street from the Drake Hotel.

A man got out, and started to remove his coat. Immediately, Special Agents of the FBI closed in on the car. The occupants—a Chicago lawyer named Norton I. Kretske and a man who gave his name as Gus Manoletti—were seized. In the rear of the car was a long tubular package wrapped in heavy brown paper.

It contained four of the stolen paintings, including "The Flaying of St. Bartholomew."

Kretske was taken into custody. Two of the Special Agents got into the Cadillac with Manoletti, and drove to an address on Chicago's West Side. There, they found and arrested Joseph De Pietro, a deputy bailiff in the Municipal Court of

Chicago. A few days later, Kretske and De Pietro were indicted by a Federal Grand Jury. The case came on for trial October 1, 1953. Assistant U.S. Attorneys Daniel J. Ward and John D. Schwartz appeared for the Government. Myer H. Gladstone appeared for Kretske, and Joseph E. Green represented De Pietro. U.S. District Court Judge John P. Barnes presided.

The first witness called was Monsignor Willett, who identified the stolen paintings. The appearance of the next witness was visibly distressing to the defendants. He answered the call for "Jean Pierre Lafitte," but Kretske and De Pietro had no difficulty recognizing him. He was the man they'd known as Gus Manoletti.

Lafitte gave his name as Jean Pierre Lafitte, his residence as San Diego, California, and his occupation as Special Investigator for the Federal Bureau of Narcotics. He said he'd held that position for three years, but during the past fifteen months had been working for the Federal Bureau of Investigation. For thirteen years before his connection with the Bureau of Narcotics, he was engaged abroad on special missions for the U.S. Government. In November of 1952, he said, he had been specially assigned to the investigation of the theft of the Bardstown paintings.

Lafitte then testified that in the early afternoon of April 1, 1953, while in New York, he had received a long distance call from Chicago. He said the conversation went something like this:

KRETSKE: Are you Gus?

LAFITTE: Yes. What do you want?

KRETSKE: I'm the party in Chicago who wants to do business with you.

LAFITTE: What business?

KRETSKE: Well, you know—the painting.

LAFITTE: Don't talk on the telephone.

KRETSKE: I've got a picture on my hands. I can reach it in about ten minutes' time.

LAFITTE: I don't want to go on any wild-goose chase.

KRETSKE: If you want, I'll show my good faith and send you the fare.

LAFITTE: That won't be necessary. Where can I reach you?

Lafitte testified that Kretske then gave him two Chicago phone numbers—a FRanklin number at his office, and a VAn Buren number at his home. Lafitte closed the conversation with, "All right, I'll be there tomorrow, and I'll call you."

Lafitte reported the conversation to the FBI New York Field Office. The following morning he flew to Chicago. He went at once to the Drake Hotel, and registered as Gus Manoletti. He found two Special Agents from the Chicago Field Office waiting for him. In their presence, he called Kretske's office number. Lafitte told him he was in Room 964 at the Drake, and asked him to come to the hotel.

Fifteen minutes later, Kretske called from the lobby. Lafitte went down to meet him and another man whom Kretske introduced as "Mark." Lafitte's FBI associates followed the trio into the hotel's Cape Cod Room.

Lafitte said: "I can't understand why a third person is here. *I'm* alone." Kretske said Mark was a friend of his. Then Kretske gave Lafitte his business card.

Lafitte looked at it, and expressed surprise that he was talking to a lawyer. Kretske answered that there was nothing to worry about, that he "had a great connection."

Kretske was anxious to talk business. "What about the painting?" he inquired.

Lafitte put him off. "Plenty of time to talk about that tomorrow." The three men had dinner in the hotel's swank Camellia House. During dinner, Mark complained of not feeling well, and left.

Later that evening, according to Lafitte, Kretske again brought up the subject of paintings—"You know, the ones somebody talked to you about in New York."

"I'm not an expert," Lafitte said, "but I'm a little doubtful about their value."

Kretske said the *Life* Magazine article about the paintings ought to be enough information if he wanted to buy.

Then, Lafitte said, he asked Kretske, "Is there any blood on this picture?"

Kretske's answer, Lafitte testified, was: "No. My boy got the picture, and he did the job in a safe way."

The answer was of vital importance, for the question had aimed directly at proving that Kretske had been a party to the theft, and therefore knew the pictures had been stolen and transported in interstate commerce.

At 9:55 the following morning, Kretske again called Lafitte from the lobby. Lafitte came down to find both Kretske and Mark. The three had breakfast together. Then Kretske told Mark to get his car. In a few minutes, Mark drove up in an old, dark-blue Chevrolet.

Kretske took the wheel and drove to a dilapidated building which housed a tavern on the first floor. Kretske said he had some business inside. He returned in a couple of minutes, turned the car around, and drove to another building nearby.

"Go to the back of the house, and wait for me in the alley," Kretske instructed Lafitte and Mark.

Kretske went in the front door. A few minutes later, he came out the rear door and joined the others. He took a key from his pocket and unlocked an adjoining rear door, which led into a small apartment. As they entered the kitchen, Lafitte asked, "Where are the paintings?"

"Relax," answered Kretske, leading Lafitte and Mark into the bedroom. There, at the foot of an unmade bed, were two large rolls of canvas. Kretske took the rolls into the kitchen and opened them. Lafitte took one look and knew they were the paintings he was looking for. Lafitte observed that it would be much handier to have all the pictures in one roll, if they did make a deal. Lafitte and Mark left the apartment and returned to the street. Kretske came through the adjoining apartment and met them. On the way back to the hotel, Kretske asked Lafitte if he was "satisfied with the merchandise." Lafitte nodded and said he was ready to talk business.

When they returned to the Drake, Mark waited in the lobby while Kretske and Lafitte went up to Lafitte's room.

"Well," said Lafitte, "let me know the bad news."

"A hundred thousand for the four paintings," replied Kretske.

At this point, Lafitte said, he told Kretske he was out of his mind. "The pictures are good, but they're stolen. You can't expect to get what they're really worth." After more haggling, they finally agreed on a price—$40,000.

"What about delivery?" Kretske asked.

Lafitte pointed out that Kretske had a car. Kretske shook his head. "It's under my own name. I don't want to be involved in case of trouble. Why don't *you* rent one? Get a big car—a Cadillac—so we can put the paintings in the trunk." Lafitte agreed to rent a car.

Kretske left, saying he had to clear the $40,000 price with "his people." Lafitte reported this latest development to the Chicago Field Office, and asked for help in renting a car. The Bureau provided a large Cadillac, and had it parked in a parking lot opposite the hotel.

At 3:10 PM, Lafitte called a bellboy. "Boy," he said, "I've got a mummy coming up. Remember that. Here's seven dollars. Go out and buy me eight big sheets of heavy brown paper and a big roll of cord, and keep the change."

The boy performed the errand promptly.

At four o'clock, Lafitte met Kretske, and they walked to

the parking lot. Lafitte carried the roll of wrapping paper. The ball of cord was in his pocket. Kretske said he knew the town better than Lafitte, and took the wheel.

This time, he drove straight to the apartment house and parked. De Pietro met them at the front door. Kretske and Lafitte went into the apartment they'd been in that morning.

The paintings were not there, but in a few moments, De Pietro brought them in. At Lafitte's direction, Kretske unwrapped them. Lafitte looked at them. Then, with Kretske's and De Pietro's help, he rewrapped them carefully in a single roll, using four of the eight sheets of brown paper. He then tied them securely with the cord. He left the remaining four sheets of paper and some of the cord on the kitchen table. De Pietro carried the roll of pictures to the car.

The package was too large to fit into the trunk, so he put it on the rear seat. Lafitte and Kretske then drove back to the parking lot.

Lafitte got out of the car first. He started to take off his coat. This was the prearranged signal for the waiting Special Agents. Three Agents closed in on Kretske. Two others climbed into the car with Lafitte and returned to the apartment house. There they arrested De Pietro, and the Agents put identification tags on the wrapping paper and cord, which were still on the kitchen table.

The remainder of the Government's case was evidence corroborating Lafitte's story.

Special Agents had been assigned at all times to positions from which they'd be able to follow Lafitte's every movement. All were called upon to testify.

Two explained they'd been present when Lafitte made the phone call from his hotel room to Kretske's office. They noted the number he called. They heard his end of the conversation, saying he was in town and would see the person to whom he was talking in the lobby of the hotel later.

Two other Agents had kept Lafitte, Kretske, and Mark under observation in both the hotel's Cape Cod Room and Camellia House.

Three Agents saw Lafitte, Kretske, and Mark go to breakfast together the following morning, and saw them leave in a car driven by Kretske.

Two Agents were waiting in the Drake lobby when Lafitte, Kretske, and Mark returned there at 12:30, and kept them under surveillance until Kretske and Mark left again, later on.

The Agent-in-Charge of the operation testified to having talked with Lafitte after Kretske and Mark left, to having attended to the rental of the Cadillac, and to the parking of the car in the parking lot. The Agent and two others testified to having seen Lafitte and Kretske get into the Cadillac and drive away.

Five of the Agents were in the parking lot when they returned. They told of Lafitte's signal, the closing in, and the arrest of Kretske. They described the tubular package.

The two Agents who went with Lafitte to De Pietro's apartment testified. Their detailed testimony matched Lafitte's in every particular. They identified the marked and initialed tags they'd put on the unused wrapping paper and cord. The Agent-in-Charge testified that he had taken the tube-shaped package to the Chicago Field Office, and in the presence of two other Agents, put his identification mark on each of the paintings and the wrappings. He identified those marks for the jury.

Kretske had denied the charges, claiming the pictures had belonged to Mark, who was a client of his. De Pietro denied knowing the pictures were stolen. The testimony concluded, the judge charged the jury, and asked it to reach a decision.

After deliberating for three and a half hours, they returned a verdict finding Kretske guilty as charged, and De Pietro not guilty.

The paintings, cleaned and reframed, are back in their places on the walls of St. Joseph's Cathedral in Bardstown.

Blood Money

by RAY BRENNAN

Ray Brennan is a top crime reporter. He feeds copy to the Sun-Times in the city that is to crime what New Orleans is to jazz—Chicago. He's written a good many bullet-ridden magazine pieces, and is the author of a best-selling book, The Stolen Years. Telling us now of a case which he covered as a reporter, Brennan relates a dramatic story of the results of some brilliant deductive reasoning.

CHARLES S. ROSS was a handsome, blue-eyed gentleman of seventy-two. He had a rugged, you-can-trust-me face, and square shoulders. Everybody who met him liked his quick, friendly smile.

For some, another attractive thing about him was his money. A manufacturer of greeting cards, he had retired in the middle 1930's with his assets in cash, real estate, and good securities. With his wife, Mary, he lived in a comfortable apartment at 2912 Commonwealth Avenue, Chicago.

The Ross' serene, well-ordered lives blew up on September 25, 1937. Ross went out to dinner that night, but he didn't take his wife. Instead, he helped his secretary, Miss Florence Freihage, into his car, and drove her to the famous dining room of the Fargo Hotel in Sycamore, Illinois.

361

Miss Freihage was blonde, attractive, and about twenty-eight years younger than Ross. Just before midnight, Miss Freihage—alone in the big car—drove up to a gas station in Franklin Park, a suburb of Chicago. She got to the phone and screamed for police.

Her escort had been kidnapped.

Near Franklin Park, a sedan had driven alongside and forced Ross' car off the pavement. A man with a gun hopped out of the sedan. As he approached, Ross said in a shaky voice,

"I've often thought of being kidnapped."

Miss Freihage said the man snatched her purse, threatened Ross with the gun, and took him away. She couldn't describe the kidnapper, except to say he was dark, curly-haired, and had thin features and a long nose. There was a second man in the sedan. She was certain of that.

The police put out a radio alarm. Nothing came of it. The newspapers didn't think much of the story. It sounded too pat. The next day, though, it sounded less so. Ross didn't come sneaking home with a lame explanation and hangdog expression.

He didn't come home at all.

Miss Freihage was as good a friend of Ross' wife as she was of the old gentleman. Mrs. Ross had not accompanied her husband and Miss Freihage to dinner that Saturday night because of a headache.

A check was made at the Fargo. Results were discouraging to scandal. Ross had had dinner there with Miss Freihage. That was all. He had never been one to drink or chase after women, and he wasn't starting at seventy-two. The only thing unusual about his heart was a tricky fluttering, for which he had to take medicine several times a day.

Mrs. Ross wept as she said, "If he's been kidnapped, my husband can't live long. His doctors say he must have constant attention."

Some Chicago police and newspapermen, however, still wouldn't take the case seriously. Then, D.M. Ladd, Agent-in-Charge of the Chicago FBI Field Office, went into the case—and came out without any doubts. He informed J. Edgar Hoover that it was a genuine kidnapping.

So, to Chicago went Special Agent Earl J. Connelley, Special Assistant to Hoover.

Like all Special Agents, Connelley's mind was open to suspicion of everybody. First, he put a couple of Agents into the Ross apartment. They were to intercept phone calls and protect Mrs. Ross. This busy pair accumulated fingerprints of every visitor, including a reporter who got in as a Western Union messenger, but was quickly tossed out.

Connelley also dug into the missing man's background, hunting for an enemy, a business double-cross, a scandal. He found nothing. Meanwhile, the FBI's policy of secrecy was slapped onto the case for press and public.

On September 30, the first break came.

A friend of Ross, Harvey Brackett, retired real-estate dealer, got a letter at his country home at Williams Bay, Wisconsin. Written in Ross' fine script, the letter read:

"I am held for ransom. I have stated I am worth $100,000.
Try and raise $50,000."

The note had been posted in Savanna, Illinois. It was re-layed by Brackett to Mrs. Ross, who turned it over to Connelley. He told her to get the money ready. Then he called on Edmund S. Cummings, a lawyer who'd served Ross. At a local bank, they packaged one thousand $20 bills, two thousand $10 bills, and two thousand $5 bills. The package was put into a bank vault to await developments.

There was a second note, also to Brackett, two days later. Written in pen by Ross, it gave Mrs. Ross complicated instructions for informing the kidnappers of how much money she could raise. It also instructed her to retain a motorcycle rider "for a very dangerous mission."

In response, this classified ad—coded to the kidnappers' instructions—was placed in two Chicago papers:

> FOR SALE: 1934 Dodge sedan. $250. William
> Gegenwarth, 5043 South Western Avenue.

The $250 meant $25,000, the ransom offered. Mrs. Ross wanted to offer $50,000, but the FBI pointed out that the kidnappers might demand double the amount offered. The Gegenwarth of the ad was a motorcyclist who had been retained by attorney Cummings.

Meanwhile, Mrs. Ross received a third note. This was addressed to her through Elton C. Armitage, another lawyer. It had been typed by a skilled typist. There were no errors or erasures.

> "Please keep this confidential. You are Charles S. Ross' last hope, his own choice as middleman. Somehow, contact Mrs. Ross, using a third person or some other devious means. At any cost, don't let the Feds suspect your part. Conclusive proof of Ross' well-being will be tendered before payment."

FBI men now were working furiously in the background. Connelley sent this report to Director Hoover:

> "All notes bear Ross' fingerprints, or partial prints. There are also unidentifiable prints. These do not match those of any relatives, associates, servants, etc. Presumably, the unidentifiable prints are those of the leader of the kidnap gang. The typed notes show he has a fair education, and is a trained typist. We know he has lately been in Savanna, because the notes were mailed there. The typewriter is a new portable."

At the time he made his report, Connelley had two hundred Special Agents working in Chicago on the case. He put one hundred and fifty of them to checking typewriter shops. It was a long-shot—but it paid off. On Adams Street, a clerk recalled selling a new portable four days before to a thin man with curly hair and a long nose.

The Agent phoned Connelley. Soon, a dozen Agents were checking the area. At a small hotel nearby, the Agents picked up the trail. A curly-haired man had been living there under the name of Peter Anders. He had checked out that day— October 4—carrying a portable typewriter.

The Agents went to his room. They dusted for fingerprints. They found some. One was a perfect match for a print on one of the ransom notes.

The typewriter salesman, the hotel clerk, a hotel maid, and a neighborhood bartender built up the wanted man's description. He was slender, probably about one hundred forty pounds on his 5-foot 9-inch stature. His nose was long, his eyes large and dark. He was a little stooped. His voice was sharp and high-pitched. He smoked cigarettes constantly. He drank beer, but drank it sparingly. He studied horse-race results in the papers.

The FBI was now getting a clearer picture.

Mail from "Anders" continued to arrive. He asked $50,000, doubling the ante, as Connelley had foreseen. He wouldn't accept Gegenwarth. Instead, he directed,

"Go to Joe and Rudy Dolezal motorcycle agency, 1661 Blue Island Avenue. Ask for the name of a brave, reliable man with a good wheel."

The Dolezal brothers turned out to be entirely innocent. "Anders" apparently had picked them at random from the classified phone book. Anyway, the Dolezals put Cummings in touch with George Kukovac, a sharp-eyed, long-chinned young man. The lawyer offered him $250 for a dangerous motorcycle ride.

"For that money," George replied, "I'll ride a motorcycle any place an asbestos squirrel can go."

Cummings took him to the FBI offices. There, George settled down to sleeping, reading, and playing cards with Special Agents. The G-Men took charge of his motorcycle, put on new tires and tubes, then painted it a dazzling white.

Meanwhile, the postman left another letter at Armitage's house. This one contained exact orders for the ransom payment. It also contained a claim check on a local photo-developing shop.

Soon Connelley was examining a roll of developed film from a small camera. The pictures showed the white-haired Ross, a little gaunt, but looking well. The kidnapped man was holding a copy of a Chicago paper, dated October 2, 1937. This was what the kidnapper had promised—"conclusive proof of Ross' well-being."

He was standing in a clearing. In the background were beech and birch trees, their branches bare of foliage. The Agents took the pictures to an expert in the U.S. Forestry Service. They wanted to know where such a woodland scene could be found within five hundred miles of Chicago.

"That's easy," the expert said. "Early frosts have knocked the leaves off those trees. I'd say this picture was taken in northern Wisconsin or Minnesota."

Mrs. Ross placed another used-car ad in the *Chicago Tribune*. This time, the code amount was $500. That meant she agreed to the $50,000 demand. The auto owner was listed as George Kukovac. Next day, a curt note came from the kidnapper:

"Put plan into effect Friday night."

Cummings went to the bank with Connelley and Ladd. They got the $50,000 and crammed it into a zipper bag. The three men then drove in an unmarked FBI car to the Chicago suburb of Oak Park. In the early autumn darkness, three Agents awaited them. They moved aside to show the ransom party a strange sight.

Young Kukovac stood there in white coveralls, white gauntlets, and a white helmet, beside a shining white motorcycle.

The costume and the paint job had been specified by "Anders." The messenger would be easy to see at any time in the long night ahead. And, in the event of an FBI ambush, the man in white on a white motorcycle would give his life in forfeit. He made a perfect target.

The Agents strapped the black zipper bag to the motorcycle. Then, Connelley handed Kukovac carefully printed instructions.

"I know," Kukovac said impatiently. "I've been studying the orders for two days. Your Agents have driven me over the entire route three times. I won't make any mistakes."

Kukovac swung onto the cycle and kicked the starter. He waited until his watch—set by Western Union time—showed exactly 6 PM. Then he was off to deliver the $50,000 ransom, and to earn his fee.

At a roadside restaurant, Kukovac stopped for a sandwich, spent exactly twelve minutes there, and rode away. After another twenty miles, he pulled in at a gas station, spent exactly five minutes checking his tires, then rolled on again.

As the lights of Rockford, Illinois loomed ahead, the young cyclist noticed a car behind him. The headlights were bathing his all-white suit and cycle in glare. The car's lights blinked. Once, twice, three times.

Kukovac cut his throttle, reached behind, and released the zipper bag. The motorcycle coasted for about three hundred feet. Then Kukovac drove it off the road into a ditch. He jumped clear, and walked straight ahead, not once looking back.

At Rockford, he called Connelley.

"All OK. I made the delivery."

Then George Kukovac went home. His job was done.

Connelley relayed the news to Mrs. Ross. She and her companion, Miss Freihage, were greatly relieved. The next day, Mrs. Ross got another note. This one had been posted in Chicago the previous day. It read:

"Your husband will be back for Sunday breakfast, if I collect, and if I have an opportunity to get rid of the bills by that time."

Connelley told Agent Ladd flatly, "The kidnapper is lying. Where could he possibly get rid of $50,000 in currency today, Saturday? The job would take days, or maybe even weeks. 'Anders' is probably smart enough to know we've recorded the serial numbers of the bills. He'll want to get rid of all the bills before we make our list public. He'll stall Mrs. Ross as long as he can. If we let him go long enough, he'll be rid of every ransom bill, and then . . ."

In the FBI office, a mimeograph was turning out 100,000 copies of the list of serial numbers. Stenographers placed them in envelopes addressed to banks, currency exchanges, police departments, railroad lines, steamship agencies, radio stations, and various Government bureaus.

On October 18, ten days after the blood money had been paid, Mrs. Ross finally gave up hope. "I believe that those responsible are unable to deliver my husband," she declared.

Next day, Ladd called a press conference at the FBI Field Office. He read a statement saying only that $50,000 ransom had been paid, but Ross was still missing. Then he handed each reporter one of the mimeographed lists.

The day after the list was published, a woman in the suburb of Blue Island came across one of the bills in her purse. She telephoned the FBI. Agent Ladd was ready. On a wall of his office was a huge map of the United States showing every city, town and village. Into the dot that represented Blue Island, Ladd stabbed a pin with the figure one on its head.

Two hours later, there was another phone call. Ladd pushed pin number two into a spot that represented Chicago's South Side.

A drugstore in the suburb of Evanston made the next pinprick. Number four was a gas station in Racine, Wisconsin. A Milwaukee bank cashier spotted four $5 bills and a twenty. Then banks in Winona, Minnesota, came through with $75 in hot money.

Now the pins on the big map began spreading. Ransom bills turned up in Indianapolis, Detroit, Toledo, Cincinnati, Cleveland, Pittsburgh, Philadelphia, New York, Washington, Birmingham, Atlanta, Mobile, Miami and Palm Beach. "Anders" was getting rid of the Ross blood money almost exclusively in gambling houses and at race tracks.

"Only one person—Anders—is passing the money," Ladd remarked. "What about the other man Miss Freihage says was in the kidnap car?"

Connelley thought a minute, then replied, "My guess is that 'Anders' killed Ross to keep from being identified, then killed his accomplice in order to hog all the ransom money for himself."

After "Anders" enjoyed himself at Hialeah, he headed west. In East St. Louis, Illinois, he gave a bookie $125 in hot money. In Little Rock, Arkansas, he left $65. In Denver, he purchased a wire-haired terrier for $15.

Ladd and Connelley studied the pathway of pins. Then they called Director Hoover. "Anders" was heading west, and the Santa Anita Race Track, near Los Angeles, had a meeting coming up.

The FBI moved in on Santa Anita, with Hoover and Connelley bossing the job.

Special Agents were put behind every pari-mutuel ticket window and cashier cage. On January 14, 1938—less than four months after the Ross kidnapping—a curly-haired man stepped up to the $10 window. Special Agent Murray B. Myerson was working the window. One flash look at the bill was enough. He had spent weeks memorizing serial numbers.

Myerson grabbed for his hip pocket. Not a gun. Instead, he pulled out a handkerchief. That was the signal.

"Curly Locks" must have thought he was hit by the Notre Dame backfield. Four husky G-Men grabbed him. In sixty seconds, they had him in a track office, and were emptying his pockets.

Agent Thomas M. Mulherin flipped open the prisoner's billfold. A driver's license and other papers were made out in the name of "Peter Anders." His pockets also held $495 in cash, a claim check for a car in the track parking lot, and a key for a room in a Los Angeles hotel.

In the parked auto was $2,000 cash. In "Ander's" hotel room was $14,400, making $17,345 recovered in all. Of that money, $11,200 was in ransom bills.

At the Los Angeles FBI Field Office, "Anders" first denied knowing anything about the Ross case. Then Hoover said, "We've got your fingerprints, and they tally with prints on the ransom notes."

They showed him an enlargement of the fingerprints, and matched them.

"I'll be damned!" said "Anders." "I didn't know you could get a print off paper. Glass, metal, wood, sure—but I didn't know about paper."

Then he confessed. He was John Henry Seadlund, age twenty-seven, from a good family in northern Minnesota. At seventeen, he'd burglarized a cafe, and been caught. They put him in jail, but he broke out and became an outlaw, of sorts. He rolled drunks, stuck up a few grocery stores, broke into homes.

Hoover interrupted this story of a career of crime to ask, "Where's Mr. Ross?"

"Dead, of course," Seadlund said. "I shot him. I also killed the fellow with me, a punk named James Atwood Gray. They're dead in a hole up in Wisconsin."

A stenographer typed the confession. Seadlund signed it. His only comment was, "Will I get hanged or fried?"

The G-Men loaded him into a plane next day, and took him to St. Paul, Minnesota. On the way, he talked to Hoover. "We were only going to rob Ross that night," he confided. "Then the old guy mentioned something about being kidnapped, so I grabbed him."

Seadlund knew little of Gray, except that his partner in a series of holdups was about twenty-two, and had come from Kentucky.

From St. Paul, Seadlund directed the FBI to Emily, Minnesota. In a woods there, he'd buried the typewriter case. It contained $30,000 of the Ross money. Hoover was astounded. This made $47,345 recovered. And the entire ransom had been only $50,000.

"I was lucky gambling, particularly at the tracks," the murderer explained.

From Minnesota, Seadlund led the Agents across the state line into northern Wisconsin. The snow was deep, and the party rode on sleighs the last sixteen miles into a forest north of Spooner. Seadlund pointed to a spot, and said, "Dig there."

In a boarded-up pit were the chains that had held Charles Ross. Also in the pit were the frozen bodies of Ross and Gray.

I wrote one of the last newspaper stories ever published about the Ross kidnapping and murder. It began this way:

"John Henry Seadlund died in the electric chair at Cook County Jail at 1:12 AM today.

"He died without ever having said one word of repentance for having killed two men. He was—right up to the last —the man described by J. Edgar Hoover as 'the most vicious, cold-blooded killer I ever knew.'

"Only a dozen official witnesses saw the execution."